HOMES
& GARDENS

A YEAR IN THE GARDEN

HOMES
& GARDENS

A YEAR IN THE GARDEN

Andi Clevely

HAMLYN

For Meg, who has shared all the joys and frustrations of twenty-five
years in the Garden – thank you.

This book started life in response to an invitation by Amanda Evans,
editor of *Homes & Gardens* , to expand my monthly Offshoots pages,
where some of the material first appeared. My thanks are due to her
for letting me reproduce, reconsider and rewrite many of those
original articles; to her efficient team of sub-editors with whom over
the years I have happily discussed commas, clauses and opaque
garden jargon (the glossary of terms is not my revenge – perish the
thought); to Anna Mumford, Selina Higgins, Robin Whitecross and
Michael Whitehead, who between them have created a book from
my text; and to The Owner, Mrs Pat Mitchell, who regularly reminds
me she prefers the title 'Assistant' to 'Boss'.

Art Editor Robin Whitecross
Executive Editor Anna Mumford
Designer Michael Whitehead
Editor Selina Higgins
Production Sarah Rees
Picture Research Claire Taylor and Anna Smith
Colour illustrations, and black and white illustrations on pages 29, 58
and 96 Vicky Emptage
Black and white illustrations, Jill Hedges' Specialist Garden Book Library

First published in Great Britain in 1993
by Hamlyn an imprint of Reed Consumer Books Limited
Michelin House, 81 Fulham Road
London SW3 6RB
and Auckland, Melbourne, Singapore and Toronto

© 1993 Reed International Books Limited
Text © 1993 Andi Clevely
Design © 1993 Reed Consumer Books Limited

Produced by Mandarin Offset
Printed in Hong Kong

ISBN 0 600 57737 6

A catalogue of this book is available at the British Library

I had a visitor last week who knows a great deal about gardening and has had much practical experience. When I heard he was coming, I felt I wanted to put my arms right round my garden and hide it from him; but what was my surprise and delight when he said, after having gone all over it, "Well, I think you have done wonders." Dear me, how pleased I was! It was so entirely unexpected, and such a complete novelty after the remarks I have been listening to all the summer. I could have hugged that discerning and indulgent critic, able to look beyond the result to the intention, and appreciating the difficulties of every kind that had been in the way. After that I opened my heart to him, and listened reverently to all he had to say, and treasured up his kind and encouraging advice, and wished he could stay here a whole year and help me through the seasons. But he went, as people one likes always do go, and he was the only guest I have had whose departure made me sorry.

from Elizabeth and Her German Garden

Contents

A YEAR IN THE GARDEN

Introduction

During their long apprenticeship, gardeners were traditionally nomads travelling from one place to another. After spending a couple of years learning how to grow fruit or raise pot plants under glass perhaps, journeyman gardeners, as they were known, moved on to fresh challenges, often to different parts of the country or to areas with unfamiliar soils, until they had learned the basics of the craft and could finally settle down.

The garden I look after has enticed me to finish wandering and strike root at last. It is a small, artlessly dishevelled country estate near Stratford-upon-Avon, in the heart of the English Midlands. Tucked in the loop of Shakespeare's Avon, it lies on fine, mildly alkaline river-terrace soil, workable hours after a thunderstorm but quickly parched in dry weather, and constantly hungry.

Winters are cool, damp and often wrapped in fog, while summer is an unpredictable mixture of strong winds, sullen drizzle and many days when it is good to be alive. Autumn is always glorious but spring can be contrary, especially when the fruit trees flower: the proverbial greengage summer occurs about one year in ten.

The garden is planted with old-fashioned flowers and shrubs, hedges of formal box, Portugal laurel, yew, holly, elm suckers and brambles, and many mature trees, including an elderly cedar of Lebanon that is in decline and regularly lacerated by gales, and riverside willows that are pollarded for fuel, fencing and garden poles.

The lawns take two hours to mow, even longer to edge, and are usually speckled with flowers that should not be there. We are gradually reviving the kitchen garden, which is large and ever changing, with beds divided variously by gravel paths, rows of soft fruit, and poles for trained roses, vines, top fruit and hops. A small range of old greenhouses has been salvaged from a Black Country demolition site for re-erection here, and is heated erratically by a solid-fuel stove.

So much for 'The Garden' of the title: 'The Year' can be any time, although now will do. Years gone by mingle freely with the present as they always must, and while working in this garden I am as aware of the footprints of my predecessors, as of our plans for tomorrow and the seasons to follow.

This book is not an exhaustive manual of the tasks to be done during this hypothetical year. Based on articles that were first written for the 'Offshoots' column in Homes & Gardens, it is a potpourri of divergent ideas, practical experiences and insights relevant to any year and every garden. If it inspires anyone to go outdoors and try something new, reveals a little of the hidden life of plants, or simply shares a few of the joys of spending a year in the garden, it will have done its job.

Early SPRING

An unmistakable SIGN OF SPRING'S IMMINENCE USED TO BE THE FRUSTRATED AND PROLONGED CURSING BY HARRY, MY FORTHRIGHT ASSISTANT ON ONE ESTATE, AS HE FOUGHT UNSUCCESSFULLY TO REVIVE OUR ANCIENT 90CM (36IN) MOWER FROM ITS LONG WINTER COMA. THERE WAS NONE OF THAT TROUBLE IN THE OLD DAYS, HE'D LAMENT ANNUALLY; THE MOWING TEAM WOULD JUST HONE UP THEIR SCYTHES AND BE OFF.

Although a keen scythe, when properly balanced and set, is still the best tool for felling nettles and thistles, short-mowing a lawn was a skilled art acquired only after long, strenuous and sometimes painful experience. Each scythesman cut his own strip, working behind the man in front, so the team was staggered diagonally across the lawn; novice gardeners were placed in the middle, and if they did not keep up the pace that was set the men behind were soon slicing at their heels. As single-bladed tools cut closest on firm, erect grass, the scything teams started well before breakfast, finishing tired and thirsty about mid-morning when the dew had dispersed. Cylinder mowers, on the other hand, cut best when the lawn is dry, and on damp mornings someone used to be sent in front of the machine to sweep off the dew with a long, flexible cane.

In mild winters lawns continue to grow and may need 'topping' once a month, always on a dry, windy day to avoid damaging both turf and machine. From this month onwards more frequent mowing is necessary. Few gardeners admit to enjoying this chore, which is on a par with hedge clipping and weeding asparagus beds, but I tend to treat the lawn as a crop in itself and willingly harvest the clippings each week for use around the garden. I use the first batches to mulch the rows of raspberry canes, which revel in the cool, slightly acid root run that an accumulation of clippings produces. Once they are tucked up, I spray the lawn for perennial weeds, walking up

Primroses IN BRIGHT CLUSTERS BENEATH TREES AND SHRUBS, BLOOMING TO GREET THE SPRING EQUINOX

THE FAMILIAR SCENT OF *freshly cut turf* AS THE MOW-ING SEASON RESUMES

STOUT GREEN SHOOTS ON EARLY *seed potatoes* TO BURY NOW TO ENJOY FOR SUMMER SALADS

A TASTE OF *asparagus* AS THE FIRST TENTATIVE SPEARS BREAK THROUGH THE SURFACE OF THE SOIL

and down the stripes to 'spot treat' plantains and dandelions with a systemic lawn herbicide; clippings from the next two or three mowings are contaminated with weedkiller, but they can be added safely to the compost heap.

Thereafter we use the clippings to mulch crops that are drought-sensitive or difficult to hoe – carrots, parsley and dib-bled leeks, for example – or to surface paths between vegetable rows and keep them weed-free. Grass from the last cuts in autumn is mixed with autumn leaves to speed their decay. It is a good accelerator for compost heaps, because it heats quickly, but for the same reason grass mulches must be built up gradu-ally from thin layers about 5cm (2in) deep.

INSPIRATION

VARIATIONS ON A LAWN Opponents of lawns condemn them as 'green deserts', because of their apparent monoculture, although in fact only dedicated enthusiasts can boast a perfect turf. One day last autumn I counted nearly two dozen attrac-tive species of toadstool on our lawn, while a week in summer is long enough for its surface to sparkle with white daisies, blue speedwell and yellow silver-weed. The turf stays green all sum-mer, its resolute drought-resistance largely due to the high moss population. So even though the presence of moss may cause offence in a perfect lawn, it does have its benefits.

When in my first private service position, I was surprised to hear my employer defend the daisies, clover and moss that threatened to take over her lawn. Then I noticed that in a dry summer her lawn, with its pleasant elasticity underfoot, stayed fresh long after others had been scorched to motley shades of brown, and eventually I learnt to accept the virtues of what are normally regarded as weeds.

Although this will be heresy to orthodox green-keepers, moss on its own makes an attractive springy lawn, which with-stands moderate wear and may be mown occasionally to keep it looking neat. In some instances an effective moss lawn can be developed simply by abandoning operations such as spiking and scarifying, for these discourage moss in conventional lawns; water unwanted grasses and broad-leaved plants with a general weedkiller, which rarely affects the moss.

If you want a conventionally praiseworthy lawn, start the intensive annual routine now: treat the surface with moss-killer, scarify it to remove layers of thatch and dead moss, improve drainage by spiking and then brushing top-dressing into the holes, and give a spring feed once it is growing steadily. Live moss is worth raking out to use later for lining hanging baskets. Set the mower blades high for the first cut or two, and over the following four to six weeks gradually lower them.

Above *Springtime* **by James Bingley. Right Cowslips growing in the lawn, where they enjoy a cool root run**

For neatness edges need trimming whatever your standards. Bare patches can be prepared as seed beds for re-sowing next month with a seed mixture that matches the level of use and sunlight it gets. If you have any seed to spare, sow pathways between rows of fruit, and cut once or twice during the summer, then skim off the top 5-7.5cm (2-3in) next spring with a spade to make turves. Use these for repairing the lawn; for stacking to rot into potting compost; for covering a shed roof like the traditional sod-barn; or for building retaining walls.

The sides of our large cold frames were built from turves six years ago, and still exclude all but the harshest frosts, which even then only penetrate through the polythene lids rather than through the thick walls. Save old mats and pieces of carpet to insulate frames, especially now when they are filling up with trays of hardy annual seeds, such as cornflowers, calendula, mignonette, godetia and scabious. In cold districts, sow leeks, calabrese, summer cabbage, Brussels sprouts and cauliflowers in a frame, as soils may still be too cold for even germination, if not for mowing.

PLANNING

HOME-GROWN WILD PRIMROSES Take an old punted wine bottle (clear or light green), carefully make a small hole in the middle of its base, and knot one end of a piece of string around its neck. Early in the morning, stealthily slip away to the nearest running water, and gently lay the bottle in shallow water, its neck facing upstream. Then wait patiently for the first inquisitive minnows to find their inevitable way into the trap.

Above Candelabra primulas bring a touch of oriental mystery to the damp garden in early spring. Below Some primroses grow in woodlands, others by streams or in bogs, some are natives of meadows, and many are found on mountain sides

Thus in England did pre-war Black Country lads catch bait with which to start the day's fishing – it never failed, my father-in-law assured me. Had he lived in the countryside, where wild flowers still grew in profusion, his catch might have been more welcome in the kitchen to make 'minnow tansies', a traditional delicacy recommended by Izaak Walton. Prepare them like whitebait, and then fry 'in yolks of eggs, the flowers of cowslips and of primroses, and a little tansy; thus used they make a dainty dish of meat'.

Self-sufficiency fostered a resourcefulness that found uses for most wild plants, among them the various native primulas – primroses, cowslips and oxlips. The short, stout rhizomatous stems of the last two were used to produce tonics for colds and chest conditions, and even today homeopathic medicine uses an essence prepared from cowslips for the treatment of kidney complaints.

For most of us, though, these gems of spring rekindle childhood memories of picking armfuls of flowers, then a legal if ultimately destructive pastime. In recent years travellers down country lanes will have noticed the return of drifts of primroses or sprinklings of the more solitary cowslips, especially where verges are left unmown until plants have seeded at mid-summer. Nevertheless, countless plants have disappeared, as their habitats have been destroyed by thoughtless clearance of hedge, ditch and copse. Guard patches that are once more thriving, and resist any temptation to pick or plunder.

If you really want to have a lot of primroses, oxlips and cowslips in your garden, you must grow them yourself. They are not hard to raise, and if content with their situation will remain with you always, seeding themselves in dense colonies wherever they fancy. The true wild species have a simplicity and resilience absent from the blousy vivid hybrids which resent wind and rain, or from the pretty little pot primroses which soon fade away outdoors.

Naturalize them where they are happy – primroses like leafy soil in a shady place, perhaps beneath trees or shrubs, while cowslips prefer grassland, whether in full sun or semi-shade, and grow best in turf left uncut until bulbs have died down. Oxlips thrive on either site, as long as it never dries out. Keep the different kinds apart if you are a purist, for they are wanton beauties and hybridize with each other to produce false oxlips and other droll offspring.

THE WIDER FAMILY Many primula species interbreed freely, a blessing for gardeners because polyanthus and other familiar garden hybrids all result from their promiscuity. There are more than 500 wild species in existence, many with greatly differing requirements. Some will break your heart, for although a few grow as rampantly as weeds where happy, others are wildly contrary away from their natural habitats. Most, however, will thrive if their few simple requirements are met.

Candelabra primulas – those species with tall spires of flowers arranged in whorls – and other marginal kinds must dabble their root tips in damp soil: grow them beside water, or in a 'bog' bed of spongy soil kept moist by a perforated sheet of plastic buried 30cm (1ft) below ground. Most other species prefer perfectly drained, organic soil that nevertheless stays moist. If your ground lies wet, open it up by forking in a generous amount of garden compost or leaf mould and then, after planting, mulch thickly with gravel or small chippings: this protects the necks of crowns from winter wet, as well as deterring voracious slugs.

The technicolour display of gaudy hybrid primroses on sale each spring has temporarily outshone some traditional garden primulas, now long overdue for revival. Gold-laced polyanthus, for example, have been grown since the eighteenth century and remain the daintiest kind of polyanthus, guaranteed to attract attention. Plants bear neat heads of small flowers, in shades of mahogany red, each petal edged with a fine gold line; as a bonus, batches of seedlings usually contain a few, equally charming silver-laced specimens. Border auriculas are confident, buxom flowers in sumptuous

PLANT HIGHLIGHTS OF THE MONTH

Kale **Don't despise the plebeian kale, a hardy and reliable brassica to harvest from late winter. Sometimes listed as borecole, its many varieties include a giant, the Jersey walking-stick or 'Chou Cavalier', whose stems make poles up to a record 5.5m (18ft) high. The earthbound 'Dwarf Green Curled' is the most decorative and was once popular for winter bedding schemes. Feed plants now and start cutting the tender young shoots; at the same time sow next year's crop in a seedbed or cold frame.**

Coleus **A vividly marked foliage plant, coleus (now *Solenostemon*) was a Victorian classic for growing in pots, or as monochrome bedding. Named cultivars still survive, but most have been ousted by modern seed mixtures. Sow now under glass and prick out all seedlings, whose full colours only develop later in the year. Pinch growing tips regularly, remove the spikes of insignificant flowers, and over-winter the best plants like other tender perennials. Growth resumes about now: shorten stems to induce bushiness and use the prunings for cuttings.**

Hops **In spring established hop plants produce masses of young shoots; they should be thinned when 15-20cm (6-8in) high to half a dozen per plant; the rest are a hop-grower's tasty substitute for asparagus spears. Let the 'bines', with their shapely leaves, scramble up poles and arches, with clematis and rambler roses for dramatic impact, and then train overhead (contented hop-bines reach 4.5-5.5m (15-18ft) if allowed). Leave clusters of green flowers until brown and fragrant in autumn, and then gather for use.**

colours ranging through butterscotch yellow, clotted cream, strawberry pink and rich velvet red to an almost midnight burgundy, most with large contrasting eyes. These bold and easy-going plants need moist, but not waterlogged, soil, and benefit from occasional division when they sprawl too languidly. Tidier by far are the double primroses, with their perfect blooms like polyantha roses. Although named plants are increasingly available, gambling with a packet of seeds is an adventure few can resist. Cherish every seedling; only a proportion of the resulting plants will be fully double, and they might not reveal all in their first season. Any you do find, though, will lavishly reward patience and prayers.

Fresh primula seed is best sown in autumn as soon as it is ripe, but foil-packed supplies germinate readily in spring, provided neither seeds nor seedlings are allowed to dry out as temperatures rise. Sow thinly in pots of seed compost, pressing the seeds into the surface without burying them, then stand the pots in saucers, each with a little water in the bottom. Prick out seedlings 5cm (2in) apart into boxes of potting compost and leave in a shaded place outdoors; keep them moist until the plants are ready to be planted out.

FRAMEWORK

WALLS AS HABITATS Virgil, that resourceful Roman countryman whose savings found ultimate security stashed in his beehives, roused little enthusiasm among us bored schoolboys. Daily we stumbled through chunks of his *Aeneid*, line by line, though most of the immortal verse was meaningless to us and we made nothing of such rhetorical sentiments as 'Happy those whose walls already rise!' Years later I grew fond of that classic line, the passionate cry of Virgil the gardener, rather than Virgil the epic poet. Over the intervening centuries, generations of gardeners have rejoiced when discovering a plot already snug within a weathered 3m (10ft) enclosure, or groaned at the expense of building from scratch that most desirable of assets, a walled garden. Four, or perhaps three, surrounding walls are certainly cause for elation, though even one should not be disdained for the shelter, warmth, privacy and support that it offers. Plants seem seduced by walls, either scrambling up their face or growing contentedly in their nooks and crannies. It only takes a moment's work to hammer a nail into a convenient mortar joint, should any plant need support.

When building a garden wall aim to blend materials with the local character, and make sure the wall is high enough to sport climbers comfortably: 1.8m (6ft) is the practical minimum. If budgets permit, use second hand bricks and stone in preference to new; reclaimed from building sites, they are widely available and already look pleasantly weathered. New brickwork can be aged by painting it with a slurry of manure and water, or you could use lime-wash to reflect heat and light and to transform gloomy surroundings with a Mediterranean brilliance. Ordinary garden lime will do, mixed with water to an emulsion and then daubed on liberally with an old distemper brush. For an intense white finish re-coat the wall each spring, otherwise every three years will do.

Old walls are often studded with nails where gardeners tied in growing stems. This may be sufficient support, but where plants are trained symmetrically, or must be dropped at times in order to repaint the wall, it is best to arrange permanent trellis, pig-netting or strong horizontal wires, fixed to nails or vine-eyes driven into wooden plugs. Tie in stems as they grow, at an oblique angle where possible, as this helps to cover an area more rapidly, and also stimulates flowering or fruiting – plants such as passion flowers often only flower on stems that are trained sideways.

Early maturity is achieved by growing in situ natural crevice plants such as valerian, stonecrop, aubretia, yellow corydalis, wallflowers, *Erigeron karvinskianus*, herb robert and dainty ivy-leaved toadflax. Leave them small gaps between bricks and stones while building, or chisel out strategic slots in mortar joints in the top few courses. Ram in soil-based compost, preferably stiffened with a little clay (peat dries too quickly), and either plant seedlings in spring or sow pinches of seed in the autumn. Contented plants will then seed themselves in other convenient cracks.

GARDEN SURGERY

GALLING PROBLEMS The blackcurrant gall mite, alias 'big bud' mite to most gardeners, chooses new sites in early and mid-spring. For the rest of the year it leads a secretive life inside fat, unproductive flower buds, feeding on sap and, much worse,

spreading incurable reversion disease from one plant to another. Once inside a bud the mites are safe, and the only time that it is possible to catch them is when they migrate on foot from one bush to the next. During winter and spring pick off and burn any of the inflated buds and then spray the bushes thoroughly with derris once or twice during the migration period. If the case is very severe, try cutting back all growth to ground level and then burn the cuttings.

Blackcurrant big bud is just one of the many plant malformations collectively known as 'galls', which are all produced by insects or bacteria as a shelter for their young or for their own predations. Not all are as sinister as the big bud mite or the organisms that cause brassica club root and potato wart disease and some mites build decorative galls that are relatively harmless. The knobbly woody growth on trees that appears as densely figured burrs in veneer is a benign form of brown gall; some miniature tree cultivars originate from witches' brooms (a type of gall) on full-size hosts, while the spectacular red mossy balls that appear on rose stems are robin's pin cushions, home to the larvae of the bedeguar gall wasp.

A few kinds of galls are even beneficial. You will never see a fig tree in bloom, because the flowers lie buried deep inside the tiny immature fruits. Figs cultivated in cold regions are all parthenocarpic – that is, they will produce fruit without fertilization, whereas varieties grown in warmer climates must be

Left In a mild garden baby figs survive the winter to ripen in mid-summer followed by a second spring generation.
Below The fig's palmate foliage makes a dramatic contrast with natural stone. Opposite left Candelabra primula.
Right Armeria and aubrieta are ideal for growing on walls

pollinated, and for this they need the assistance of a minute fly, whose infancy is spent inside galls within the fruit. Male fig gall wasps hatch first and then crawl around looking for females with whom to mate, after which they die without leaving the fig. A fertilized female wasp emerges from her cell, passing male flowers on her way to the outside world, and in doing so collects a dusting of pollen. In her search for somewhere to lay her eggs, she enters a baby fig through the hole in its nose. Once inside, she will find that some of the female flowers are fertile, and that others are sterile. To complete the process, the wasp pollinates the fertile blooms in passing and lays her eggs in the sterile ones, which she also injects with a growth hormone. This stimulates the ovaries to grow into galls which will protect the next generation.

Big bud infestation on blackcurrants might seem less fascinating than the fig wasp's life cycle, but they are both examples of the complex relationships that flourish behind the scenes in every garden, and illustrate the ambiguity of gardening, in which there is as much interference as creativity.

BLINDNESS IN BULBS Dense clumps of daffodils and narcissi, especially those naturalized in drifts within a lawn, may eventually refuse to flower. They are then often said to have gone 'blind', but this is not always accurate, as blindness refers strictly to the loss of a main growing tip, usually as a result of physical injury. Bulbs seldom go blind in this sense; their failure to flower is rarely due to damage or disease, but is most often caused by starvation. Overcrowding is the likeliest reason for this, unless the foliage is mottled or shows other visible signs of disease. After many years clumps become densely congested and although they are still vigorous, they produce fewer flowers. Affected groups should be dug up and split, replanting the largest bulbs 10-15cm (4-6in) apart on the same site or elsewhere after first adding a little bonemeal to the soil.

Below Hosts of naturalized daffodils relieve the uniformity of a sweeping lawn in spring, but their foliage must be left to ripen naturally before being cut down

Dwindling flowers and leaves are a common result of mowing naturalized bulbs too early in the season. At least six weeks should elapse after flowering before the daffodil foliage is cut down; this allows the full transfer of food from leaves and stems to the bulbs, to fuel future growth and flowering. Avoid removing leaves too soon as this will gradually exhaust the bulbs, as may a series of early droughts – low rainfall in spring, especially on light soils, weakens bulbs and discourages flowering the following season. After a succession of such seasons bulbs sometimes fade out completely.

DOWN TO EARTH

PLANTING SUMMER BULBS As spring bulbs get into their stride, summer-flowering kinds such as tigridia, camassia, brodiaea and gladioli become due for planting. Start now, rationing the work over the next six weeks or so for successional flowering. When taken from storage gladioli need a spring clean first: rub loose pieces of dry 'tunic' from around the corms, and gently prise off the shrivelled remains of last year's corm at the base of each bulb. Plant about 7.5cm (3in) deep in a sheltered place. If you plant at twice that depth and protect the area with a mulch in the autumn, gladioli can be left out in cold gardens over winter. As with most bulbs, efficient drainage is a vital factor in their survival from one year to the next. Heavy soils need to be opened up by digging in large amounts of coarse sand or ashes over the whole area; improving individual planting holes alone may simply create waterlogged drains for the rest of the site. All this, of course, is laborious work, and a useful alternative on poorly drained soils is to plant near a hedge or at the base of a tree, where existing root systems will tend to remove surplus water. To insure against too much competition from other plant roots and to help provide a cool moist environment in summer, topdress the area in late spring with a mulch of rotted leaves, garden compost or shredded bark, together with a dusting of sulphate of potash to build strong bulbs for the following year.

It is because of the structure of their bulbs that lilies are more sensitive than most to wet soils, as water tends to collect between their loose scales instead of being shed, as happens with smooth-skinned bulbs. Nestling each lily on a bed of coarse sand and packing more around its sides will help prevent water from collecting, and planting bulbs on their side is a further insurance in wet soil. Another important consideration is shelter, especially from high winds. It is better to choose a suitable site where lilies and gladioli can grow naturally, rather than to plant them in an exposed patch and hope to stake them unobtrusively for support. Such is the slender habit of their stems that canes

and other props would always detract from their grace, whereas adjacent shrubs and bushy herbaceous perennials can provide discreet support and also shade the base of lilies from hot sunshine. Remember, though, that other strong colours can diminish the impact of summer bulbs; check that their flowering time coincides with a fairly neutral background.

FOCUS ON FOOD

POTATOES During the early years after their introduction to France, potatoes were widely considered to be fit only for cattle and for 'the most wretched of human beings'. Louis XVI used to wear a nosegay of the flowers to encourage his countrymen to accept the new tuber, but the story goes that the French only did so when the king had a palace garden walled in and planted entirely with potatoes. Sentries guarded the 'king's treasure' by day, but artfully were withdrawn at nightfall. Louis knew his subjects: as curiosity triumphed over prejudice, the whole crop disappeared over a few nights, and so potatoes were dispersed throughout ordinary French gardens.

Some gardeners are still reluctant to grow their own potatoes. True, at first sight they are not the most decorative of plants; they need space, but not as much as might be assumed; if the crop is not thoroughly cleared at harvest time, 'volunteer' plants from overlooked tubers will grow like weeds, though they often crop earlier than planted tubers. But these are minor objections, when set against the delight of eating 'new' potatoes, packed with flavour, compared to bought supplies which are still expensive and lack flavour.

Potatoes vary considerably in habit. The best kinds for forcing or for growing in restricted spaces are those with short compact growth (eg 'Arran Pilot'); vigorous varieties (eg 'Desirée'), on the other hand, are ideal for helping to break new ground. It is often said that potatoes 'clean the soil', but this is not strictly true, for while dense top growth suppresses some weeds it is the gardener who does most of the work – harvesting a crop at the same time simply makes the effort seem much more profitable.

There are several ways to enlist the aid of potatoes in cultivating waste or weedy soil. If the ground is to be dug, make sure you work with a clear trench. At the start of each row, slice off the surface weeds with a spade and then transfer them to the bottom of the trench, burying them beneath the soil thrown forward as you dig down across the bed. Every third or fourth row, space maincrop potatoes (ware tubers from a greengrocer will do) 30-38cm (12-15in) apart on the layer of weeds in the trench, and cover these as you continue digging. Level the surface to make hoeing easier until growth is 15cm (6in) high, when you can start earthing the soil up in a ridge. Eventually the potato haulm will be dense enough to provide ground-cover. In autumn it is a simple matter of forking out surviving weeds while lifting the crop.

Another technique, which is gaining in popularity and is valuable where there are not too many tough perennial weeds, is to cover the ground with black polythene, bury the edges with soil, and then plant seed tubers, with a dibber, through cruciform slits cut in the plastic. Another option known as the 'lazy bed' method involves setting the potatoes in a layer of compost or rotted manure spread on the soil surface; these are then covered by skimming off a layer of top soil on each side of the row with a spade and folding the layers, weedy side downwards, over the tubers. The exposed soil can then be cultivated and used to earth up the crop as it grows.

SPARROW-GRASS Explore any neglected kitchen garden and among the tangle of weeds you will probably discover two robust survivors from earlier times: potatoes that sprout each year from undug tubers, and asparagus, which seems equally indestructible. On the estate where I work the annual reappearance of new season 'sparrow-grass' on the table is cause for celebration, and any time from mid-spring onwards, The Owner may be seen prowling the beds, her knife at the ready for cropping precocious spears.

There is no truth in the claim that modern gardens have no room for asparagus. The traditional raised asparagus beds, which are 1.5m (5ft) wide and a labour of love to maintain, are undoubtedly an extravagance where space is precious. Commercially, though, crowns are now planted in single rows on flat ground like any other vegetable, while in small gardens they can be grown as specimen plants in flower borders.

Gather spears for the kitchen until the longest day of the year, when cutting must cease to avoid exhausting the plants; they will then produce masses of tall graceful fern, which lasts all summer and justifies their inclusion in herbaceous borders. Asparagus will grow well in most soils but good drainage is essential. Plant a few crowns now, or sow a row of seeds outdoors and transplant the strongest seedlings in the autumn. Choose a moist day for planting and never let the crowns dry out. F_1 hybrids such as 'Lucullus' and 'Franklim' yield heavily when young, but trials suggest they might be shorter-lived than standard varieties ('Connover's Colossal' or 'Martha Washington') that crop for 30 years or more if well-managed.

Cut down the fern or 'bower' in late autumn after it has turned gold and started to disintegrate. Plants are either male or female, the latter sporting bright red berries as the bower assumes its autumn tints; if your interest is strictly culinary, rogue female plants because unproductive seedlings from the berries may eventually take over the bed. Once cut down, weed and mulch plants with rotted manure every year, to ensure fat spears throughout the cutting season.

NEW PLANTS FROM OLD

HERBS FROM SEED Perennial leafy herbs such as lovage, sweet cicely and angelica, are grown from seed, whereas shrubby herbs are normally started as cuttings; this is the only way to multiply variegated kinds and ensure they stay true to type. Many gardeners, though, find that perennial woody herbs grow more vigorously from seed, a sound and inexpensive way to introduce a large number of plants to the garden; if sown now they will germinate quickly as temperatures start to rise. Chives, lemon balm and other herbaceous kinds can be sown outdoors where they are to grow, whereas thyme, marjoram or sage are sown for convenience in trays under glass, for pricking out individually into pots. The growth rate of a few herbs, sweet marjoram and oregano in particular, seems to slow down after seedlings emerge from the soil, so it is a good idea to bring them on in warmth until they are planted out in summer.

Annual herbs (including parsley, which is strictly a biennial) must be grown from seed sown every spring. With their lush foliage and rapid growth, they prefer richer conditions than woody perennials, and for this reason are often grown in the kitchen garden. Some need sowing once only, because they self-seed freely – borage seedlings will pop up here and there each year for transplanting to more convenient flowering positions, while chervil can produce two or three generations a year from seed and maintain a permanent carpet of plants.

Above Planted with flair herbs can refute their reputation for formality and monotony, and have all the motley beauty of a wild garden. **Opposite left** The female asparagus bears red berries in the autumn. **Opposite right** Asparagus spears

Although grown as a perennial in pots in Mediterranean courtyards, basil needs special treatment in less genial climates, where it is vulnerable to cold and dampness. Sow any of the attractive varieties early under glass and grow in pots. They can be grown either in the conservatory or outdoors in a sunny spot sheltered from winds; keep the sensitive leaves dry by watering from below. Seed-bearing herbs like coriander and dill, on the other hand, can be sown outdoors, in rows between vegetables, where they are left to flower and ripen their seed heads. It is often cheaper to buy culinary seeds from herb suppliers, but make sure you have the kind you want: there are two types of coriander, for example, one grown for its pungent seeds, the other as a green leaf crop for Indian cuisine.

UNDER GLASS

REPOTTING AND POTTING ON Unless specially formulated to release nutrients slowly, the fertilizers in soilless composts are exhausted after about six weeks of active plant growth, whereas the loam content of soil-based mixtures will continue feeding plants for a little longer, after soluble fertilizers are exhausted. Supplementary feeding every week or fortnight then becomes necessary to sustain plants for the rest of the season.

After a year of root penetration and regular watering, the structure and freshness of the compost changes and so most plants need repotting in spring as they start the new season's growth. Tap a mature plant out of its pot and gently tease a little soil from the sides and surface of its rootball, before repacking it with fresh compost in the same size pot. You can restrain more substantial plants from growing too large by trimming back some of the thicker main roots at the same time as repotting. Topdress the plants that are too large to remove from their containers by scraping off the top few centimetres of old compost, and replacing it with a fresh one. Take care not to damage the roots or expose too many of them.

Younger, vigorous plants soon fill their pots with roots and need to be transferred to larger containers ('potting on'), in many cases more than once a year, if their steady growth is not to be checked. The easiest method of potting on is that used by blind gardeners and some commercial nurseries. First spread a layer of compost in the bottom of the new pot, centre the plant (still potted) as a template on this and pack compost around its sides. Twist the potted plant gently to free it from the compost, knock it out of its original container and then fit the rootball back into the perfectly shaped cavity. Settle the contents by bumping the new pot lightly on the table.

19

Mid SPRING

Everyone REVELS IN THE GARDEN THIS MONTH, NOT LEAST BECAUSE IT EXPLODES INTO COLOUR AND LIFE WHETHER WE TOIL OUTDOORS ALL WINTER OR HIBERNATE SNUGLY UNTIL THE LAWN NEEDS MOWING ONCE MORE.

Spring gardens 'happen' quite unaided, whereas for the rest of the year success depends on conscientious planting, watering, feeding and clearing, and if we fail to do these on time our neglect is sure to show.

My old garden foreman pretended never to see anything in flower. Once a plant reached maturity, he argued, he had done his bit, and he was far too busy planning ahead to enjoy the results of his skill and hard work. When I enthused about a magnolia in full bloom, he reminded me to sow the Brussels sprouts; if I pointed out a choice primula in flower, he told me to divide the violets. Such an attitude is perhaps extreme, but even as you admire the spring shrubs and pear blossom, it is worth checking that your secateurs are sharpened ready for pruning, to take with you wherever you walk. At this time of year there is always something to prune (providing it is not frosty). Evergreens such as yew hedges and laurel banks can be clipped to shape – next month might be wiser in cold gardens, but if you wait until hawthorn buds begin to burst, you will not go far wrong.

Eucalyptus should be cut back hard, sawing branches down to bare stumps, to stimulate plenty of young decorative growth. Prune buddleias hard too, or leave a few longer stems in the centre if you want taller bushes. Trim forsythia as soon as flowering ceases, removing a few of the older branches completely and shortening other flowering shoots. Pinch the ends from stems of flowering quince (chaenomeles) to divert energy to the flower buds, and once blooms fade, cut the exhausted shoots back to one or two leaves.

WHAT TO WATCH FOR THIS MONTH

Fruit trees and bushes SWATHED IN BLOSSOM, GAMBLING WITH SPRING FROSTS

Hedgerow buds BURSTING — CUE TO SOW HARDY FLOWERS AND VEGETABLES

FLOWERING *lilac* TO GATHER IN BUNCHES AND THEN PRUNE HARD AFTER BLOOMS FADE

Seedlings MATURING RAPIDLY INTO YOUNG PLANTS FOR HARDENING OFF AND PLANTING AS TEMPERATURES RISE

When he wasn't preparing us for the next task in hand, the old foreman would test us on vinery management, one of his favourite topics. Vineries are exalted places, and few of us are blessed with them now, but a grape vine is worth growing, whether in a greenhouse or conservatory for fruit, or outdoors for shade and vivid autumn colours. Plant now before it is too late, choosing 'Muscat of Alexandria', the supreme dessert grape for a warm conservatory; outdoors plant the ornamental 'Brandt', 'Millers Burgundy' ('Wrotham Pinot') against a dark background, or 'Purpurea' on paler walls and pergolas.

INSPIRATION

VINE GROWING TODAY For centuries the grape vine was a symbol of economic security. When Charles II addressed his countrymen in England in 1684, he revived the Biblical image (Micah, IV, 4) of the independent householder sitting beneath his own vine and fig tree. Yet, today, despite the remarkable renaissance of British vineyards, vines are still usually seen in the context of stately homes and large hothouses rather than in more modest back gardens. This is a pity, for many vines crop reliably outdoors in temperate climates, while a small greenhouse or conservatory provides enough protection for some of the more classic dessert grapes to be able to produce fruit with little or no heat. Moreover, many gardeners do not appreciate or are unaware of how docile and attractive vines can be when they are grown as ornamental climbers. They can support themselves by their twining tendrils

and often develop brilliant tints in the autumn.

Although reliably hardy, outdoor vines are most often grown as decorative climbers or for wine; in a good year some varieties achieve dessert quality, but this is best accepted as a bonus. There are only a few hardy black grape varieties available. Dessert grapes are most likely to ripen on a warm sheltered wall trained like an espalier – that is, with a main vertical stem and several evenly spaced horizontal branches, from which fruiting sideshoots are produced each year. Wall-grown vines need watering frequently as the soil near walls dries out rapidly.

The decorative virtues of grape vines are most obvious when they are grown less formally. A vigorous variety such as *Vitis coignetiae* (above), will rapidly clothe a wire netting fence, trellis or archway, transforming it into a riot of autumn colour, especially if combined with an ivy such as cream and green *Hedera colchica* 'Dentata variegata'. The reddish-purple leaves of the Teinturier grape (*V. vinifera* 'Purpurea') blend regally with a richly coloured rambling rose such as 'Crimson Shower' or 'Violette'. Try this partnership on a pergola or over a garden seat to transform it into a seductive arbour, and add annual blue morning-glories for spectacular contrast.

A gaunt or unfruitful tree is the perfect site for energetic *V. coignetiae* or *V. amurensis* grown together with 'Paul's Himalayan Musk' rose, planted 60-90cm (2-3ft) from the trunk and trained up to meet the tree branches, after which they should need no encouragement to climb. The less vigorous parsley leafed vine (*V.* 'Ciotat') can be used to transform a tree stump into a charming mound of finely cut foliage, while white-felted 'Dusty Miller', *V. vinifera* 'Incana', creates a dramatic impact when scrambling through purple-leaved shrubs.

Both the last two vines make graceful weeping standards, when trained on a simple framework to support the heavy trailing growth. Erect a sturdy pole 1.8-2.4m (6-8ft) high and cap it with an old bicycle wheel, using a carriage bolt where the axle would be. The main stem is trained to the top of the pole, where the growing tip is cut off together with all but the topmost sideshoots. Alternatively, support the vine with a cane at the centre of a pair or trio of vertical posts whose tops are linked by a stout wire hoop. Allow about five or six branches to grow from the top and over the rim of the wheel or hoop. Pruned back to 30cm (1ft) every autumn, these will produce a mass of pendant growth annually, the young stems reaching right to the ground in a cascade of foliage.

FOCUS ON FOOD

REMARKABLE BEAN FEASTS After retraining young runner bean plants unravelled from their canes by wind, I wrote to a magazine with a wide overseas circulation and asked whether beans twined themselves in the opposite direction south of the

Above A vine such as *Vitis vinifera* 'Purpurea' is an ideal companion for climbing roses, it's flamboyant foliage hides any bare stems that would otherwise be visible

Equator, in the same way that water swirls the other way down Antipodean plugholes. Many readers sent the results of experiments with both beans and bathwater, confirming a phenomenon they had not previously noticed.

Runner beans are just as remarkable below ground. Their thick roots are perennial and gardeners blessed with a frost-free garden can mulch them over winter to save them for another year. In cooler climates, roots can be dug up and stored like dahlias for replanting early the following summer. Like most legumes, the roots also make their own fertilizer, by courtesy of soil-borne bacteria that penetrate the root hairs and produce gall-like structures, called root nodules, in which they manufacture a steady supply of nitrogen. Wise gardeners cut down exhausted peas and beans, leaving the decaying roots to release their nitrogen into the soil, like the farmer's break-crops of clover, lucerne and sainfoin, legumes that are dug in to raise fertility. In some parts of the world it is normal to grow beans among rows of sweetcorn for their mutual benefit: the corn thrives on the surplus nitrogen, providing the less robust beans with shelter and support in return.

In our village, runner beans are best known as a prime topic for gossip and competition. At this time of year, rumours start circulating about whose beans are already 7.5cm (3in) high in pots and which sluggard has not yet sown them. Next month bamboo cane rows appear and wigwams sprout in every vegetable garden, but by mid-summer anticipation regularly turns to dismay as flowers start dropping and beans refuse to set.

Most of us in fact sow too early, so that vines begin flowering when the summer air is still dry. While spraying blooms with water and keeping roots consistently moist may help, delayed sowing is the best policy – aim for late spring – for late summer is prime runner bean time, when the sultry heat and evening humidity ensure rapid growth and certain pollination, not to mention a prodigious yield that can daunt the keenest appetite. Surplus pods may be frozen, but results are a poor imitation of fresh crops. Salting is the traditional method of preserving, and preferable if you have the patience and are careful to use crock pots or dark glass jars, together with coarse sea salt. Soak salted beans overnight before cooking. If you cannot wait a few weeks, sow runner beans now in small pots or boxes for planting out in a month's time under cloches or some other protection against late frost.

Sweet, wrinkle-seeded peas, such as 'Kelvedon Wonder', 'Little Marvel' and 'Douce Provence' can be sown safely now in a sunny bed or where the soil has been warmed with cloches for a couple of weeks. Sowings this month often avoid attacks by the pea moth, which ruins pods with its grubs that are most active on plants flowering from mid- to late summer. Peas need plenty of space, so don't expect to grow enough for freezing: just sow short rows to eat raw in salads. Even short varieties benefit from support such as twiggy hazel sticks or canes and netting, best provided before the tiny plants develop their first tendrils and search for something to climb. Picking should begin four weeks after full flower.

Where you have room in a greenhouse or polytunnel sow a few climbing French beans such as 'Climbing Blue Lake' in pots under glass, to plant in late spring for heavy pickings while you wait for the first scarlet runners to set and fatten. Once runner beans start cropping, pinch the tips from the French crop and strip off all the leaves to deter red spider mite. If you continue watering and feeding the vines, sideshoots will appear and start flowering for a second autumn crop after the runner beans have been killed by frosts.

IMPROVING ROOT CROPS Although renowned for growing the best root crops, light soils do have their disadvantages. Swedes and turnips, for example, are really members of the brassica family and so prefer to fatten their roots in more substantial ground; sandy soils produce only second-grade crops that often split in a dry season. One solution is to grow turnips fast in well-manured ground with a mulch of garden compost or grass clippings as a buffer against rapid drying; the yellow turnip 'Orange Jelly' yields an acceptable substitute for swedes on the plate, and reaches a good size and quality if the soil is well enriched with humus and contains ample water.

PLANT HIGHLIGHTS OF THE MONTH

Fritillaries **Fritillaries, with their demure charm, offer a graceful celebration of spring's arrival. Crown imperials (*Fritillaria imperialis*) are the beaux of the family, handsome and regal with clusters of pendant bells – scarlet, vivid orange or golden yellow. Other less flamboyant species range from *F. persica***

'Adiyaman', tall and sultry purple, to *F. michailovskyi*, with flowers like red and green elfin caps. Plant snake's head fritillaries (*F. meleagris*), chequered purple or pure white, in drifts on well-drained soil beneath deciduous trees.

Melons **Where greenhouse space is rationed, don't bother growing cucumbers: home-grown crops either sulk or produce an embarrassing glut. Instead try sowing the bush melon 'Minnesota Midget' which bears small juicy fruit in 20cm (8in) pots or grow-bags. For training up netting the F_1 hybrid 'Sweetheart' crops**

early, and is easy to grow in a soil border or planted one at each end of a grow-bag. Germinate seeds now in small pots in warmth, and keep plants growing fast for a long fruiting season.

Gaillardias **Perennial gaillardias flower zealously until the frosts, but their lives tend to be short unless clumps are divided now for replanting in rich soil. Cherish them, for their large cheerful daisies – rich burgundy, or red and orange in concentric rings – are indispensable to the summer border. In cold or**

wet gardens, cut young side pieces in autumn and pot up for wintering under glass, or buy a packet of seeds as insurance; if sown now, plants often flower in their first season.

You are on safer ground with other roots grown in light soils. Perfect shape and quality depends upon easy penetration, and deep cultivation for longer-rooted varieties. Fork the ground thoroughly before sowing, pulverize clods by tamping them with an upright rake, and then remove as many larger stones as possible – on very stony ground, rake them to the side of rows and leave on the surface as they can by put to good use as temporary paths.

Accessible fresh manure is notorious for causing roots to divide into fangs, but it is a mistake to assume therefore that root crops need little sustenance: either bury fully-decayed manure below the first spit, or if possible follow a manured crop such as legumes or brassicas with carrots, parsnips and other roots, which can then mop up nutrient residues.

Sow an early carrot variety now (eg 'Tip Top'), and then repeat every three to four weeks until late summer; maincrop carrots (eg 'Autumn King') for storing are sown next month. Keep all the sowings together so that they can be enclosed in a 30-38cm (12-15in) high 'fence' of clear polythene as a barrier against carrot root fly, or build up a thick mulch of grass clippings to deceive the pest and to keep the soil evenly moist.

Parsnips can be sown as late as mid-summer for small sweet roots, but if you want large ones start now, when the seeds germinate faster than earlier sowings. Any parsnips still left from last year can be dug up and buried in a group out of the way, where they will stay usable for several weeks; once they begin growing again, roots become too woody for the kitchen but they can be used to make potent wine.

While sowing parsnips, add a row of salsify or scorzonera as an alternative for winter use. Choose root varieties to match the depth of top soil; you need two spits of friable soil for the longest kinds, but even the shallowest ground will support a stumpy carrot like 'Rondo' or the short parsnip 'White Gem', which is also blessed with canker resistance.

PLANNING

ANNUALS TO THE RESCUE Like paprika and penetrating oil, annual flowers are for keeping near at hand to resolve problems and inadequacies as they arise. Most varieties germinate eagerly any time during the growing season, and can be used to fill gaps or sustain a display when other plants begin to fade. Summers are not always as genial as we would like, for exam-

ple, and just in case main bedding displays are washed out or burnt up early, you can plan now for an autumn surge of colour by sowing zinnias, rudbeckias and annual asters (properly called Callistephus). Compact and tall varieties are available for bedding.

Save seeds of more precocious kinds (some flowering when only six to eight weeks old) to sow as mid-summer approaches for successional colour from late summer onwards. Asperula, limnanthes, clarkia, godetia, *Dimorphotheca aurantiaca* (Star of the Veldt), linaria and night-scented stocks will all bloom soon after sowing and last until the first frosts. Scatter candytuft and Virginian stocks to fill the gaps in between herbaceous perennials, and to succeed bulbs as their foliage dies down; they rarely fail to self-seed for future seasons.

Taller annuals such as *Chrysanthemum tricolor*, gypsophila, cornflowers, larkspur, *Centaurea moschata* (sweet sultan) and scabious make long-lasting cut flowers, worth sowing for this purpose in lines among vegetables to rest overworked soil as a break-crop or to follow crops as they mature: try sowing scarlet poppies to infiltrate raspberries or potatoes, for example. Phacelia, Sweet Alyssum and nemophila can be sown direct in rows to make a pretty, dwarf edging for beds; broadcast patches of alyssum in sunny spots for its pervasive scent of ripe honey on hot afternoons, and leave in place to volunteer seedlings thereafter in every nook and cranny.

OF TREES, TUBS AND WATER LILIES Growing outdoor plants in pots is an ancient and enduring art. Around 1480BC the ambitious Egyptian Empress Hatshepsut sent a botanical expedition up the Nile to the neighbouring kingdom of Punt (Somalia). They returned with 'many fine plants and green myrrh trees' to augment her already extensive collection. According to contemporary accounts, these trees were planted in baskets for the journey home to Thebes, there to be potted into large tubs and arranged in enclosed courtyards.

Nearly 3500 years later the practice survives, and some years ago I was given the intriguing job of repotting two dozen tall laburnum trees, kept at the council nursery for the rare royal visits to the city. On such occasions the trees would come into their glory, enclosing the obligatory red carpet in an avenue of gracefully arching branches and golden blossom. Most of the time, though, they passed sheltered lives plunged in the soil at the back of a border, where they quietly flowered

Opposite Blue is a rare but desirable flower colour; introduce gems such as *Centaurea cyanus* dwarf blue to relieve brighter colours. Below Hardiest of the citrus family, lemons still need protection in British winters but revel in full sun outdoors for the rest of the year

unnoticed. They were dug up every few years for us to clean the 38cm (15in) pots in which they were confined, renew some of the compost, and prune the roots and branches before returning them to their seclusion.

Do not be dismayed by traditional claims that successful cultivation in pots is the test of a true gardener. If you remember the basic principles of good drainage, regular watering and feeding, and protection in winter, any mystique surrounding the craft will soon evaporate. Experience shows there are few plants that cannot be grown in pots, at least for a large part of their lives. Even though there is a wide choice of containers, habit and caution still restrict the range of plants attempted.

With understanding and a little confidence, the possibilities are unlimited. For centuries, Chinese gardeners have grown all manner of plants in pots, sometimes creating whole potted gardens, with shrubs arranged as hedges, and trees flourishing in larger containers. Citrus fruits in white wooden Versailles boxes are a classic European combination, but many other trees are equally suitable. In partial shade acers are excellent; weeping trees, too, are outstanding features in pots, especially the popular Kilmarnock willow, *Salix caprea pendula*, from whose silky grey buds golden catkins burst in early spring. The silvery-green weeping pear, *Pyrus salicifolia pendula*, with a cream froth of blossom in spring, grows slowly to a height of 3-3.6m (10-12ft) and thrives in a 45cm (18in) container, as will *Betula pendula* 'Youngii', the weeping birch whose limp branches cascade to the ground. To fully appreciate the corkscrew hazel (*Corylus avellana* 'Contorta'), grow it in a decorative pot raised up so that the bare winter stems, curiously twisted like Harry Lauder's walking stick, are silhouetted against a clear blue sky.

If you have difficult soil such as clay or chalk, containers can house plants that might quickly languish in the open garden. Not only will familiar lime-hating shrubs such as hybrid rhododendrons, azaleas and the many beautiful kinds of pieris, all revel in a chalk-free ericaceous compost, but other less obviously fussy plants will welcome their own special patch of acid soil. Our pearl bush, *Exochorda racemosa*, grew quickly from seed, and twice we watched the pure white blossoms shimmer in the spring sunshine before unaccountably fading. We discovered its low tolerance of lime too late. A tubful of acid compost might easily have prolonged its life.

A half barrel will house any of these trees and shrubs comfortably for many years. If it is made totally waterproof with a lining of plastic sheeting, you can also use one at this time of year to make a small courtyard water garden, complete with miniature water lilies and other aquatic or marginal plants. Soil discolours the water, so spread a layer of clean gravel at the bottom, and grow the plants in baskets of water lily compost covered with gravel. Select one of the restrained pygmy water lilies for the centre and stand its basket on the bottom. Around this arrange two or three choice marginal plants (blue-flowered pontederia, menyanthes or bog bean, and dwarf irises, for example), their baskets raised on bricks to bring them to just below the surface.

UNDER GLASS

POTTED FRUITS With blossom all around, mid-spring is the natural time to consider adding fruit to the garden. Most fruits adapt to pots and ornamental containers; even normally large trees such as apricots, peaches or tender pear varieties are suitable. Immense skill was once needed to restrict vigorous growth, but modern dwarf rootstocks combined with basic pruning to maintain an open compact framework of branches, has considerably simplified cultivation. A 30-38cm (12-15in) clay or plastic pot is usually large enough at first; use a small tub or planter for bigger specimens. Rich compost is essential, preferably a soil-based mixture such as John Innes No 3. This should be rammed firm when potting, by using the handle of a trowel or a piece of broomstick to pound the compost into place. Repot late every winter, teasing compost gently from the outer roots with a plant label and then replacing it with fresh soil; in larger containers, only the top 7-10cm (3-4in) of compost need be renewed.

Some of the most popular trees for pots are the various citrus fruits, especially lemons and oranges. These are often grown as houseplants but seldom fruit indoors; in a greenhouse

or conservatory with good light and a minimum temperature of 5°C (40°F), however, they can flower or fruit, sometimes both at the same time, all the year round. Most types of citrus can be grown as bushes or half standards. Thin fruits while tiny, leaving those intended to ripen deep in the bush, and pinch out the ends of shoots when fruits have set. Stand the plants outdoors in summer, first moving them on a mild still day to accustom them to the open air.

In Germany, gooseberries are often grown as small weeping trees, and a dessert variety trained this way makes an ornate addition to a greenhouse collection. Choose a naturally lax, good flavoured variety (red kinds are particularly tasty when ripened under glass, try 'London') and either order a ready-shaped grafted standard, or grow your own from a cutting, pruned to form a tall single stem; at the required height pinch it out to encourage sideshoots from the top. The main stem needs a stout cane for support, topped by a wire hoop over which the sideshoots are trained. These lateral branches are permanent and should be kept tied in place, so that they will radiate like the ribs of an umbrella. Arch the branches gracefully downwards and secure their tips with twine to the main stem for a season or so, until they remain naturally in position. Sideshoots (one-year-old or more) from these branches bear the gooseberries; prune new sideshoots back to about 15cm (6in) in mid-summer and then again to 5cm (2in) in winter to retain the weeping shape.

Apples grown as cordons or small pyramids are excellent pot plants, but a naturally non-branching type recently made available might prove even more adaptable. In 1960 a Canadian apple 'sported' an unusual form with no sideshoots, its flowers and fruit all appearing on short spurs on the single stem. This has been developed into a race of columnar trees, usually grafted on MM106 (semi-dwarfing) rootstocks, which can grow to 3.6m (12ft) high but may be kept much shorter – after five years they will be about 2.4m (8ft) tall. They are naturally compact and need no pruning, other than to maintain the final height. When grown in 30cm (12in) pots, they make unique flowering and fruiting pillars among other conservatory shrubs. Remember that, like all other greenhouse fruits, they need to be pollinated by hand if they remain under glass while in bloom. Tap or gently shake flowering stems, transfer pollen from one flower to another with a soft paint-brush, or simply stand the pots outdoors if the weather is mild. Most fruit trees and bushes benefit from a summer holiday in the open air, which helps ripen new stems, reduces the threat from red spider mite, and improves the overall health of all pot plants.

DOWN TO EARTH

HARDENING OFF Though fashionably branded as a menace in our diets, sugar plays a crucial role in the metabolism of plants. It forms part of their basic food reserves, assists pollination and seed-dispersal by tempting birds and insects to forage, and is largely responsible for the vivid leaf tints we enjoy in autumn.

The survival of plants in cold weather also depends on the protective level of sugars deep inside leaves and stems: a higher sugar content reduces the likelihood of their cells freezing in frosty weather. Plants that are grown under glass in artificial heat have a watery sap that confers little immunity to low temperatures. Even nominally hardy flower and vegetable plants, if removed abruptly from the warmth of a greenhouse in spring, are liable to succumb to cold weather outdoors unless first tempered by 'hardening off'.

A coldframe with an adjustable opening light to allow gradual exposure to fresh air is the ideal aid for hardening off, but you can acclimatize plants effectively without one. Choose the hardiest young plants – early brassicas, broad beans or hardy annuals, for example – and during a mild spell, perhaps occurring as early as mid-spring, stand their trays outside in a sheltered place. Bring them back under cover as afternoon temperatures fall, and repeat this process on successive days, leaving the plants out for a little longer each time. After a week or so, they should be able to withstand a frost-free night outdoors. Two or three weeks of this gradual exposure will prepare them for planting out, but once you have done this, it is still a good idea to cover them for a few more nights should temperatures plummet.

Hardening off in a cold frame follows the same routine. Protect the plants by keeping the lid closed at first, and cover with mats or old carpets if frost intervenes. Starting with just a crack of air by day, increase the ventilation until the contents are completely open to the elements, after which they can safely be planted out. It is best to wait until late spring before preparing half-hardy annuals and tender vegetables, starting about three to four weeks before the last expected frosts, as no amount of hardening off will render them totally immune to sub-zero temperatures. Houseplants and greenhouse perennials need a similar, though shorter, introduction to the open air when transferred outdoors for the summer; choose a mild day to stand them out at first, and be ready to re-house them during the first week if the weather turns cold.

FRAMEWORK

FURNITURE OUTDOORS Seats, fences, arches and pergolas require some kind of seasonal maintenance if they are to last. Stone needs little attention apart from an occasional clean, and its appearance steadily improves with age, but other materials should be given regular protective treatment for long life. In spring, clean deposits of algae from metal and painted wooden structures with a stiff brush and repaint every two to three years, taking care first to touch up exposed patches with rust inhibitor or the appropriate primer. Seats made from finished timber are best moved under cover for the winter, a task made much easier if they are fitted with wheels and handles. With the exception of durable species such as elm, paint bare wood annually with preservative or a wood oil when quite dry, and stand the legs of seats and tables in containers of preservative to soak for 24 hours.

It is rarely worth the effort to treat rustic timber unless the bark has been stripped, for this normally protects the wood for several years, and broken or rotten pieces can be easily replaced. Felled or fallen timber of all kinds is a valuable material for turning

Wood is perhaps the most adaptable material for seating; whether used as finished timber in the intimate seat at Wyken Hall (above) or in its natural fallen state as a trunk supported on two butts (below)

into simple and serviceable structures that harmonize instantly in most gardens. Even slender branches can be used for furniture provided they are sound and well-supported. Members are best nailed into place, but blunt each nail first so that it tears a hole when driven in – a sharp nail may split the wood for quite a distance. The thinnest branches can be used for infilling on furniture; try weaving long willow, hazel or ash stems into the back and seat of a rustic chair to form decorative basketwork.

When felling a large tree, cut it higher than usual to leave a stump tall enough to shape into a simple chair, treating the cut surfaces with a suitable herbicide to prevent re-growth. To make a bench, use the horizontal length of a tree trunk, either firmly bedded in the ground or raised at each end on a vertical piece of the trunk. To transform a thicker trunk section into an armchair or settee, use a chain saw to make two longitudinal cuts through to the heart wood, one parallel with the back

Above Of all the available colours, a truly lilac syringa variety, such as 'Louis Van Houtt' is the most fragrant and prolific

and another to define the seat; by cutting into the log a few centimetres from each end, a quadrant of wood can then be removed. There is no need to apply a preservative.

GARDEN SURGERY

LILAC MAINTENANCE Until experiments to breed ornamental cut-leaved varieties reach fruition, we must accept that lilac is glorious in spring, with the intoxicating fragrance of its flowers and the oddly matt intensity of its colours, but it is rather dreary for the rest of the year. As though overcompensating for its dullness, it attracts attention instead by its energetic growth, especially if grown in open positions in fertile chalky soils, and either by producing annual crops of suckers or by blooming in alternate years when very tall.

Most lilacs need regular pruning every year if they are not to change quickly from elegant shrubs into spreading trees 7.5m (25ft) or more high. They are normally pruned immediately after flowering, by shortening the old stems that have just flowered: cut just above a pair of buds slightly below the height you want to maintain. Each of these buds will produce a stem that should flower the following year, but if this grows too vigorously, pinch off the tip in late summer to divert energy into further sideshoots.

Overgrown bushes and lilacs with a tendency to flower biennially need hard pruning back to size when they are dormant. This usually results in the growth of a thicket of soft, sappy shoots, the weakest of which need early thinning to leave an open arrangement of strong branches; these may have to be shortened in summer if they become too long. The shoots which then break from the pair of buds immediately below each cut should form flowering stems for the following spring. Replacing the top growth lost by pruning and hard cutting back, absorbs a lot of energy, and if this is not to be diverted away from the blooms, you must feed the bushes. The most profuse flowering results from annual top-dressings of rotted manure, but a spring application of bonemeal, or a slow-release granular fertilizer, is an acceptable substitute.

Try to avoid cultivating deeply around lilac bushes, because injuring the shallow roots with a spade or fork is the commonest cause of persistent suckering. Once you get suckers, there is little to do except cut or pull them off annually, although you could dig them up with portions of root attached to move elsewhere as new plants. Even if the resulting plants turn out to be the common lilac-coloured *Syringa vulgaris* from the rootstock of a grafted tree, their sweet fragrance will certainly make it a worthwhile exercise.

PRUNING

BENDING THE RULES There are countless stories, apocryphal and otherwise, of gardeners who cheerfully abandon pruning dogma with impunity, while the rest of us, bewildered by the niceties of this apparently complex science, snip away cautiously to no avail. Once, while quietly tidying up an avenue of 'Queen Elizabeth' roses, I was interrupted by the local milkman, who stopped his float and demanded to see my secateurs. 'No good,' he snorted contemptuously, 'they are much too flimsy. I broke two pairs like this on my roses. Took the chainsaw to them in the end. The missis thought I'd murdered them, but didn't they flower that year, though!'

His was a healthy attitude to a technique that has become needlessly mysterious. Pruning is a simple skill, invaluable for shaping and rejuvenating plants, or for improving yields of fruit and blossom; it deserves none of the obscurity with which it is usually approached. Nor in practice is there a closed season for pruning. The almost legendary Fred Streeter, seldom seen without his secateurs, insisted that pruning should be continued throughout the year, not just when a plant needed it but above all whenever the gardener felt like doing it.

Inclination is one important requirement, confidence another. The first rule of pruning is never to cut without a good reason, for a severed stem cannot be replaced except by the plant in its own time. It is better not to prune at all than to remove either too much or the wrong parts altogether. Some plants are very forgiving, or even thrive on savage surgery, and pruning certain kinds of rose severely is now approved by some authorities. Do the same to an apple or pear tree, however, and you may sacrifice much of the fruit crop, rather like gardeners of an earlier generation who believed in strict training and sculpted apple trees into perfect goblets or similar conceits; every branch or spur ruining the symmetry of a row was cut off, regardless of the potential fruit that might be lost.

There is no best way to prune, apart from making sure that your tools are sharp and every pruning cut clean; otherwise the rules are infinitely adaptable. If you are afraid that pruning an apple tree in winter will cut off all the fruit buds, wait until it flowers and then trim it to size and shape with an eye to leaving enough blossom for a crop. If the tree flowers during hard frost, trim off the tips of spurs where the first blooms have opened, in order to conserve energy for the later flowers at their base which may have escaped injury. On the other hand, keep things as simple as possible when tackling a densely overgrown tree or shrub, and saw off one or two complete branches to open up the centre, as opposed to snipping aimlessly at every twig.

Concentrate first on removing dead, diseased and exhausted growth, and follow this with cosmetic pruning to maintain a pleasant shape. As confidence is gained in the basic techniques of ensuring the good health, productivity and appearance of your plants, you will start to discover some of the subtler methods of finely tuning a plant's habit and performance. Its flowering season, for example, can be delayed by pruning later than is normally recommended, or advanced a little by not pruning at all. Showmen have developed this to a precise art, and know, often to the day, when to stop pruning and pinching out shoots so that plants will flower on a given date. Experiment with a buddleia, pruning a few stems at a particular time every month from late winter to late spring to give a prolonged succession of bloom.

Late SPRING

Gardeners IN PRIVATE SERVICE HAVE TRADI-
TIONALLY LIVED 'OVER THE SHOP'. THIS MEANS THAT YOU
ARE NEVER QUITE OFF-DUTY, BUT THERE ARE PERKS, SUCH
AS FINDING THE FIRST RIPE NECTARINE BEFORE ANYONE
ELSE, AND POSITIVE ADVANTAGES, ESPECIALLY THIS MONTH
WHEN FROST IS STILL A CONSTANT MENACE.

Late spring is both winsome and treacherous, and many times I
have been lulled into a false security by a benign weather
report at teatime, only to hear the late forecast predicting sharp
frost, thus prompting a dash outside by torchlight to close
frames and ventilators.

Tender plants in cold frames are the likeliest victims, especially if they are left exposed overnight in the last stages of
hardening off. Fine afternoons with clear skies should find you
prepared to close frames and greenhouse windows, and to keep
young potato haulm tucked up with soil to protect against the
frost. After a chilly night, bright early morning sunshine thaws
frozen tissues too fast and can be lethal, but it is sometimes possible to reduce injury by 'washing' frost off plants: unless the
yellow centres of early strawberry blooms have been ruinously
blackened, try spraying the frost away with a hose before the
sun reaches them. Above all, don't plant out summer bedding
too early, however blithe the weather: nurserymen love
impetuous gardeners, whom they expect to welcome back for
more plants after late spring frosts. The end of this month is
soon enough to set out most bedding plants, but wait another
two to three weeks before risking sensitive salvias, geraniums
and dahlias, especially if you live in a cooler district.

A head gardener working in North Yorkshire for a keen
English patriot was ordered always to plant geraniums early this
month, the same time as at Buckingham Palace. Being so far
north, frost inevitably killed them, until the gardener cunningly planted them very deep, so that at least the buried stools
survived the Yorkshire spring to grow again. In Warwickshire,

Bees and butterflies FORAGING FREELY WHERE THEIR FAVOURITE FLOWERS HAVE BEEN PLANTED

New leaf ON HEDGES, A REMINDER TO START CLIPPING AND TO PLANT NEW ONES

STRONG *clematis* STEMS EXTENDING DAILY FOR TRAINING OR LAYERING TO MAKE NEW PLANTS

A fresh vitality IN THE AIR UNDER GLASS, A SIGN OF GROWTH SURGING AHEAD

England, I move out fully hardened early varieties of runner beans ('Kelvedon Marvel'), sweet corn ('Kelvedon Sweetheart') and celery (self-blanching 'Celebrity') at about the middle of the month, but keep some kind of protection nearby for emergencies, because all are sensitive to frost – recycle bottomless 4.5 litre (1 gallon) plastic milk containers to make ideal improvised cloches.

In moist soil or just after a spring shower the plants are set out without further watering, but sometimes late spring is dry for days on end, and if that is the case you should give the ground a thorough soaking immediately after transplanting. During a drought, the old practice of 'puddling in' can be used as this normally prevents any check to growth: plants are positioned in their holes, which are then filled with water and left to drain, before being refilled with soil and firmed.

FRAMEWORK

FRAMING VEGETABLE BEDS In the days when appearance mattered as much as productivity in the kitchen garden, vegetable beds were edged with rows of plants intended as a permanent frame for the constantly changing contents. Due to their easy accessibility from the paths, flowers for cutting were a popular choice and is one worth reviving; use tidy, long-flowering annuals or hardy perennials to provide colour both outdoors and for vases. One dependable perennial is the double yellow coreopsis 'Sunray', 45cm (18in) tall and flowering all season. Equally pretty and prolific are the 'Jewel' strains of erigeron,

available both as individual colours or in a blend of pink, rose and pale blue. Although becoming a cliché in other parts of the garden, the luxurious grey-green foliage of *Alchemilla mollis*, or lady's mantle, makes an unusual and decorative kitchen garden edging for most of the year, its sprays of greenish-yellow blooms a popular bonus for flower-arrangers.

In formal vegetable gardens, beds were sometimes enclosed with miniature fences of apples. They were trained to about 30-38cm (12-15in) above the ground along horizontal canes or a wire stretched taut. Neat and permanent, this edging is easy to construct and maintain provided the right type of tree is used. Grow the apples as single-tier espaliers (one horizontal branch extending to each side) and choose varieties grafted on the most dwarfing rootstocks of all, M27 for rich soil or M26 on poorer ground. Planted about 1.5-1.8m (5-6ft) apart, these are trained and pruned in the same way as upright cordons, but look a great deal more decorative with their ankle-high froth of blossom in spring and a potential fruit crop of 1.8-2.3kg (4-5lb) in autumn. Rambling roses can be used in the same way, although they need occasional attention during the season to keep them tidy as new canes develop.

Some crops are themselves ideal for edging. Parsley is commonly used in this role, but as demand for it from the kitchen is limited, it is only really economical for small beds. A worthwhile crop of haricot beans, on the other hand, needs a lot of plants and these can be grown from seeds sown outdoors towards the end of this month, in a single row around the perimeter of a large vegetable bed. There they will form a compact and attractive hedge all season until cleared for harvest, leaving the ground free for winter cultivation.

A traditional hedging plant for kitchen gardens is dwarf box, *Buxus sempervirens* 'Suffruticosa', which can be clipped to less than 15cm (6in) high, although if left to grow naturally will slowly mature into a 60cm (2ft) shrub. Box hedges are notorious for harbouring slugs and snails, and also host woolly aphids in summer, but when looked after they make a pleasingly formal frame for a vegetable bed of any size. Larger box specimens are sometimes available, but are expensive due to their great age, and may be difficult to plant close together for hedging because of their large unmanageable root system. To start a formal hedge, choose young plants 15-20cm (6-8in) tall and space them 10cm (4in) apart; order bare-root stock from a specialist nursery, as container-grown plants can cost three times as much.

INSPIRATION

FLOWERING VEGETABLES Gardeners who delve into botany soon discover it is a joyously bizarre subject. Any reverence I felt towards my favourite science disappeared on learning that the proper name for nasturtium is *Tropaeolum*, whereas the botanically approved *Nasturtium* is what everyone else knows as watercress. Other oddities followed: the fruit of the strawberry is not a true fruit, it seems, because it wears its seeds on the outside, and no-one has ever seen a fig tree in flower, for its blooms hide deep inside the baby figs.

Above A single-tier apple espalier surrounding a bed.

Left *Box* is hardy in most areas and tolerant of all soils and sites except where drainage is poor

Plants, of course, are not to blame for the eccentricities of botany. Any absurdity lies within the system by which scientists group and classify the plant world, although they are no more illogical than gardeners who insist on segregating their plants into flowers, vegetables and fruit. It is because of this deep-seated habit that many people are surprised to find that garden flowers may be edible and that their vegetables bear attractive blooms. Exhorted to pull up crops the moment they 'bolt', we rarely give them a chance to reveal their finery.

Late spring is the time when overwintered vegetables come into flower and by mid-summer their seeds will be ripe. It is also the prime time for vegetable seed sowing and each year brings with it the chance to try new and alternative varieties. Some years ago I re-introduced seakale to a private estate. This is grown solely for its blanched stems and any flowers that appear are usually cut off, but as I needed the seeds to grow many more plants I left the remarkable 60cm (2ft) wide flower heads to set. Each seed was enclosed in a round white capsule, and I had to admit that the complete heads looked very handsome as they hung drying in the potting shed. My employer clearly thought so too, for one day shortly before Christmas they all disappeared up to the House, where I later found them sprayed with festive colours and arranged in vases.

In summer many crops tend to bolt and run to seed. On dry soils radishes are certain victims of hot weather, but do not despair, for their pods are worth saving, both for seed and for eating cooked or raw as a crunchy savoury; the variety which has the fattest, spiciest variety is 'München Bier' and it is grown specifically for this purpose. When past their prime leeks also produce decorative flower heads. If you grow 'Blue Solaise' with its stiking purple-blue foliage in cold weather, leave a few plants for their large drum-stick blooms. These can be dried and added to an indoor arrangement.

Some vegetables bloom in the normal course of cultivation, although their flowers seldom get the appreciation they deserve. In fact, gardeners are often advised to remove flower stems from crops such as chives and rhubarb in the belief that the plant will otherwise be weakened. If plants are fed annually, however, the neat mauve pompons of chives may safely be left for bees and butterflies. As commercial fields with their spectacular flowers testify, well-nourished rhubarb will come to no harm; its broad sculpted leaves and proud yucca-like flower stems add an exotic element to pool-side plantings, the ideal place for this ornate plant.

Although ordinary kinds of Jerusalem artichoke rarely flower in summer in cooler climates, the shorter variety 'Dwarf Sunray' regularly produces numerous sunny golden daisies. Perhaps the most brilliant impact in the kitchen garden, however, is provided by a row of runner beans in bloom,

PLANT HIGHLIGHTS OF THE MONTH

Raspberries **Energetic raspberry varieties have a habit of hiding their fruit amid a thicket of lofty new canes that will bear crops next year. Some training systems separate the two generations on parallel wires, but these take up too much room in smaller gardens. Simplify matters now by cutting to ground level all young canes that have appeared this year, thus leaving the fruiting stems unobstructed; a fresh crop of canes will soon follow, growing to a more manageable height after the summer harvest is finished.**

Forget-me-nots **Chosen by Henry IV as a personal emblem, forget-me-nots will soon be in full flower, carpeting woods and gardens alike with their dainty blue stars. Self-conscious gardeners call them myosotis and grow deep indigo strains as strict edging, but the ordinary sky-blue forget-me-nots are cheerier, planted in drifts on their own or beneath an early tulip such as 'Princess Irene'. Let existing plants seed themselves, or sow now and line seedlings in a nursery bed; plants are perennial and chance pink- or white-flowered seedlings can be kept going by division.**

Laburnum **Sophisticates may dismiss it as common, and alarmists condemn it for its toxic seeds (in fact all parts are poisonous if eaten), but Golden Chain undoubtedly remains one of late spring's unfailing glories. *L.* x *watereri* 'Vossii' is the loveliest, with long heavy racemes of bright yellow flowers; Scotch laburnum, *L. alpinum*, comes into its own later and has gleaming leaves and very fragrant blooms. Grow them in abundance over arches and pergolas, fan-train flat against a house-wall, or keep a specimen shapely in a courtyard tub.**

and it is easy to understand why they were once grown chiefly for ornament. Exploit their flamboyance by planting double rows, one each side of a path, and joining their 2.4m (8ft) canes overhead to create a tunnel; scarlet, white and pink/white bicolours are available, and mixed together make a startling tapestry of colour.

The predominantly mauve flowers of purple climbing beans and tall peas are almost as colourful as the crops themselves, and are ideal for creating tunnels and covering screens. There are dwarfer purple beans for ground-level use, while lowliest of all is the outstandingly pretty asparagus pea, *Tetragonolobus purpureus*. Though not a true pea, in summer this vigorous ground-cover plant is studded with brilliant red blossom, followed by the short winged pods coveted by connoisseurs. The same rich colour was once to be seen in some varieties of broad bean, but despite their beauty all but one red strain seem sadly to have disappeared.

NONCONFORMIST HEDGING In late spring, plant growth really takes off and nowhere is this more obvious than in lawns and garden hedges, where it will be impossible to delay the start of regular clipping. Improving a conventional hedge can help compensate for this chore. The same few familiar species are usually suggested for hedging: privet, beech, hornbeam, hawthorn, or various conifers, most of which grow much too fast and look alien in a garden context.

There are a great many other hedging plants which are adaptable to a variety of sites and positions and yet are not so widely used. For tall divisions, try growing the purple hazel, *Corylus maxima* 'Atropurpurea', which must be trimmed at mid-summer; forsythia, to be pruned late in summer and again after flowering; the evergreen *Photinia* x *fraseri* 'Red Robin' with crimson young growth; or *Prunus laurocerasus* 'Herbergii', an erect cherry laurel which must be pruned at mid-summer like the red photinia.

For opulent colour, choose *Berberis thunbergii* 'Atropurpurea', a deep purple shrub with yellow flowers in late spring. It can be clipped to shape until the autumn, when the foliage first turns an intense crimson and then falls to expose red berries. A hedge of this kind will grow to 1.2-1.5m (4-5ft) if allowed, but its dwarf cousin, 'Atropurpurea Nana' is only half the height and a perfect substitute for box as an edging for vegetable beds. Another low hedging plant is 90cm (3ft) high *Euonymus alatus* 'Compactus', a dense slow-growing spindle bush with pink or scarlet autumn tints and purple fruits.

Herbs make versatile hedges too, their use for this dating back to medieval times when washing was draped on them to dry and capture a little of their perfume. Lavender is always popular, especially the robust *Lavandula spica* 'Grappenhall', with strong flowering stems up to 1.2m (4ft) tall. In full sun, the dwarf French hedging lavender (*L. stoechas*) is easily raised from seed and flowers prolifically with an intense fragrance.

Opposite Scarlet Chilean glory vine relieves the sobriety of the yew hedge without destroying its classic formality.

Above Although grown for its winged pods, the asparagus pea is equally successful as decorative ground-cover

Rosemary, hyssop, germander, steely-blue rue and cotton lavender (*Santolina chamaecyparissus*) all tolerate being clipped into dwarf scented hedges around beds, or between them as divisions in the style of old knot gardens.

Privet hedges are generally disliked, not so much for their appearance as for their extensive greedy root systems which prevent much else from growing nearby. One stalwart survivor which carpets the ground beneath our golden privet hedge is sweet woodruff (*Asperula odorata*), a dainty woodland herb spangled with brilliant white stars in early summer, whose dried flower stems can be used to perfume tea and linen.

Many plants, in fact, relish the shelter and dry soils typical of hedge bottoms, and flourish despite competition for water and nutrients – some of the prettiest wild flowers, after all, are found beneath wayside hedges. Numerous bulbs are happy there, especially crocuses (*Crocus flavus* and *C. tommasinianus* are outstanding) snowdrops, winter aconites, bluebells, colchicums and the variegated *Arum italicum* 'Pictum'. In more moist soils trilliums and erythroniums are also reliable.

Hedges that are only trimmed once a year can support a number of climbing plants, such as tall nasturtiums, which scramble cheerfully through the foliage and flower more profusely in an elevated position. Dark-leafed hedges are ideal hosts for *Tropaeolum speciosum*, the perennial crimson flame flower, or for the scarlet and yellow Chilean glory vine, *Eccremocarpus scaber*; this may be killed by hard frost, but seedlings usually appear the following year. The small summer-flowering clematises, *Clematis tangutica* and *C. viticella*, are both suitable and bloom all the better if cut back together with the hedge in spring.

GARDEN SURGERY

FIREBLIGHT The approach of summer brings with it a growing threat of fireblight, the fungal disease that affects members of the *Rosaceae* family and which seems to have been on the increase in recent years. This is partly because gardeners regard it as some kind of normal die back rather than as an insidious and disabling complaint. Hawthorn is one of its principle hosts, and in parts of the country where this species is widely used in hedgerows, spread of infection is inevitable.

Apples and pears, together with cotoneasters, pyracanthas and related ornamental shrubs, are most at risk. The pear variety 'Laxton's Superb' has been banned from cultivation in parts of Britain as it produces late blossom in summer when fireblight spores are most prevalent. Shoots of other susceptible species are just as vulnerable to spore invasion as the flowers, and it is there that the most obvious symptoms are seen.

Young shoots die for no apparent reason, and assume a brown scorched appearance – hence the name of the disease. Leaves turn dark brown and hang there, except for hawthorn whose leaves often fall prematurely. Symptoms appear in summer, often after heavy rain which distributes spores down the stems from their initial sites. Insects also play a part in spreading the bacteria. The extent and impact of infection varies: sometimes a complete tree will be killed by the disease, sometimes a single bough or just a few shoots. Cutting these off usually reveals a dark staining beneath the bark, on which a white slime, rich in spores, also appears in humid conditions.

Treatment must be surgical. Infected stems and branches must be cut off, working back until the exposed tissues are free from stain. Keep a pot of disinfectant solution nearby, and dip tools in this frequently during and after use. Burn all prunings, together with fallen leaves around the victim, as these may carry spores and cause re-infection.

POLLINATION PROBLEMS There is more to producing a good crop of fruit than simply planting a tree and waiting. No matter how well it blooms, fruit will not follow unless the flowers have been fertilized, and there are several factors that can prevent this from happening. In a cold, late season when spring is slow in coming, there may be few insects around to effect pollination, and keen fruit-growers are known to keep or hire hives of bees to reinforce their numbers. Gardeners can encourage bees to their gardens by growing

the insects' favourite late spring flowers, such as golden alyssum, crocuses, wallflowers, aubretia, and by avoiding spraying open flowers while pollinating insects are active – even spray drift onto nearby dandelions may harm foraging bees.

To fertilize flowers, bees and other insects need a supply of suitable pollen, which is not always readily available. Most flowers and soft fruit are self-fertile, that is they will set seed with their own pollen, but many fruit trees are less obliging and need a suitable neighbour with which to exchange pollen. Triploid varieties must be planted near two non-triploid varieties as they have no viable pollen of their own to offer in return. Sweet cherries and plums are notoriously self-sterile and most must be planted with a companion for effective fertilization – good nursery catalogues will guide your choice by listing compatible groups. Self-fertile varieties are the kind to choose when planting a single fruit tree. Some crop well in isolation (the cherry 'Stella', for example), while others fruit adequately on their own, but more heavily if cross-pollinated by another variety.

If you cannot plan for more than one fruit tree, there are ways round self-sterility. Ornamental crab apples are good sources of pollen for large-fruited varieties, the prolific and attractive 'Golden Hornet' probably being the best of them. Alternatively you might revive the old ploy of 'planting' a pollen source within your lone tree; pick a few sprays of open blossom from a compatible variety and suspend them in jam jars of water among the branches of your tree, and the bees will do the rest.

PLANNING

THE GARDEN ORCHARD When gardening begins to lose its appeal as a physical activity and age brings thoughts of laissez-faire, you might do worse than turn a part of your garden into a small orchard which begins to bear rich rewards of blossom and fruit at this time of year.

Festooned cherries, plum trees in pots and low, 'step-over' apple espaliers have had good publicity since the advent of dwarfing rootstocks, illustrating the infinite possibilities of including fruit in the smallest garden scheme. Old varieties too, the kind we used to scale and scrump in childhood days, have found recognition in a campaign to save old orchards. But it is the fruit trees of intermediate size – bush, quarter-standard, spindle and pyramid among others – that have been neglected by comparison, and yet they too could find a place in many gardens.

If you have room for a specimen acer on the lawn or if you intend planting the corner of a field with native trees, consider the rival claims of the apple. It is attractive in leaf, blossom and even winter deshabille; trees thrive and crop on most soils with little encouragement; according to variety, the fruit can be stored successfully over a long season, right up to the

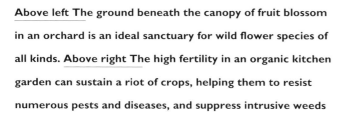

Above left The ground beneath the canopy of fruit blossom in an orchard is an ideal sanctuary for wild flower species of all kinds. Above right The high fertility in an organic kitchen garden can sustain a riot of crops, helping them to resist numerous pests and diseases, and suppress intrusive weeds

appearance of the first spring rhubarb or gooseberry. Apples are not just native but truly local, with English regional varieties ranging from 'Beauty of Bath' to 'Yorkshire Robin'.

Grafted on a semi-dwarfing rootstock, trees can be planted as close as 2.4m (8ft) apart or as much as 6m (20ft) depending on the style of pruning, if any, that you decide to follow. Choose a balanced selection of varieties, one tree of each except for long keepers such as 'Dumelow's Seedling' and 'Bramley' cookers, or dessert 'Ashmead's Kernel' and 'Suntan'. Make sure they pollinate each other, or interplant one or two pollen-donors such as the ornamental crabs, 'Golden Hornet' and 'Aldenhamensis'.

Keep the base of the trunks weed-free for the first few years to eliminate competition and to get the young trees off to a head start. Afterwards you could undersow them with a meadow seed-mixture of wild flowers and selected grasses, which will enhance the orchard landscape with further colour in late spring or summer and need mowing only once or twice a year. Self-sufficient gardeners might also fence the area and run geese or fatten lambs under the fruit trees. Ideally the site should be frost-free and sheltered from strong winds but in cold districts choose late-flowering varieties and enclose the orchard with a damson hedge for shelter (but leave gaps for frost to 'drain' away). Growing trees on dwarfing stocks is another option as they can be easily protected from the cold. Finally add a comfortable rustic seat, for somewhere to rest and to taste the fruit in comfort, and to meditate on the mysterious and timeless atmosphere that permeates every orchard.

DOWN TO EARTH

NATURAL GARDENING Fanaticism is the original sin, according to the Hungarian writer George Paloczi-Horvath, but fashion must be a close second, for they often appear together. Both tendencies have conspired to turn 'organic' issues into political and moral dogma, thus bewildering numerous gardeners who have more or less followed its basic principles all along for the sake of economy and common sense.

The majority of gardeners do not spray large quantities of chemicals on plants: they are too expensive, for one thing, and also too much bother to mix and apply when there are so many more seductive jobs to do outdoors during the growing season. Nevertheless, the shrill controversy continues to prick consciences, and when pests, diseases and weeds start appearing in earnest at this time of year, they bring with them the usual angst about whether to use chemical controls or not.

We use few sprays in this garden. Experience has shown that roses survive black spot, natural predators arrive in time to reduce aphid populations to tolerable levels, and the best control for cabbage white caterpillars is to pick them off by hand, as some of us did years ago to earn our pocket money. Since compromise is essential in a large garden, we reduce the workload by using weedkillers on paths, and on fallow vegetable beds before digging in dead weeds to produce humus.

The most valuable lessons to be learned from organic gardeners are not concerned with the treatment of problems, but with their avoidance, and here traditional practice blends with modern science. Gardeners used to be scrupulous about returning to the soil more than they took, and adding manure or compost to sustain soil fertility. This all encourages healthy growth and so remains a sound priority. Pruning out dead or diseased stems, and thinning growth so that air and light can penetrate to the centre of plants, are further time-honoured ways to maintain positive health.

One important modern development that helps us guard against pests and diseases has been the breeding of resistant varieties: lettuces unaffected by root aphids, raspberries that withstand viruses and canker-resistant parsnips, for example. Wherever a problem recurs annually, it is sensible to concentrate on planting disease-resistant varieties, especially if you are unwilling to use chemical remedies even as a last resort.

Non-chemical gardening demands an informed acquaintance with plant and pathogen behaviour if you are to dodge troubles. There is no approved organic spray for gooseberry mildew, for example, and since this is prevalent in our garden we use a combination of stratagems to help prevent it. As stagnant air favours the disease, I prune out all but the main well-spaced branches to open up the centres – according to tradition you should be able to rest your straw hat in the centre of a pruned gooseberry bush. It is also important to mulch heavily to keep the soil moist (mildew likes hot dry conditions). I use bracken and wood ashes for mulching, because they are rich in potash and stimulate more resilient growth compared with manure which encourages soft vulnerable stems. A proportion of the berries are picked early for culinary use before the disease strikes, and this helps to reduce congestion on the branches. Finally, we are gradually replacing the more susceptible varieties with mildew-resistant 'Invicta', which has proved its worth over several years.

FOCUS ON FOOD

A PERNICIOUS WEED The traditional preparation of horseradish is a painful chore – even the coarse leaves of the plant contain a mild irritant. In my wife's family her father was always the unlucky 'volunteer' charged with cleaning the roots – under running water to dilute the violently acrid fumes – and then grating them finely for the sauce, while hot tears streamed freely down his cheeks. Growing the plant is far less

Above A cosmopolitan greenhouse collection grown at high density needs good light and a buoyant atmosphere to maintain vigour and good health. Opposite Where content and established clematis is impressive in full bloom

distressing, although you need a firm plan of campaign to forestall its wilfulness, because if given the chance, it will quickly develop into a weed.

Before praising horseradish as a fine vegetable, William Cobbett condemned its loutish ways. 'As a weed, I know of nothing quite so pertinaceous and pernicious as this; I know of nothing but fire which will destroy its powers of vegetation; and I have never yet seen it clearly extirpated from ground which had once been filled with its roots and fibres.' Many gardeners would agree, especially if they have planted and then forgotten it in a secluded corner. Once established it is virtually ineradicable unless sprayed with a total weedkiller several times, for every fragment of broken root will revive to grow again and recolonize the patch. The way to tame it, as Cobbett implied, is to treat it as a vegetable, not a perennial herb to be plundered now and then.

Roots are dug up in late autumn and stored like maincrop carrots in boxes of moist sand. Take the fattest ones to the kitchen when required, and save slender straight 'thongs' for replanting. Trim the latter to 15cm (6in) long, and to distinguish one end from the other, cut the top straight across and the bottom obliquely. Plant them in spring, top end uppermost, at the same time as early potatoes, in similarly prepared ground (see page 17). Draw the soil into a ridge, like a fully earthed-up potato row, and thrust the thongs 30cm (12in) apart into the sides of the ridge. You can dig up the best for use during the season if you wish, and clear the rest for store in the autumn, making sure nothing is left behind to revive pertinaceously next spring.

UNDER GLASS

TESTING THE AIR If you step inside any greenhouse or conservatory and take a deep breath, you will know instantly whether the plants are content. When grown in pots under glass, plants are totally dependent on us for their welfare, and this means providing them with a genial atmosphere to sustain their health, as well as seeing to the more mundane necessities of watering, feeding and repotting.

In winter the air in a greenhouse ought to smell fresh, clean and dry. Even on the foulest days, you should open a ventilator for ten minutes or so to change stale air; a damp, stagnant atmosphere encourages fungal diseases which may be lethal to a plant when it is not growing actively. Greenhouses are mostly ill-equipped with ventilators, small structures often having a single opening light, and it is a good idea to install one or two more for choice so that you can ventilate on a windy day without admitting a violent draught. Watering is best done early in the mornings in winter to allow time for any surplus water to evaporate before nightfall.

Once growth resumes in spring, plants need a more buoyant environment – warmer, brighter and slightly more humid. You will need to water and ventilate more often to compensate for dramatic changes in temperature. As sunlight increases from late spring onwards, start coating the outside of the glass with thin layers of white liquid shading paint. This will prevent plants from scorching and help keep up humidity.

Later in the season, it may be necessary to leave all the vents open, including the door, to keep temperatures down. Check whether you need to water every morning and evening, and damp down daily: this involves spraying or watering the greenhouse path and the staging in between plants. Neglect this in summer and the air will smell dry and sterile, even though all the plants' other requirements are catered for.

During autumn, growth declines and with it the need to maintain a 'growing' atmosphere. It takes time to trust your nose as the shrewdest judge of how much to increase or reduce watering, damping down and ventilation, but this is an infallible skill well worth acquiring.

NEW PLANTS FROM OLD

THE DEMAND FOR CLEMATIS The genus *Clematis* attracts more than its fair share of enthusiasts. If you grow one of the less familiar varieties or species, friends seem to arrive at flowering time with the sole purpose of enviously admiring your plant. Yet despite their slightly exclusive appearance, clematis are in fact very simple to propagate and you could multiply enough plants to satisfy covetous visitors. The most foolproof method of doing so is known as serpentine layering, for obvious reasons. After the clematis has flowered, one of the long stems is laid out at ground level over a series of shallow depressions, scooped out about 30cm (1ft) apart. Start from the end nearer the parent plant, press the stem into each hollow and then cover it with the excavated soil. Every buried portion will root to form a new plant by the following year, and when it is growing strongly, it can be separated from its neighbours for potting up or transplanting. As an insurance, scrape the underside of each buried section just below a pair of leaves to expose the inner tissues, which will accelerate rooting.

Cuttings root faster, especially if given bottom heat in a propagator, but the success rate may be lower, partly because layers are sustained by the parent plant while rooting, whereas cuttings must fend for themselves, initially without any roots. Soon after flowering, choose a straight vigorous shoot that is still supple, and cut off a 60cm (2ft) length just above a pair of leaves. Discard the top two or three pairs of leaves as this part of the stem will be too soft to use. The remaining section should then be divided into cuttings using a very sharp knife on a piece of glass. Cut through the stem 0.5cm (¼in) above every pair of leaves to produce a number of segments in the shape of the letter T. Trim the stem of each to about 3.5cm (1½in) long, and remove one of the two leaves, taking care not to damage the bud at its base. Use a proprietory rooting compost or a 50:50 mix of peat and grit, and insert each cutting so that its buds sit on the surface. A 10cm (4in) pot will hold six cuttings around its rim, while 40 can be arranged 5 x 8 in a standard seed tray. To avoid the risk of rotting, try to prevent adjacent cuttings from touching each other (the reason for removing one of the leaves). The ideal rooting temperature is 21°C (70°F) in a propagator; alternatively enclose the containers in polythene bags, keeping the plastic clear of the leaves, or stand them in a shaded cold frame, spraying occasionally with water to maintain humidity. When they are about 10cm (4in) tall, well-rooted cuttings can be potted up, at the same time pinching out tips to encourage bushy growth.

Early SUMMER

Everything DONE IN THE FLOWER AND KITCHEN GARDENS SO FAR THIS YEAR STARTS TO MAKE SENSE NOW. ALL THE PLANNING AND PREPARATIONS – DIGGING, SOWING AND GROWING ON, OFTEN IN UNKIND WEATHER – SHOULD HAVE PRODUCED AN ERUPTION OF COLOUR AND CULINARY DELIGHT THAT DESERVES CELEBRATION.

Cynics might regard it merely as a good feed with a view, but the uninhibited enjoyment of the fruits of your labours, preferably in good company at a table amid the flowerbeds, is a worthwhile festival I can recommend. It was a former employer who introduced me to her annual 'summer feast', when the family would gather early in the season and share platters of home-grown vegetables to welcome the long days and warm evenings. Fortunately the housekeeper gave me this alarming news just in time to give me the chance to plan how I might persuade a wide variety of succulent crops to precocious maturity and so justify my recent appointment as gardener.

It was with the aid of cold frames and cloches, together with the good fortune of congenial weather, that I was able to wheel a barrow load of fresh vegetables up to the House on the appointed day. The secret of success was using the fastest maturing ('early') varieties: 'Early Nantes' carrots, 'Pilot' peas ('Meteor' in cold gardens), 'The Sutton' broad beans and 'Snowball' turnips, for example. They are invaluable for both early feasts and successional crops, and there is still time now to sow a few rows for late summer indulgence. Add asparagus, blanched seakale, new potatoes and French beans grown under glass, together with forced rhubarb, green gooseberries and the earliest strawberries, and you have all the ingredients for a perfect summer meal, ideally enjoyed while contemplating your recently planted summer bedding display.

WHAT TO WATCH FOR THIS MONTH

EARLY *strawberries*, THEIR RUNNERS BEARING TINY PLANTLETS TO ROOT NOW FOR NEW STOCK

Bedding plants IN FLOWER TO SET OUT IN PATTERNS AND PATCHES FOR SUMMER COLOUR

Vegetable seedlings EMERGING, A SIGNAL TO SOW MORE FOR SUCCESSION

Fruits OF ALL KINDS SETTING AND SWELLING; STEEL YOUR-SELF TO THIN THEM FOR THE BEST CROPS

PLANNING

BEDDING WITH FLAIR When frosts are a melancholy memory, even the most cold-susceptible subjects – begonias, cannas, salvias and heliotrope, for example – should be safe outdoors. Remember, they must have been hardened off for a week or two before being planted out. Early summer temperatures may still fall rather low for sensitive plants that have been raised in constant warmth, and just one or two chilly nights may disfigure cosseted flowers and foliage. If in doubt, keep some form of emergency cover handy: cloches, large pots or bottomless plastic 4.55 litre (1 gallon) milk containers are ideal.

Planting up a bed is a hallowed routine. When the soil has been forked over, weeded, fed and raked until it is level, start by positioning the 'dot plants', those bolder central features such as marguerites, dahlias and castor-oil plants, or asparagus and cardoons if you feel adventurous. Edging plants should be set out next, together with any used to divide blocks of colour. Lastly fill the intervening spaces with your main bedding plants, the 'groundwork'. Knocking batches of plants from their pots or trays and spacing them individually on the soil helps to assess positions and density, as they need enough room to develop healthily but not so much that they do not cover the visible soil by mid-season. As a guide, plant compact varieties 10-15cm (4-6in) apart, those of medium height 23-30cm (9-12in), and tall kinds 38-45cm (15-18in) apart.

The addition of one or two dot plants can transform a bedding scheme. It is a way of creating dramatic impact and their contrast and height reduces the risk of a formal design looking too uniform, so it would be worth investing in a few standard fuchsias, pelargoniums or heliotropes, or training your own (*see* page 49) for the purpose. Tall tobacco plants, variegated *Abutilon pictum* 'Thompsonii', coloured maize, and even large foliage houseplants enjoying a summer break outdoors, are all suitable for strategic prominence in a bedding design.

Try experimenting with divergent ideas. Ivy-leaved pelargoniums were a Victorian favourite for bedding, with their sinuous stems pegged to the ground in whorls to produce carpets of bloom. Trailing lobelia, usually grown suspended, is equally successful at ground level; exploit its great froth of blossom as informal edging, or for a little frivolity grow it among more restrained plants. Annual climbers such as morning glories, cup-and-saucer vine and the annual variegated hop will scramble through evergreen shrubs in a warm corner. Trailing helichrysum, lysimachia and glechoma, often sold for hanging baskets, will similarly brighten up heathers and other prostrate spring plants that have finished flowering.

WATER PLANTS Rising temperatures should now be warming the water in garden ponds, and you can confidently add new plants to your collection. Choice may be a problem because, although diversity is preferable to dull uniformity, it is easy to plant too much and produce a cluttered impression or, worse still, an unmanageably chaotic tangle.

Plants need space to grow, so allow at least 60cm (2ft) for each to spread, and if there is room plant two or three of each

Above Marginal plants are as important as floating aquatics for creating a balanced water garden. Right Smallest of all water lilies, *Nymphaea pygmaea alba* can be grown in a tub

type, rather than a mixture of many kinds. Study catalogues to assess the potential vigour of plants: varieties of the water lily *Nymphaea pygmaea*, for example, will thrive for years in a water tub, whereas *N. alba* can colonize a small lake. Depth is important. The most rampant plants need 60-90cm (2-3ft) of water, whereas others like water forget-me-not prefer just to touch the surface. Grade the pond's depth, therefore, by leaving a shallow shelf at the edge for marginal plants, and gently slope to a full depth of about 45-60cm (1½-2ft) in the centre (note that most pond accidents involve children under 3 years old, so make sure they are supervised and that pond margins are shallow).

Pond maintenance is easier if all submerged plants are grown in perforated containers, but remember to include the height of the pots when calculating the depth at which the plants are to grow. Contrast adjacent plants so that prostrate species such as the beautiful bogbean intermingle freely with tall irises or zebra grass. For a healthy pond environment, add plenty of oxygenating plants, but leave at least one-third of the surface clear for sunlight to penetrate.

Beside an informal pond make a small bog garden by burying a section of pond liner, perforated a few times for drainage and filled with soil. If the pond edge is lowest at this point, water can overflow to keep the bog moist. This type of garden is ideal for valerian, astilbes, bergenias, scarlet lobelia, marsh marigolds, meadowsweet and candelabra primulas. Don't overlook the choicer wild flowers that like moist, but not waterlogged, soils. Fritillaries, primroses, cuckoo flowers (lady's smock) and the graceful, honey-scented grass of Parnassus are ideal here. Include a small shrub or two for winter interest – a Japanese maple, perhaps, dogwoods with coloured stems, or a dwarf willow such as *Salix lanata*. Larger trees should not be allowed to overhang the water, as their shade can suppress flowering, and falling leaves need immediate clearing before they foul the water.

FRAMEWORK

A SEAT IN THE GARDEN At the nursery where I first trained, we did everything standing up. To sit, even for a moment's respite, was the cue for the foreman to appear, breathing fire and thunder, and sentence any offender to the usual banishment of washing down the glasshouses. Older gardeners, on the other hand, spent hours sitting on upturned buckets as they riddled the soil or tied up chrysanthemums, all the while putting the world to rights. No doubt they had earned the privilege, for they never had to wash glass.

Many garden tasks are far less arduous if done in comfort, and every keen gardener should have some kind of portable seat to help the work along. Even more important is somewhere to sit at leisure and enjoy the fruits of one's labours, because a garden is also a sanctuary in which to relax, whether alone or in company. For this, something more inviting than an upturned bucket is obviously needed. A wealth of designs exists from which to select your garden seat, but remember that once installed it will be an integral part of the garden, as much as any other decorative feature, and should blend in with both the site and your particular style of gardening. Intricately ornamented metal furniture, ideal for a semi-formal patio setting, would seem fussy in a cottage garden, where the simplest of improvised seats, perhaps made from rustic poles, might be just the thing to fill an intimate niche among a riot of traveller's joy (old man's beard) and wild flowers. Shakespeare was not being fanciful when he laid Titania on 'a bank whereon the wild thyme blows, where oxlips and the nodding violet grows', for the earliest garden seats were simple turf or herb banks. You can make a cosy bench with the base, back and sides built from live turves, lifted while creating a new border, and its seat put together with a few square stone slabs. Clip the grass with shears periodically and plant violets and primroses here and there, to add to the general charm.

Herbs make ideal 'furnishing' material, especially durable woody kinds such as marjoram and thyme, but even the much softer chamomile is suitable for occasional use. If you think that sitting on plants is disrespectful or impractical, place them decoratively beneath and around more conventional furniture. A plain bench will be transformed into a romantic

PLANT HIGHLIGHTS OF THE MONTH

Aquilegia Cottage gardens always sport 'granny's bonnets' in pink, white or pale blue, growing wherever they will. These are basic *Aquilegia vulgaris*, often reverted seedlings from exhausted hybrids, and not to be despised for their simple fragile grace. Other columbines are equally attractive, including gorgeous hybrids like 'McKana Giants' or the fashionable double 'Nora Barlow' in a blend of pink, cream and green. Explore the many species: scarlet *A. canadensis* or blue *A. caerulea*, State flower of Colorado. Sow now and transplant in early autumn in sun or light shade.

Edible roses As well as making classic potpourri, rose petals are used in jams or fritters and to flavour ice cream or mousse, while their buds can be pickled. Always use old-fashioned fragrant kinds, brightly coloured for best effect (or blend white petals with a few coloured ones). Choicest are pink 'Queen of Denmark' and 'Great Maiden's Blush'; deep purple 'Cardinal Richelieu'; red 'Hansa' and white 'Blanc Double de Coubert', both producing large and valuable hips; and heady white 'Alba Semi-plena', traditionally used to distil attar of roses.

Lupins Versatile plants, lupin species are used agriculturally for oilseed production, as green manure to add nitrogen to the soil, and for unfailing early summer colour in borders. Wild lupins on railway embankments are usually pink or blue, common usurpers that will take over from brilliant, often bicoloured garden hybrids unless you prevent seeding. Take cuttings from spring shoots, deadhead plants promptly after flowering and keep free from aphids to perpetuate the best forms.

arbour if enclosed by a framework of trained honeysuckle, rambling roses or espaliered apples and pears, and nestled amid marigolds, ferns and wild strawberries. Plant sweet woodruff all around for its invigorating scent and pretty flowers; cut and dry its stems to add as a fragrant tonic to Indian tea.

FOCUS ON FOOD

SUCCESSIONAL SOWINGS Feast freely on the tender summer crops that will be crowding the rows of your vegetable garden now, but remember to sow more for salads later in the season. Maintaining unbroken supplies is a difficult art learned only from experience, and even then it is fraught with problems. Subtle changes in weather will delay some crops, and force others to mature simultaneously or bolt to seed before they are edible. Sowing little and often is the only insurance.

Radishes are best sown in a moist shady spot because they detest dry heat which forces them to flower while roots are still thin. Since lettuce seeds remain stubbornly dormant in high temperatures, sow them in rows in a bed located in a cool part of the garden and thin surplus seedlings with the least disturbance – transplanting lettuces in summer heat seldom works. Keep salad plants watered for fast, even growth, and as soon as seedlings are through sow again, as catch crops between other vegetables if space is precious.

Iceberg lettuces revel in the heat, and in rich moist soil are dependable for summer crops. If you have difficulty raising good hearted lettuces though, try sowing seed mixtures for repeated cutting while immature. Many loose-leaf blends of plain, frilled and coloured varieties such as green and red 'Lollo Rossa', 'Lollo Bionda', and 'Black Seeded Simpson' are available, or you can mix your own with any surplus lettuce

Above A cool stone seat in the shade is an ideal position from which to contemplate sun-loving annuals such as multi-coloured clary

seeds. Sow broadcast or in a block of rows 10cm (4in) apart, and leave unthinned. When young plants are of a usable size, pick individual leaves or crop with scissors but make sure 2.5cm (1in) or so of growth remains to fuel further supplies. An early autumn sowing of these mixtures in a greenhouse border will crop all winter if protected from frost.

Peas, French beans, beetroot, kohl rabi and dwarf broad beans can be sown for a second time, together with vegetables such as Chinese cabbage and Florence fennel that prefer to grow when the day-length is dwindling. There are early, non-bolting varieties of these, but for the best crops sow as mid-summer approaches for use in autumn. Endive and heading chicory sown now will add variety to salad bowls later in the year. Beans, celery and other tender crops, raised under glass and fully hardened off, will be safe once frosts are over, but guard against cold nights for a week or two after planting.

EARLY STRAWBERRIES While producing their first and largest fruits for summer feasts, strawberry plants are also preparing to multiply themselves, their young runners rapidly creeping in all directions to colonize neighbouring ground. Several plantlets form on each individual runner, and although the orthodox practice is to keep only the largest for propagation, all will develop into useful plants. Even the tiniest plantlet at the tip of a runner will root if detached and pressed into moist soil in a closed cold frame or a covered seed tray. Provided parent plants are healthy, you can soon increase stocks in this way.

If the strongest plantlets are rooted in early summer and grown on in pots, they can be forced in a cool greenhouse to fruit early the following spring, sometimes six weeks before outdoor plants. Peg down plantlets in small pots of rich compost or transplant them if already rooted in the ground, and as they grow move them on into 12.5-15cm (5-6in) pots; water and feed regularly, keeping them outdoors in a shaded place. Any time after the shortest day, you can start to bring the pots indoors, in fortnightly batches, for succession. Tidy the plants, removing faded leaves and stems, check for aphids, clean the pots before housing them, and then arrange near the glass for maximum light. You need to keep the plants frost-free, although crops are much earlier if you can maintain a temperature of 10°C (50°F). When flowering starts, fertilize blooms by brushing the centres gently with a soft paintbrush or a wad of cotton wool. Water regularly, and feed when fruits start to form, supporting the trusses on small forked twigs. For the largest fruits, leave only the first three or four to form. After fruiting transplant outside to fruit next year at the normal time, although some prolific varieties may bear again in late summer of the same season.

NEW PLANTS FROM OLD

IRIS DIVISION   Before planting new stock of iris, it is worth checking that the site suits their needs because there are so many different kinds belonging to this cosmopolitan family. *Iris unguicularis* (which most gardeners still prefer to call by its former name, *I. stylosa*) appreciates an annual dressing of garden lime and dusting the soil with 50g per 0.836 sq metres (2oz per sq yard) will help to ensure healthy growth. Do the same before planting flag (bearded) irises, as they are seldom happy in acid soils. Most varieties will grow readily on fairly light soils, in a sunny position.

Existing beds of flags often become congested as their surface rhizomes spread in every direction; weeding among the decaying old roots and matted young lateral stems becomes difficult, and vigour diminishes as nutrients are exhausted. The remedy is to fork up all the rhizomes, divide them and replant in refreshed ground every few years. This is best done after flowering, when plants rest for a short while before starting to make new roots. The end few centimetres of firm young rhizomes are used for replanting, each piece with at least one good fan of leaves. Cut these ends from the main rhizomes and discard the rest, including the old decaying portions. Prepare a free-draining bed, mix in a dressing of lime and general fertilizer, and rake the surface to a fine tilth. Plant the rhizomes with their tips facing the sun, 30-38cm (12-15in) apart, at or just below the surface, and make sure their roots are firmed in – in windy gardens you might have to trim the leaves by half or support them with canes until roots are established.

DOWN TO EARTH

COPING WITH DROUGHT   Among its many functions, the soil in your garden acts as a vast reservoir for rain water. The amount that can be stored depends on the nature of the soil: the particles that comprise clay are minute compared with those of sandy soils, and so there are many more spaces between them to hold water, which is one of the reasons why heavy ground is slow to dry out in spring. On average clay holds three times as much water as light sandy soil, which dries more rapidly and so becomes warm earlier in the year and is therefore suitable for the cultivation of early crops. During the growing season it may need a few centimetres of rainfall every week or so to keep its reservoir topped up sufficiently to meet plants' demands. However, since rain seldom falls when we want it, watering becomes necessary, especially for groups of plants at particular risk.

Some gardeners delay irrigation on the grounds that plants ought to fend for themselves, and that once begun watering must be sustained. Certainly there is no virtue in starting too early, as this often causes waterlogging or stimulates the development of shallow roots that quickly succumb to dry weather. If you neglect watering when plants need it, they may not fully recover during that season from the resulting check to growth.

Below If it is to flower as lavishly as this, *Iris stylosa* needs a sheltered position at the base of a sunny wall, annual liming and occasional division

Left Watering in the evening is one of the best times of day to ensure that your plants get a thorough soaking.

Above Hoverflies are attracted to flat-headed species such as helichrysum. As well as being a predator, the insect also acts as a pollinator

There are ways to delay the start of watering. Adding organic material to any soil dramatically increases water retention, because the spongy humus it forms after decay is highly absorbent; mulching the surface substantially cuts evaporation, as does close spacing, which eliminates bare ground between plants. Ground-cover plants are effective as a mulch: on a dry day lift the sprawling stems of any dense prostrate plant, whether it is a garden pink or a clump of chickweed, and you will find the soil still moist. Even a layer of stones raked from cultivated soil and gathered round the base of fruit trees will conserve ground water.

Unless appreciable rainfall intervenes, some plants will eventually show typical drought symptoms: flagging or yellowing leaves, limp stems, reduced growth rate and smaller foliage, discontinued flowering or a tendency to bolt to seed in the case of vegetables. First victims, which should be top priority for watering, are plants that have been moved or recently set out, those growing at the foot of walls, leafy crops, and any in full flower or with maturing fruits and pods.

Suffering plants must be soaked thoroughly, using as much as 18-23 litres per 0.836 sq metres (4-5 gallons per sq yard), a hasty sprinkle barely quenching their thirst. Leave a hose to trickle gently at the roots of trees and shrubs, bury a pot or short drainpipe nearby that you can fill to direct water to the

roots, or confine it in a depression scooped around stems. Watering plants individually with cans or a hosepipe is more precise than using a sprinkler, which scatters water indiscriminately, but is only feasible on a small scale. Using sprinklers during cloudy weather, in the evening or early morning will help reduce rapid evaporation; try to adjust the spray so that it is not heavy enough to beat a hard cap on the soil surface, nor so fine that most of it drifts away. Finally, mulch after watering to maximize the benefit of your efforts.

THE GARDEN SURGERY

BIOLOGICAL PEST CONTROL Not everything that creeps or flies around our plants is necessarily hostile. Many insects prey on others, and some of these are allies in our annual struggle against the various pests certain to arrive sooner or later. It is the assistance of these natural predators that makes it possible for us to demote the tedious and questionable spraying of pesticides to a last resort in the event of serious infestation.

The Royal Botanic Gardens at Kew, London, has enlisted the help of lizards and Australian ladybirds to control greenhouse pests, and banished chemical sprays to a locked cupboard. This approach, while undeniably more wholesome and environmentally sound, is not altogether straightforward, especially outdoors. No predator can survive in the absence of its prey, for example, and once food supplies are exhausted, predators will die out. Until pests are present they will not appear of their own accord in the garden.

Patience is a virtue: predators arrive in due course, but if you panic and spray the first wave of pests, you will either deter or destroy the predators. In the USA enterprising nurserymen have been known to give away quantities of ladybirds as a bonus with larger orders, but most of us have to encourage them into our gardens, together with the hoverflies, lacewings, rove beetles, and parasitic wasps that all thrive on a diet of pests. Inaction is one way to attract them, for just when aphids look like taking over, you will find ugly and voracious larvae quietly feasting on them at a rate of one or more a minute. A single hasty spray would upset the whole balance, and might possibly aggravate the situation because many pests have evolved resistance to common garden chemicals and would therefore survive, whereas the predator larvae would not. Growing certain flowers favoured by our allies is another useful enticement. Adult ladybirds and lacewings feed, like their young, on aphids, but the many valuable species of hoverfly thrive on flowers rich in

nectar. Their tongues are short, which confines browsing to easily accessible flat-headed species such as fennel, parsley, achillea, sedum and most kinds of daisy. It is also useful to remember that robins, wrens and the tit family relish insect pests, so encourage these smaller birds with food and nest-boxes.

Winter usually reduces the pest population outdoors, but there is no such natural remedy under glass. Most gardeners find that glasshouse whitefly is the worst villain, its waxy armour and chemical tolerance making it difficult to destroy. It multiplies rapidly, especially on fuchsias, cucumbers and tomatoes, unless you move quickly to control them. The parasitic encarsia wasps (harmless to us) feed on whitefly larvae and lay their eggs inside them, but they must be introduced first, usually as pupae ordered from specialist companies. These same sources can also supply the predator *Phytoseiulus persimilis*, which is useful for controlling the red spider mite, a tiny creature that thrives in dry conditions on the underside of leaves, turning them yellow and eventually draping them with fine webs. The mites detest high humidity, and gardeners used to dissuade them by spraying plants with water each day. When they get a footing, though, control is difficult; their resistance to chemicals is high, and introducing predators is your best recourse against these pests. Cucumbers, melons and impatiens are prime targets.

Once dismissed as eco-freakish, biological alternatives to chemical treatments are now widely used by organic and commercial gardeners alike, for a number of reasons: they are clean, simple, inexpensive and, in many cases, self-sustaining. But their success depends upon maintaining a delicate balance. There will always be insect pests in the garden – even the most rigorous chemical spray routine has never resulted in total elimination. As with weeds, we must learn to tolerate a low level of pest incidence for the sake of the overall welfare of the garden community.

OVERCROPPING   For a number of reasons fruit trees may fail to set a crop, even though wreathed in blossom during spring, but this is an unavoidable hazard that must be accepted when growing fruit. A less obvious problem is overcropping, when ideal conditions result in too many fertilized flowers setting fruit. In our natural joy and relief at a potentially heavy harvest, it is easy to forget the risks of overcropping and the precautions that need to be taken against it.

Above The perils of overcropping are amply illustrated here, luckily in this instance just as the fruit is ready to harvest

Thinning is pleasant, leisurely work that helps reduce the risks of overcropping, and as a bonus it improves fruit size and quality. Many fruits, especially gooseberries, peaches and grapes, remain small or worse still, never ripen if a large crop is left intact. The immature thinnings need not go to waste. Gooseberries, for example, can be picked when green to make 'fool' for summer feasts, leaving other fruits 5-7cm (2-3in) apart to mature to full size. Grape thinnings are excellent when cooked in a pie, in the same way as gooseberries.

Peaches and apricots should be thinned to 15cm (6in) apart, and damaged and misshapen fruits removed from clusters of apples and pears, together with the large central 'king' fruit, because its retention often suppresses the development of others in the cluster. Some apple varieties are naturally biennial, producing far too much fruit one year and none the next: removing half will encourage annual cropping as well as help to avoid the problem of an embarrassing glut.

It is always wise to thin plums if there is a heavy set, otherwise they will remain small and may start rotting if densely packed – 'Victoria' is notorious in this respect, commonly shedding overladen boughs. The fruit should be thinned to approximately 2.5-5cm (1-2in) apart, and the branches supported with clothes-poles or forked sticks, as they could collapse and leave ugly wounds that invite entry by disease organisms. If breakage does occur, trim the tear to a clean wound and then dress immediately with pruning paint to reduce the threat from silver leaf disease.

PRUNING

CUTTING BACK   In the ideal garden shrubs never step out of line, nor can age and disease ever ravage their youthful good looks. According to purists, conscientious pruning and routine care will keep plants in some state of suspended perfection, and they condemn 'cutting back' as an admission of past neglect. In reality hard pruning, sometimes back to bare stumps, is a valid way to rejuvenate many shrubs that over a number of seasons have only produced flowers and young growth at the top of gaunt tired stems. Cutting these back during the dormant season to induce growth lower down is sometimes too drastic and may result in a shrub's death, whereas hard pruning in summer when growth is surging ahead is often quickly followed by a flush of new shoots. These should be thinned while still small enough to be pinched out or rubbed off with your thumb, leaving a few of the strongest evenly placed to make the new framework of branches.

Try reviving top-heavy shrubs and climbing roses, magnolias, camellias and rhododendrons in this way, by cutting out all thicker old wood early this season, but beware of subjects such as cytisus, lavender and rosemary, whose old stems resent pruning. I have successfully cut back billowy specimens of 'Nevada' and rugosa roses, in whose mass of stems dead and live growth were indistinguishable and so I waited until they were in full leaf before cutting them back. Saw each stem off cleanly just below the bottom fork, trim off any ragged edges from the wound, and give a feed of general fertilizer.

Older fruit trees, too, can be sawn off where the main stem first branches, to produce a mass of new shoots for thinning in late summer. Threadbare plum and damson trees, wall-trained peaches, and old apples and pears usually respond to harsh surgery any time from mid-spring onwards, but summer is the best season when frosts are past and wounds heal quickly. Cutting nicks in the trunk, deep enough to penetrate beneath the bark, is another way to modify lateral growth by redirecting the flow of sap. A nick below a bud will starve and so suppress its development, while cutting the bark above a bud diverts energy into stimulating the bud to grow. Try nicking a stump in a few places after hard pruning, to induce lower branching. Experiment with roses or fruit trees that are not irreplaceable if you doubt your pruning skills, and then move on as your confidence increases – remember that many currently unorthodox practices were once commonplace, and that a faint heart never produced an inspired garden.

TRAINING

THE STANDARD METHOD A simple and inspired way to fit a lot of plants into a small space is to combine them at different levels. When arranging pot plants, for example, stand one or two on inverted pots and tuck others beneath them. Outdoors many plants can be trained as standards on clear stems of various heights so that their bushy heads stand well above their neighbours and their branches radiate in all directions.

Below *Wisteria sinensis* excels as a standard or as here, trained on discreet supports

Rose, topfruit and weeping tree standards are created by grafting or budding the chosen variety high on a sturdy rootstock, a method sometimes used to counter slow growth, since the vigour of the rootstock affects the whole plant. The demure houseplant *Hoya bella*, for example, is far more exuberant if grafted on a rooted stem of its robust cousin *H. carnosa* and trained as a standard. Most standards, however, start as a rooted cutting that is trained with a single vertical stem until it reaches the appropriate height, where the growing tip is cut off to induce a selected number of sideshoots to develop and build up a bushy head of growth. Whether it is a wisteria, grape vine, red currant or a fuschia, the same method applies. Permanent staking is necessary to support the main stem, together with annual pruning to maintain a balanced, uncongested head. It is sensible to have a second stake driven in at an angle to the main stake and bound to it as further temporary support.

Some tender bedding species can be trained as standards to make dramatic dot plants, or flowering topiary for pots and urns. Vigorous varieties of fuchsias (those with leaves in threes make the densest heads), pelargoniums, heliotrope, coleus and marguerites all lend themselves to this treatment. Start now by rooting a sturdy straight cutting and tie it at frequent intervals to a thin cane to keep it growing vertically. Pot on as necessary until you end up with an 20-23cm (8-9in) container. Retain leaves growing on the stem but pinch out any sideshoots as they form. Cut off the growing tip at the desired height, which can vary from between 30cm (1ft) for houseplants to about 90cm (3ft) for full standards for outdoor use. If plants take all season to reach this height, overwinter them in the usual way and then start training the head when growth resumes in spring. Removing the growing tip will prompt the appearance of several sideshoots; keep those at the top of the stem and pinch off their tips after two or three pairs of leaves to induce further branching. Continue stopping shoots in this way until a full bushy head has evolved. Once you have achieved this, the only requirement is to prune or pinch shoots to maintain the shape and keep the stem clear of any growth. It will pay to occasionally check supports for firmness as the heads of mature standards can be very heavy and unstable, especially outdoors when in full bloom.

Mid SUMMER

Why, THE OWNER COMPLAINED AS WE TOILED IN THE THISTLY ASPARAGUS BEDS, DO WRITERS NEVER SAY ANYTHING HELPFUL ABOUT THE UNIVERSAL PROBLEMS OF GARDENING? SHE SAID THAT BUDDING ROSES, THINNING GRAPES AND HANGING UP MELON NETS MIGHT BE AMIABLE OCCUPATIONS FOR ENTHUSIASTS BUT JUST THEN SHE WANTED TO HEAR THAT 'IT IS TIME TO PULL YOUR THISTLES AND THEY WILL NEVER REAPPEAR'.

The presence of weeds is inevitable even in the best of gardens, and dealing with them has none of the charm of training stephanotis or gathering alpine strawberries. Yet control them we must if they are not to host pests and diseases, or totally swamp choicer plants in their competition for light, water and nutrients. Rivalry for limited food can be a virtue, of course. Letting the grass grow around vigorous trees restrains their energy (but always keep young trees weed-free for two to three years, to encourage maximum growth). Years ago my daughter planted onion sets in her first little garden, but quickly lost interest, as children will; the bulbs promptly vanished in a jungle of weeds whose competition for nitrogen ultimately produced onions that kept rock solid until late the next spring. However, usually weeds mean trouble. Most kinds are particularly lusty around mid-summer; neglect them now and you lose any advantage gained from your efforts made earlier in the year. Hoe infant weedlings and hand-pull larger specimens where it matters, but try not to become too paranoid about every weed in the garden – speedwell, campion and scarlet pimpernel, for example, are pretty and harmless. Concentrate instead on persistent perennials such as nettles, ground elder and creeping buttercup, and beware of twining species that sneak craftily through other plants. Haul them out before they can flower because if given the chance, they will multiply alarmingly. Spray alloxydim-sodium on otherwise inaccessible grasses such as couch where it invades other plants, and glyphosate on other perennial species (apply on a humid evening for best effect).

Main crops of *soft fruit*, especially red and white currants, the most luscious of all

Suckers from rose roots, to cut out or use for producing new stock

The first sun-warmed *tomatoes* on strong plants needing regular training and direction

Mint to add to garden peas; cut back now for tender leaves in autumn

Only you can judge how much housework of this kind is necessary, or even desirable, in your garden. Heartsease and pimpernels look at home in herbaceous borders, whereas thistles in asparagus beds are intolerable: keep pulling them from the moment they appear in spring, and by now they should be ready to surrender. Above all, never despair. Remember, the soil is full of weed seeds that will germinate wherever you cultivate; accept them as an occupational irritation, and gather alpine strawberries for relief.

PLANNING

FRUIT IN SMALL PLACES No fruit is more welcome than the first dessert apples. Commercial growers have finely tuned the cultivation of 'Cox' and other varieties, so these are available for much of the year; avoid them, and choose early apples to eat straight from the tree instead. They don't keep, which is why home-grown apples always taste better than bought ones, and small trees provide enough for immediate use. 'Gladstone', 'George Cave' and 'Stark's Earliest' (syn 'Scarlet Pimpernel') usually ripen first, and are soon followed by 'Laxton's Epicure', 'Lady Sudeley', 'Merton Knave' and 'Discovery'.

Lack of space is no reason to deny yourself fresh fruit. By choosing compact varieties on dwarfing rootstocks, for example, everyone can grow a few early apples, even in pots on a patio. Order now for autumn delivery, and specify rootstock M27 for the smallest trees, M26 for poorer soils and for cordons or espaliers, to grow against walls and fences. Small pear

trees will have been grafted onto Quince C rootstocks; plums, peaches and apricots on 'Pixy'; and cherries on 'Colt' or 'Inmil' stocks. Train them as cordons, pyramids or festoons by a combination of summer and winter pruning. So restrictive are these rootstocks that most dwarf trees will need staking for most or all of their lives, and their yields are not enormous. Size and quality, though, are supreme, and an added bonus is that they are easily netted against birds. Make sure all varieties are compatible for cross-pollination.

Currants and gooseberries also adapt readily to pruning and training to fit into small places. Red currants are perhaps the most ornamental of all fruit crops, with long heavy trusses of brilliant, glistening fruits. Although often grown as bushes, they are just as prolific and far more decorative if trained as standards, single or multiple cordons, or

Right Ideally suited to small gardens, cordons should be spaced 76cm (2½ft) apart on good to medium soils, or 92cm (3ft) apart on poor, shallow or sandy soils

Left The stems of rambling roses are flexible enough to conform closely to the framework of an arch, adding grace and colour to its outline especially if combined with other climbers such as clematis (below)

as fans on walls where they produce berries in sequence according to aspect, starting in early summer with those on the warmest walls and ending with the fruit that has been in the shade. Most varieties hang for a further month when ripe. Pick whole trusses to strip through your teeth on hot days, or in classic fashion dip into egg white and icing sugar. When mixed with raspberries they make a refreshing jam. Be sure to net them though as birds and squirrels also find them irresistible. White currants are close relatives, less popular with wild life; mix them with red currants or exploit their distinctive flavour in white currant tartlets or wine. The two best varieties are 'Red Lake' and 'White Grape'.

FRAMEWORK

ARCHWAYS WITH PLANTS Arches are important and active garden features. For all their excellence, even the best flowerbeds and borders are only displays to be admired in passing, but overhead structures invite participation, especially when plants bring them to life. You are tempted to walk or sit beneath them; when you do, another view unfolds, or you suddenly find seclusion from the rest of the garden. It is for this reason, that arches need careful siting and should be used to create or embellish entrances, divisions and passageways. They produce illusions of distance, intimacy or enclosure, even grandeur if you have room for the broad stone piers and oak cross-members once used to create Italian gardens; lavishly festooned with wisteria or an ornamental vine, such an enviable structure adds opulence to the large garden. These days, however, there is seldom either space or means for anything so substantial, but even the smallest garden will benefit from a modest archway, artfully placed to frame a view or pathway and lifting the eye above ground level.

Since arches are essentially self-effacing supports for climbing plants, the simplest frame of wire, rustic timber or wooden trellis will do, provided it is sturdy. They occupy little space and for much of the year disappear beneath foliage and blossom. Using the lightest of lattice supports, a path beside the house can become an airy tunnel of clematis or sweet peas, the garage an integral part of the garden if an arch of rambler roses surrounds its doors. Even the compost heap will seem a desirable corner when enclosed by a simple wire fence and archway draped with honeysuckle and ivy.

Roses and vines are the traditional climbing plants for overhead structures. Vigour is important to ensure rapid and

total coverage; so, too, is strong colour, for an arch of any kind is intended to be prominent and should therefore be clearly defined. A soft pink rose such as 'Phyllis Bide', lovely on a dark wall, will be inconspicuous against most other backgrounds, whereas crimson 'Etoile d'Hollande', bright 'Climbing Allgold', or scarlet 'Danse du Feu' can reinforce the shape of an arch. For narrow passageways, fragrant pink 'Zéphirine Drouhin' is benignly thornless.

When training the main rose stems, twine them while supple around the upright supports to improve their coverage. To extend the season, partner the roses with other climbers such as perennial sweet pea, morning glories, jasmine or clematis. A favourite Edwardian combination was rambling roses and hops, trained up vertical poles and festooned along chains slung between them. Common hops are too vigorous for most gardens, but the ornamental Japanese hop with its white marbled leaves is a restrained substitute. Vines, both decorative and fruiting, are ideal perennial climbers for clothing arches, which they do very efficiently. Choose varieties that colour well in autumn, such as *Vitis pulchra*, white-dusted 'Miller's Burgundy' (also known as 'Wrotham Pinot'), 'Brandt' and the strong-growing Japanese vine *V. coignetiae*.

FURTHER SPECIAL EFFECTS WITH ROSES Classic climbers and ramblers were traditionally grown on poles, either as freestanding pillars or in rows to transform kitchen garden paths into flamboyant avenues. The stems of varieties such as 'Crimson Glory', 'Mme Grégoire Staechelin', 'Blush Noisette' and 'Gloire de Dijon' can be trained spirally around the supports and soon make excellent flowering pillars; once they reach their full height you can loop ropes from pole to pole and train them along these as garlands. Rambling roses such as 'Seagull', 'Crimson Shower', 'The Garland' and the curious lilac 'Veilchenblau' can be grown in the same way; they will also gracefully drape arches, pergolas and arbours. Try planting them at the top of banks, retaining walls or in large tubs on a strong roof so that they hang down in great swags. If you take care to tie in new stems as they appear, ramblers trained horizontally on a low wire or fence make unique dwarf hedges.

Once you start using roses for floral sculpture the possibilities seem endless. A classic method with ramblers is to train the stems up a pillar, at the top of which they are fanned out and tied to a wire or metal former so that they arch down like the ribs of an umbrella, resembling a weeping tree. The only attention they need is the removal of older branches immediately after flowering. Young stems must then be tied in to replace those that have been pruned.

Climbers flower best if their main branches are trained away from the vertical, which is why they are tied in spirals on pillars. Energy that would normally surge to the tips of stems is then diverted into flowering sideshoots. If a climbing

PLANT HIGHLIGHTS OF THE MONTH

Wax flowers Like most other evergreens, hoyas are neat but unremarkable until they flower, when everyone stops to admire the clusters of immaculate pink and white stars that resemble iced cake decorations. Climbing *Hoya carnosa* is the best known of the many species, its long sinewy stems are often trained round a wire hoop and are studded with pendant flower heads in mid-summer, each perfect blossom weeping a great tear of sweet nectar. Train it up into the rafters in the conservatory to enjoy the flowers from below.

Blue hydrangeas Hydrangeas are very sensitive to soil conditions, producing blue flowers only in acid soils; even nominally blue kinds react to traces of lime by tending to turn red. When grown in pots they prefer the ericaceous (lime-free) compost designed specifically for rhododendrons, azaleas and other lime-hating plants, and should be watered with rainwater to maintain the right balance. To counter soil alkalinity, dress plants with 'blueing' agent, available from garden shops.

Greengages Perhaps the elite of the plum world, gages need more warmth than other kinds to set and ripen well. The real greengage is a notoriously shy bearer and needs a compatible pollinator, but 'Early Transparent Gage' has the same rich melting flavour and crops well on its own. 'Cambridge Gage' is also partially self-fertile and flowers late, thereby escaping the spring frosts that often disable the true 'Greengage'. All are best grown as fans on a warm wall and coddled for best results.

rose blooms only at the top of tall bare stems, try tying them down sideways into arches to stimulate sideshoots. A young climber planted on a wall is better trained as a fan or espalier for the same reason, more prolific flowering compensating for any delay in gaining height.

UNDER GLASS

CACTI WITH CHARACTER Domestic collections of cacti often consist of too many anonymous green plants that sit on windowsills collecting inaccessible dust and seldom, if ever, flower. Some species undeniably lack visual interest, especially if their simple routine care is neglected, but to brand all cacti as boring is to overlook some easy and spectacular plants that deserve to be cultivated by everyone.

While differences between cacti are largely botanical, it is important to distinguish native desert dwellers from those species that prefer to live in forests, often as epiphytes growing in plant debris lodged on the branches of trees. Desert cacti must be kept dry and cool from autumn until early spring, but they require regular watering and feeding with tomato fertilizer for the rest of the year, together with full sunlight. Epiphytes, on the other hand, must be kept constantly moist, and often flower in partial shade or even at night.

To convince yourself of the merits of desert cacti, you should concentrate on species that flower reliably while still young, or columnar kinds that sport attractively shaped and coloured spines. Free-flowering cacti include astrophytum, chamaecereus, echinopsis, gymnocalycium, mammillaria, notocactus and rebutia species; cereus, cephalocereus, cleistocactus and epostoa are a few decoratively armed kinds. All kinds like free-drainage, so grow them in potting compost mixed with an equal volume of grit.

Tropical epiphytes prefer a richer, moisture-retentive mixture. It is due to their normal aerial existence that they make excellent hanging basket plants for conservatories, where their pendant flowers can be fully appreciated. Christmas cacti (schlumbergera) and Easter cacti (rhipsalidopsis), together with the even showier epiphyllum hybrids, are typical of this group. After flowering the baskets can be suspended outdoors until early autumn, provided you remember to water them freely and feed them every fortnight.

Another group of epiphytes, bromeliads this time rather than cacti, also benefit from aerial cultivation, and can be used to make a novel tropical feature in a greenhouse or conservatory. These so-called air plants – aechmea, guzmania, tillandsia and vriesea, for example – all form a central funnel of leaves which in the wild acts as a reservoir for rainwater. Their roots are chiefly there to provide anchorage. Instead of growing these air plants in pots, collect them together on a tree branch, preferably gnarled and pleasantly twisted, and wedged firmly at

Above Victorian conservatories were sometimes devoted to collections of cacti. Rebutias (left) are some of the easiest as well as the most attractive, with their intricate tracery of spines, scarlet buds and orchid-pink flowers

an angle across a shaded corner of the house. Thickly wrap the roots of the plants in damp sphagnum moss and bind them with copper wire to nestle securely in forks and crevices on the branch. Add one or two delicate ferns for varied leaf texture. Keep the plants' funnels filled with rainwater and add a little diluted feed every few weeks; occasionally spray the moss with water if it looks as though it is drying out. Plants normally flower annually, after which some species die, leaving young offsets to take over for the next season.

NEW PLANTS FROM OLD

HOUSEPLANT AND SHRUB CUTTINGS This season most houseplants will root quickly from cuttings, as will shrubs such as fuchsias, hydrangeas, philadelphus and weigela. Perfectionists identify ideal times for propagating specific plants, but in practice gardeners take cuttings as the opportunity occurs, or perhaps when a shoot is accidentally broken. Some types of cutting material are only available at a particular season – hardwood cuttings, for example, are by definition taken in late autumn or early winter, when the plant tissues have hardened. There are some perennials that are reluctant to grow from cuttings and so these must be layered, grafted or divided, but there still remains a wide range of shrubs, herbaceous plants and houseplants worth attempting to propagate from soft stems, tips or leaves.

Softwood cuttings: these are taken from the tips of the current year's shoots. Trim them to 7.5-10cm (3-4in) long, cutting just below a leaf joint and stripping leaves from the lower half of the stem. Enclose the containers in which the cuttings are placed in plastic bags to maintain humidity.

Semi-ripe cuttings: sturdy sideshoots pulled off the main stem, sometimes with a 'heel' of bark, are best for these. They may take longer to root, but often succeed in a cold frame or when plunged into the ground beside the parent plant, as well as in pots under glass.

Leaf cuttings: many houseplants can be multiplied from whole leaves or prepared fragments. Saintpaulias, for example, will grow from whole leaves, complete with stalks, inserted in compost or water. Begonias will root wherever the severed veins of a leaf are in contact with moist compost. Large leaves, such as those of streptocarpus and mother-in-law's tongue, are best cut laterally into strips whose lower edges are then inserted into the compost.

Always use a sharp knife when preparing cuttings, and make sure the material is chosen from healthy, vigorous plants. Select the best colours when propagating variegated cultivars. Some gardeners like to root cuttings in water, others in a coarse free-draining compost; use whichever method works for you. Hormone rooting preparations can accelerate the development of roots, but will make no difference to species unlikely to root from cuttings (always keep hormone powder in the refrigerator and replace after a few months).

PROPAGATING ROSES From now until early autumn is the period for grafting budding roses onto suitable rootstocks to make new plants. There is no doubt that it is easier to root cuttings from many kinds of roses in early autumn, and spend your summer afternoons instead lightly pruning exhausted stems back to two leaves to prompt a further flush of blooms. However, if your rose collection includes grafted plants, you will probably have to tackle the annual problem of suckers arising from their rootstocks. The easiest way to get rid of them is to cut them off at ground level, but they will reappear, often in greater numbers. To eliminate the current crop altogether, you must scrape away the soil to reveal the origin of

Flowering time for old fashioned roses is also the start of the outdoor tomato season; both of these plants benefit from regular attention such as deadheading, stopping sideshoots, feeding and watering during a dry spell

each sucker and tear it from the plant's root. They are a resource and it is a waste to discard them: shrub and species roses growing on their own roots can be propagated from suckers, as can the rootstocks of grafted varieties if, instead of pulling the sucker free, you cut through the root from which it is growing, and transfer the rooted sucker to a nursery bed.

Turning these rootstocks into budded rose plants is simple surgery that will cause great elation the first time you succeed. To do this you need a very sharp knife, a stem (called a budstick) from your chosen variety, and a steady hand. Make sure the budstick has several plump buds at the base of the leaves, and trim off each leaf but not its stalk. Make a T-shaped cut through the bark of the rootstock, close to the ground for bush roses or higher up to form standards – three or four buds are usually arranged around the stem of a standard, just a single bud for other kinds. The upright of the 'T' should be cut about 2.5cm (1in) or so long, the crosspiece a little shorter.

Cut a bud and its leafstalk from the budstick, starting the cut 2cm (¾in) above the bud and emerging the same distance below to remove a shield-shaped piece of bark with the bud in the centre. Ease out the tiny piece of wood behind the bud, gently lift the bark on each side of the T-shaped cut, and slip the bud behind it. Bind raffia around the wound above and below the bud, and keep the plant watered until the end of the season. Early next spring the rootstock stem above the graft is pruned off, and young growth from the bud should give due cause for celebration. The following autumn your home-made rose bush will be ready to transplant into the flowerbed.

TRAINING

THE TOMATO ROUTINE During high summer tomato plants, both indoors and out, need frequent attention; in fertile soil and sultry weather their growth rate can be alarming. Check indeterminate (cordon) varieties every few days for unwanted sideshoots, especially any arising from near ground level, as these are vigorous competitors and can quickly overtake the main stem. Pinch the main growing tips from outdoor plants at the end of the season to concentrate energy on fruit development. There is no need to pinch out the tips of determinate (bush) varieties because the sideshoots bear fruit and stop of their own accord after flowering, but you should keep tucking straw or some other protective matting under laden branches, to keep the fruit unsoiled. Some lax varieties need their weak stems supported to keep them off the ground; to do this drive a strong stake near the centre of the plant and suspend the branches with loops of soft twine.

Sideshoots taken from cordon plants soon root as soft cuttings, and will provide you with supplementary plants for a late crop under glass. If you are limited to just a few maincrop plants, try training one or two low sideshoots as extra fruiting stems by tying them to neighbouring canes to form a multiple cordon. In view of the tomato's boundless energy, there is no reason why a single plant, started early enough in the season, should not be fan-trained with numerous branches against a sunny wall. Given copious amounts of water and feed, a whole family's needs could then be supplied by a single plant.

PRUNING

THE ART OF SUMMER PRUNING Basic winter pruning restores shape and size to a plant, whereas summer pruning is a more subtle technique that finely tunes a plant's habit and performance. Wisteria, for example, will flower more prolifically if trimmed twice a year; shortening new sideshoots now to about five or six leaves will prevent the production of stems and foliage at the expense of flower buds. These develop on pruned shoots during the second half of the season. By further pruning these sideshoots to two buds in winter, the wisteria is kept within bounds and should produce an improved cascade of blossom the following year.

Other plants benefit from a summer trim. Late-flowering herbaceous perennials, such as the loftier kinds of golden rod and Michaelmas daisies for example, can be too tall for modern compact gardens and are easily damaged where wind is a problem. Although dwarf forms are available, you can restrain the height of tall varieties by shortening their main stems by half in summer. They react by growing numerous sideshoots, and although they flower slightly later than unchecked specimens, they do so at a much more manageable height.

Herbs, too, respond to summer pruning. On one estate I was commanded each year by the cook to hard prune a mint bed just after mid-summer so that she would have a generous supply of young growth with which to make her batch of mint jelly for the winter months. This is sound practice with a herb, such as lemon balm or fennel, that looks untidy in flower; cutting off top growth almost to ground level encourages a new flush of young attractive foliage. It is important, though, to give a dressing of fertilizer immediately after pruning to sustain the plants' extra work.

Fruits susceptible to silver leaf disease (almonds, apricots, cherries and plums, especially 'Victoria') are best pruned in summer when there are few fungal spores about. This often means thinning the stems and thereby sacrificing some of the unpicked crop, and in commercial orchards whole branches laden with immature fruits may be seen lying on the ground during the summer.

Fruits and wall shrubs trained in restricted forms, such as cordons and espaliers, must be summer pruned to flower well the following spring and to avoid losing their geometrical beauty within thickets of young foliage. This stimulates flower bud development, as well as removing surplus growth, which allows sunlight to reach ripening fruit. Specialist handbooks offer complicated advice, but a simple approach is to cut back all new sideshoots to five or six leaves; these are further shortened in winter to one or two buds, so restoring basic outlines. Start cutting back after the summer solstice, dealing first with shrubs such as chaenomeles, gooseberries and currants (red and white only), continuing with cherries and plums, and then moving on to apples and pears.

Summer-fruiting raspberries look tidier if their exhausted canes are cleared as soon as the crop is finished, instead of waiting until winter, and the new canes will then have more room to grow. Blackcurrant bushes, too, can be pruned in summer: about a third of the old dark stems should be removed each year to force the growth of new, more productive branches. Combine pruning with harvesting by cutting out whole surplus branches, taking them away to strip off the currants in the comfort of a seat in the sun.

THE GARDEN SURGERY

SETTING THE GARDEN ALIGHT The infernos of ruthless rainforest destruction have so sharpened environmental awareness that some of us are reluctant to burn any waste garden material. However, one can justify having the occasional bonfire. Apart from the incidental family fun – jacket potatoes, toasted marshmallows and hot chestnuts – a carefully managed bonfire

Right A secluded corner of the garden in dappled shade is an ideal sanctuary for wild flowers, botanical rarities or as here, traditional cottage garden flowers

is one of the most effective health precautions at a gardener's disposal, a certain way to destroy diseased plants and infected prunings. For this reason traditionalists set fire to the straw that surrounded cropped strawberry plants, as well as to that placed around rust-infected mint. Both straw and foliage are consumed, together with pests and disease spores. Research on other crops, including bulbs, suggests that by some mysterious chemistry exposure to smoke actually promotes growth, but for gardeners the main purpose is to sterilize beds and reduce some of the problems that beset even the best strawberry and mint plantations.

A flame-gun is a useful investment, which satisfies organic criteria for approved weed control and can also be used to burn off strawberry and mint foliage. Make sure that this is completely burnt and not just scorched, and also take all the sensible precautions about starting fires in the summer time. If you still have reservations about using fire, an alternative is to run a rotary mower over the exhausted strawberry plants and rake off all the debris; rusty mint may be cut down and subsequent growth sprayed with fungicide.

The joy of a flame-gun is that it consumes all the top growth, reducing it to sterile ashes without harming the buried portion of the plant, which remains protected in the soil – hence another use of a flame-gun for destroying annual weeds; perennials of course survive to grow another day.

INSPIRATION

INTRODUCING WILD FLOWERS There are so many native gems to choose from, that adding a few wild flowers to conventional beds and borders is a great temptation, but it is important to check the credentials of candidates first. A garden is a sanctuary to be protected against unscrupulous intruders, but sadly a number of wild flowers are notorious colonizers; just one apparently innocent specimen can rapidly multiply and become a persistent nuisance. Beware of cow parsley, lamiums polygonums and campanulas with unfamiliar names, until you have irrefutable evidence of their good behaviour. Bosky corners of larger gardens might comfortably accommodate such charming invaders as rosebay willowherb, greater celandine, Enchanter's nightshade, comfrey and green alkanet, but they are much too boisterous for most gardens, where sociability must be tempered with restraint.

First select those species you like and can trust, and then look up their personal preferences for sun or shade, sand or clay, dry soils or moist. Wild flowers by their very nature are 'site specific', flourishing only where the ground and exposure suits them. Since the amount of lime in the soil might also be important, note the predominant weeds in your garden, for these are usually sound indicators of soil type.

It is prudent to start gently if you are used to regarding all weeds as intruders and wild flowers as denizens of the country-side. Look again, for example, at your garden weeds, and reap-praise the dainty foliage of cinquefoils, bird's eye speedwell's sky-blue flowers, the compact growth and gem-like blooms of scarlet pimpernel, or even the dandelion's sunny brilliance. Instead of consigning them to the compost heap, ask yourself if there isn't room in a flower border where, with a little care and timely deadheading, they might earn a home.

Since their wayside beauty is lost in a formal bed, plant them instead in casual drifts between shrubs, beside a path or in an otherwise unoccupied corner. Gradually add patches of other choice species, bought as plants or raised from seed, but try to arrange them all informally. Wild flowers blend subtly with cottage garden plants, but should be kept away from the more vivid garden hybrids lest proximity should make them

Even though the traditional mixed flower border, such as that at Eastgrove (above) is only just reaching its mid-summer peak, some crops are ready to harvest, among them high-bush blueberries (right) and home-grown garlic (far right)

look pale and meagre against their gaudy neighbours. Concentrate on a few trusty kinds such as foxgloves, oxlips, bird's eye primroses, grass of Parnassus, heartsease (wild pansy), quaking grass and lady's smock (cuckoo flower).

Once these tentative plantings have proved their merit, you might want to advance beyond cautious integration and convert whole areas to wild flower gardening, such is the evocative charm and fascination of these plants. Appropriate species might even triumph where cultivated plants fail, because every kind of site has its specialized flora. There are blends for all soils and purposes: spring flowers for heavy soils, species to attract bees or butterflies, wild flower meadow mix-tures and traditional cornfield flowers. Many of these will seed themselves and so persist from year to year.

Sites in the garden are easily adapted to small collections of wild flowers. A pinch or two of mixed seed can turn a tub or urn into a unique feature with an ever-changing sequence of flowers and foliage. Another idea is to loosen stones or sections of mortar in paths and patios to make planting sites for wild thyme, stonecrop, tormentil, mind-your-own-business and mountain avens. You might even relax your normal mowing regime to let lawn species such as speedwell, daisy and black medick bloom, grow and thereby transform a green desert into a flowering meadow.

LOOKING AHEAD

SEEDS TO SOW While admiring your well-dressed kitchen garden, which should be bursting with crops, spare a thought for next year, for canny vegetable growers always have one eye on succession. In order to have nutritious greens early in the season, sow spring cabbage now and then transplant it approximately six weeks later to any vacant ground. This might seem humble fare at the moment compared with mid-summer produce, but after a long winter vitamin-rich cabbages are a refreshing tonic. You can have loose-leaf greens or hearted cabbages according to variety; make another sowing of either in three weeks' time to ensure continuity.

In very cold gardens sow spring cabbages in a cold frame, and leave some of them there in reserve where they can be covered during savage frosts. At the same time sow a few rows of a fast maturing early carrot to protect for autumn supplies. In milder gardens these can still be sown outdoors, and often miss being attacked by the destructive attentions of carrot root flies as these are between generations at the moment. During dry weather flood the carrot seed drills, and refill after sowing with damp peat or spent peat compost to retain the constant moisture essential for good germination. Mulch with grass clippings as a further deterrent to root fly.

Cyclamen take 15-18 months to flower from seed, so if you sow now they will reward your patience early the winter after next. Apart from this long nursery stage they are easy to raise, and certainly worthwhile now that several very fragrant strains are available. Soak the seeds in water for 24 hours and then sow thinly in seed trays, keeping them at a temperature of 15°C (60°F); germination takes approximately one month. When seedlings have made two leaves, transfer to trays of potting compost and maintain the same temperature or a little higher until they are visibly growing. They can then be kept cooler by being given good ventilation and shade from bright sunlight. Water carefully from below and avoid wetting the corm; keep barely moist over winter.

INTIMATIONS OF AUTUMN The fruit season is gathering momentum as currants and berries are ready to be picked by the trugful, and the earliest apples and plums about to follow. Though autumn seems far away yet, harvesting fruit wakens in gardeners a dormant squirrel instinct that will not subside again until the frosts appear. Hoarding starts with surplus fruit and summer vegetables being stashed away in freezers and Kilner jars, followed closely by garlic and shallots as they ripen and dry. Many herbs are at their aromatic peak now, and thyme, sage, rosemary and savory can all be gathered for drying in small bundles for winter use. Sow a late row of parsley which will have to be covered with cloches in winter, or potted up for the kitchen windowsill.

Seeds are also maturing from now onwards. Keep a supply of 35mm film canisters or empty spice pots in your trug for collecting crisp pods and capsules as you weed your way through the flowerbeds. Stick blank labels on containers before setting out and write down seed sources immediately as you collect them; rediscovering dry seed heads from anonymous donors in the winter will test even the most retentive memory. Seed is worth saving from most annuals and many perennials, although cross-pollination makes predicting their colours a gamble. The seed heads of F_1 hybrids must be avoided as genetics play havoc with their offspring.

$\mathcal{L}ate$ SUMMER

The restoration OF A LARGE OVERGROWN GARDEN IS BEST DONE IN REALISTIC STAGES, STARTING WITH THE MOST OBVIOUS AREAS OF NEGLECT AND LEAVING LESS CONSPICUOUS PROBLEMS FOR FUTURE ACTION.

When we were faced with this prospect, the Owner agreed that the dishevelled wilderness of trees and bulbs at the far end of her garden still had enough bosky charm to justify placing its reclamation low on our list of priorities, and so it has been explored occasionally but otherwise left untouched. Recently the subject of its clearance arose once more, to my daughter Sarah's consternation, for in the meantime she had claimed the corner for herself. The ill-defined track meandering through its dappled shade was her secret path leading deep into a magic wood. Where I saw work, she discovered alchemy. Each of our children in turn has been parent of the man, sharing their discoveries and teaching me to look again at whichever garden I was managing at the time. Gnarled faces peering from the bark of old tree stumps, butterfly eggs, broken eggshells revealing the hidden flycatcher's nest, the first daisy and the last strawberry – all these marvels, easily overlooked from adult height, were breathlessly brought to my attention.

Such finds are fortuitous and come only to those allowed to run free in an imaginative outdoors. Sadly, garden design today makes little provision for children, many of whom grow up with little more than a sandpit or swing to play with, and dire warnings not to pick the flowers. Gardens need to provide more than small, defined play areas if children's valuable creative instincts are to be fully nourished. Don't expect impossible standards of neatness – in fact, excessive tidiness spoils the fun. Logs left lying around can be transformed quickly into tables and chairs, industriously hammered full of nails, and used with a board or two to make seesaws and a precarious

Hardy annuals IN THEIR FULL GLORY NEED DEAD-HEADING FOR CONTINUITY

THE INTENSELY BLUE FLOWERS OF *borage* TO GRACE SALADS AND SUMMER DRINKS

Runner beans LADEN WITH PODS TO PICK EVERY FEW DAYS FOR MAXIMUM CROPS

JUICY *fuchsia berries* YOU CAN EAT OR PICK OFF TO ENCOURAGE MORE FLOWERS

climbing frame. Dead leaves can be turned into lacy skeletons, while nature's casualties need their own cemetery with lolly-stick crosses and jam jars of flowers. Above all, never dissuade children from picking flowers: more will grow later, and how else are they to discover posies, petals and potpourri?

PLANNING

THE CHILDPROOF GARDEN Planning gardens with children in mind should not be an elaborate exercise, for most youngsters prefer to devise their own games, often using the least likely places and materials. Far more important is a shift of focus from the garden as a formal no-go area to one that is both attractive and can be lived and played in comfortably. This need only be a temporary phase: children quickly grow up, leaving parents plenty of time to create the perfect garden.

Lawns are popular play areas, easily damaged if made from finer grasses. When sowing a lawn that might be used for foot-ball and other abrasive games, choose a seed mixture rich in hard-wearing fescues and rye grass, modern dwarf strains of which are not so coarse as wild perennial rye grass. Do not mow it closely – 3.5cm (1½in) is short enough – and limit its use in wet weather. If you have room, arrange a clock-golf 'course' with a 12.5cm (5in) pot sunk below ground level at the centre, and spots of paint to mark the hours (dip a tin or pot in white emulsion paint and press it on the grass). Paths and paving slabs can be laid with different colours or textures in geometrical patterns for chess or hop-scotch, but choose a

non-slip surface to avoid accidents. Swings can be intrusive structures and frequently work themselves loose from the ground; where there is a conveniently strong bough, suspend an old tyre instead, while a rope ladder or length of knotted rope will seduce the more adventurous (cushion falls with a deep layer of shredded bark). Line a sandpit with waterproof material so that later it can be transformed into a pond, and cover when not in use to deter pets from fouling it.

Safety is always an important consideration. Stone and metal ornaments, especially if unstable or sharp-edged, are best avoided. Garden ponds are a particular hazard, since small children can drown in just a few centimetres of water. Cover with sturdy but removable net panels, or arrange their surroundings so that they are not easily accessible, and make sure their existence is known and obvious: I once saw a child amble blithely straight into a pond that was invisible beneath a blanket of pond weed. A little common sense could prevent some of the 100,000 annual garden accidents involving children. Never leave glass and sharp

Above *The Little Gardener* by Harold Swanwick captures the magic of childhood in the garden (right)

tools around, and store chemicals and fuel out of reach (preferably in a locked cupboard). Keep fences in good repair where toddlers are liable to wander. Even plain netting or chain-link can be disguised with scrambling plants to form a decorative and functional hedge. Explain to young children the dangers of plant poisons and prickles, rather than overreact by banishing every potentially harmful plant.

Most children ask at some time for a garden of their own. Encourage this by giving them a small area of good soil (NOT a neglected, inhospitable corner), and let them do their own thing. Where space is scarce children will turn even a plastic urn or tub into a garden. Let them help in the greenhouse, too, for they love handling compost, filling trays and sowing large seeds. Work with them, but keep supervision to a minimum – an earlier generation was put off gardening for life by compulsory school allotments and weeding to earn pocket money. Radishes, linaria, sunflowers and immortelles germinate easily, but let them grow strawberries, parsley, carrots or potatoes as well, and sow tree seeds for later transplanting. It is worth investing in child-size garden tools, which can be recycled later for your own use; miniature trowels and handforks are ideal for tending pot plants, others can be used in the greenhouse or when cultivating rock gardens. Do encourage children to keep small pets: this will involve them in recycling waste bedding as compost for their own gardens, as well as collecting weeds or surplus vegetables in order to feed their animals.

BUTTERFLY FLOWERS Apart from a few moths that are serious fruit pests, and large whites whose caterpillars can devastate crops of brassicas, butterflies deserve encouragement for the sheer joy of watching them on a warm, late summer's day as they browse freely on nectar-rich flowers and rotting fruit, or sun themselves on fences and tree trunks. Planting their favourite food plants provides a certain enticement; spring species such as orange-tips and brimstones like aubretia, cowslips, golden alyssum, wallflowers and lady's smock. However, the most colourful species are more abundant during summer. They are attracted by buddleia, valerian, lavender, catmint and honeysuckle followed by Michaelmas daisies and sedum in late summer. Plant heliotrope among your bedding, for its vanilla scent is irresistible to butterflies.

Look carefully before clearing weedy areas, as some species feed or lay their eggs on ivy, brambles and nettles. The latter, a

Many easily grown species are irrestible to butterflies, though buddleias are their great favourites; 'White Profusion' (Below) attracts Red Admirals and Tortoise Shells among others

determined and well-armed colonizer once allowed a foothold, is favoured by Peacock and Tortoiseshell butterflies, whose small voracious caterpillars cluster gregariously on the foliage. The solitary young of Red Admirals spin nettle leaves into tightly curled hide-outs and unless you live near open country, it is worth sparing a few nettles in a corner of the garden for the sake of these species.

FRAMEWORK

HEDGECRAFT For some people hedges are a total nuisance, especially if they are too tall for trimming comfortably from ground level. Spare a thought, though, for the intrepid crews who clip the tallest hedge in the world. This grows on the Meikleour estate in Perthshire, Scotland and extends for nearly a mile. Planted in 1746, the beech hedge is now over 30m (100ft) high. Sensibly it is pruned to shape only once every decade, a job that can take four men, equipped with a hydraulic platform, a month to complete and cost several thousand pounds. On previous occasions steeple jacks and even the local fire brigade have been called in to help with this Herculean undertaking, which makes clipping the average garden hedge mere child's play in comparison.

Nevertheless, the majority of gardeners dislike cutting hedges, particularly those that need frequent attention throughout the growing season. Privet and *Lonicera nitida* are the worst offenders, although they undoubtedly make some of the neatest hedges when they are well looked after. If you want formality without the regular commitment, lightly clip these species in late spring and within five days of doing so spray the foliage with dikegulac ('Cutlass'), a growth inhibitor which diverts the plant's energy into bushiness. Under normal conditions, hedges will stay trim for the rest of the season.

Unfortunately, not all species respond to this treatment. Notable exceptions are box and yew, perhaps the two most traditional hedging plants. Few gardeners deliberately plant these today, partly because they are expensive to buy, but also because of their reputation for slow development. Once established, however, they can still grow too quickly for the reluctant hedger – immaculately formal box hedges in particular often need a monthly trim between early summer and early autumn. The solution is to clip annually in mid-summer, and then for the rest of the year, there is little choice but to settle for a slight softening of their crisp outlines.

Very often a hedge is no more than a simple passive barrier, planted for a variety of reasons: to create a windbreak, for example, or deter intruders, to define boundaries, or confer privacy. Decide which function your hedge serves, and then consider whether it could be transformed into a more attractive feature to contribute something positive to the overall garden design. Clipping to severe, right-angled outlines is an

PLANT HIGHLIGHTS OF THE MONTH

Lachenalias These demure South African bulbs must be grown indoors in cooler climates. To get the best from their intriguingly marked blooms grow them en masse in shallow clay pans or in hanging baskets. Pot or repot now in groups and keep evenly moist at

about 10°C (50°F); feed regularly while in active growth. There are numerous species and hybrids, flowering in late winter and early spring in white, yellow or red racemes. The bulbs need to be rested in summer in a dry warm place.

Michaelmas daisies Although renowned for their autumn display, the earliest varieties of these late-flowering asters show colour from mid-summer onwards, when mildew may also reveal its presence. Many gardeners despair of this susceptible genus, but rich soil, plenty of

moisture and airy surroundings can deter mildew, as do routine sprays of fungicide, applied regularly after the longest day: try alternate sprays of different fungicides to undermine resistance. If all else fails, substitute *amellus* and *Novae Angliae* varieties for more vulnerable *Novi Belgii* types.

Vallota Formerly a popular house-plant, the Scarborough lily has been eclipsed by monstrous hippeastrum hybrids that lack its grace and brilliance. In summer the single species, *Vallota speciosa*, produces several stems of scarlet flowers, up to ten in a cluster; 'Major' has larger

flowers, while those of 'Alba' are pure white. After they have flowered, the plants can be kept in leaf or allowed to rest until winter. Water and feed regularly, and topdress pots with fresh compost annually in spring – plants flower best when pot-bound.

Strictly clipped hedges are active design components in the garden. Whether grown to accentuate informal shrubbery (left) or to frame carpet bedding (top right), they need frequent attention to maintain a precise outline.

Below right Courgette flowers need to be picked when they are fully opened, with the immature fruit attached

essential discipline where hedges are used as formal edging to beds; slow-growing and dwarf varieties such as lavender or box are ideal for this purpose. One elderly gardener I know recalled cutting the box hedges at Blenheim Palace, near Oxford in the 1930s, when the Duke of Marlborough used to lie prone to check that they were in fact symmetrical. However, unless a hedge is used as a deliberate frame, such precise geometry is not necessary and is often inappropriate. Try moulding hedges to match or complement other features instead, using shears like a sculptor's knife. Bulky rounded contours, for example, can echo the lines of a thatched roof visible behind it.

Set your imagination free. Hedges can be clipped to create numerous topiary ornaments and archways can be cut through the hedge to reduce its otherwise plain features, so transforming a barrier into a frame for a view. With a little patience and care most species can be trained to arch over a garden path, or to form pillars beside a gateway to emphasize its importance.

INSPIRATION

FLOWERS WORTH EATING Our gardening ancestors, more widely versed in plant lore than we are, understood the medicinal and culinary value of all kinds of flowers, most of them first cultivated for their perfume or for use as natural remedies. Though some plants, such as borage and elderflowers, are still occasionally gathered for the kitchen, few gardeners and cooks today are schooled in the imaginative use of edible flowers.

In addition to borage, whose bright blue starry blooms decorate summer drinks or, minus their green sepals, add a cool sweetness to salads, a number of common flowers were once used to embellish food. Try adding nasturtium flowers to fresh fruit dishes and the spicy flower buds to green salads, using brilliantly coloured varieties such as dwarf, deep crimson 'Empress of India' or 'Peach Melba', whose cream petals are splashed with scarlet. Vivid orange pot marigold petals were once a popular colouring and seasoning ingredient for rice, custards and cooked meat; use the basic *Calendula officinalis*, which blooms right through a mild winter and often self-seeds. Always gather flowers when they are just fully opened, and preferably immediately before use, as many close after picking.

Fresh sweet violets, usually candied, can be used in syrups, salads and flower vinegars, the latter is also sometimes made with strongly scented roses, pinks, rosemary and lavender flowers. The blooms of paeonies, whose ground peppery seeds used to be made into

a condiment, add flavour to drinks and sauces; avoid the crimson cottage paeony with its unpleasant odour, and choose Chinese hybrids such as the pink 'Kelway's Supreme' or maroon 'Philippe Rivoire' instead. Garden forms of many wild flowers are also edible, particularly cowslips and primroses which are both used candied and are ideal for adding flavour to puddings. The dainty purple, yellow and white pansy flowers of heartsease have a delicate flavour and traditional medicinal value, as the name implies.

Pruning blackcurrants releases the leaves' powerful and lingering fragrance, which is shared by the flowers and flower buds, so much so that after the berries have been harvested, the buds can be stripped from the pruned stems and then used in the manufacturing of perfume. At home a few strings of open flowers can be picked in spring to flavour ice cream and sorbets. The flowers of the common yellow garden broom are often made into wine, and the almond flavoured buds can be used in pickles or salads.

While many vegetable flowers are insignificant or offensively scented, a distinguished few are almost worth growing just for their blooms, among them the neglected root crops salsify and scorzonera. The latter is a perennial, with bright yellow flowers like dandelions, while salsify is biennial and produces purple daisies in summer. Whole flowers or petals of both can be mixed with salads, and their buds can be eaten cooked or raw. Forcing chicory left to flower produces tall stems and a host of bright sky blue daisies that can be eaten raw or pickled. The marrow, or squash, family has large golden flowers which are edible if picked before they fade. Once only a Mediterranean delicacy, cookery fashion has made courgettes served complete with their flowers widely popular, but they must be picked while still small. The curd of cauliflowers is, of course, nothing more than an enormously over-developed head of flower buds; try 'Purple Cape' which has a fine flavour and a rich red-purple curd, intriguing when added to stir-fried dishes or served raw in salads. If your radishes bolt to flower quickly in the summer heat, let their fat spicy seed pods develop and eat them raw, cooked or pickled: 'München Bier' has outsize succulent pods.

FEASTING ON FUCHSIAS In one greenhouse I trained the opulent fuchsia 'Lady Boothby' right up into the roof like a grape vine, so that its blooms hung in heavy crimson and purple festoons. As its prolific crop of enormous berries ripened, an alcoholic blackbird came daily to feast on any that had fallen and started to ferment. It would then flutter drunkenly outdoors and stand beneath the garden sprinkler until sober, when the whole performance would be repeated.

I cannot promise intoxication, or even mild merriment, but the luscious berries are certainly edible and have a fruity, slightly vinous flavour when eaten raw. They can be pickled in red wine vinegar, or marinaded in brandy and icing sugar to fill soufflé omelettes, top cheesecakes or blend into ice creams and sorbets. With 1.5kg (3lb) sugar, lemon rind and yeast, 2kg (4lb) of berries will ferment 4.55 litres (1 gallon) of rosé country wine, or you can make an intriguing marmalade with them: bruise 2kg (4lb) berries and layer in a bowl with 1kg (2lb) of sugar and the juice of a lemon for 24 hours before cooking in the normal way. Particularly enticing is an old recipe for fuchsia berry dumplings. Melt 55g (2oz) of butter in 150ml (5fl oz) of water and bring to the boil. Remove from the heat, and add 55g (2oz) of self-raising flour and beat until smooth. Then beat in 1 egg until fully blended. Enclose each berry in this mixture and fry in very hot, deep fat for a few minutes until golden. Drain, sprinkle with sugar and serve.

FOCUS ON FOOD

THE GARDEN PULSE The best way to appreciate how much has been sacrificed by our dependence on frozen peas, is to grow a row or two in the garden. Shop supplies are a poor substitute, for peas rapidly lose their freshness after picking. Gathered and shucked just before use, however, garden peas have a flavour and succulence that recalls childhood days spent sitting on the back doorstep with a colander and trugfuls of crisp green pods.

Seasoned pea fanciers soon become connoisseurs, as I discovered on one estate. Naturally assuming that gardeners know best, I selected and sowed a number of modern pea varieties noted for their yield. Row by row they matured and I delivered them confidently to the kitchen door, only to be rebuked a little later by the unimpressed cook who commented scornfully, 'Not quite up to 'Kelvedon Wonder', are they?' After years of critical tasting, she could unerringly distinguish the aristocratic few from a plebeian host of indifferent peas. Only once did she recognize a worthy rival, and that was a tall prolific pea called 'Admiral Beatty'. Since then most vegetable varieties have been assessed for authenticity or duplication, and 'Admiral Beatty' is now considered a synonym for 'Alderman'. It deserves to be widely grown in gardens, even

Opposite Purple podded peas are decorative as well as edible, and bear pods that are conspicuously clear of their foliage. Below Restrained varieties of rosemary are ideal for simple artistic topiary

though it reaches a magnificent 1.8m (6ft) in height and is therefore disowned by suppliers who assume that gardeners with limited space must confine themselves to dwarf varieties.

Height is an important dimension in any garden, but is specially relevant in very small ones where vertical features relieve Lilliputian monotony. Peas and beans are ideal, for taller kinds combine an exuberant subtropical appearance with increased yield. Runner beans grown on bamboo cane wigwams are obvious candidates, but French beans can be trained in this way too. The best of these is 'Climbing Blue Lake', a white-flowered variety producing masses of fat, juicy pencil pods; grow them outdoors like runner beans, or sow under glass in early spring and late summer for out of season crops. Tall flowering peas make colourful features in the summer garden. Although edible when fresh, the 'Purple-podded Pea' has more flavour used as a dried pulse ('Alderman' is excellent for this, too), and it is also outstandingly decorative, its rich mauve flowers and deep purple pods conspicuous among the green foliage. Crimson *Lathyrus tingitanus* and mauve 'Lord Anson's Pea' are unusual pretty annuals that may be grown among climbing beans for extra colour.

When planning a supply of garden peas, it is important to remember that from sowing to the start of the harvest early varieties take 10-12 weeks, the second early crop 12-14 and tall maincrops 14-17. Some people always have difficulty germinating peas and beans, especially where soil-borne pests and diseases are present. Seeds dressed with fungicide are available from market garden sources, otherwise add a suitable dressing to a packet of seeds and shake well. Maximize space by sowing culinary peas in broad bands the width of a spade or more. In cold areas, sow peas in groups of five or six in small pots or in the cells of divided trays, planting out seedlings unthinned; sow beans singly in pots or space them 5-7.5cm (2-3in) apart each way in seed boxes. Soak all peas and beans in cold water overnight to accelerate germination. All pulses prefer deeply-dug, limed soil, and runner beans in particular like plenty of moisture at their roots; soak and bury newspapers, old woollens or autumn leaves when digging the ground prior to sowing. In dry weather mulch peas and beans with grass clippings or compost to retain moisture and help combat mildew.

When early runner beans first bloom, some gardeners spray their plants with a weak sugar solution to attract pollinating insects, but this should not be necessary in late summer, their natural flowering season. Towards the end of the crop, leave unused peas and beans on the vines to dry for seed, or as

pulses to add to stews and soups. For full-flavoured haricot beans, sow 'Dutch Brown' in mid-spring and leave unpicked until the autumn; store dry in airtight jars. Sow surplus pea and bean seeds broadcast on spare pieces of ground and dig in when a few centimetres high to enrich the soil. Finally, cut off the exhausted vines at ground level, leaving behind their nitrogen-rich roots to decay, and then plant brassicas in the firm undisturbed soil.

TRAINING

HERB TOPIARY Pruning plants restores both shape and vitality, as gardeners who may be reluctant to carry out this task will confirm, since clipping a hedge or mowing the lawn only stimulates yet more prolific growth. Perennial herbs, too, respond to frequent picking (a productive form of pruning) by making many new stems that eventually give plants a finer, closer texture. By a combination of training, clipping and pinching, varieties with small leaves can in fact be transformed into whimsical miniature topiary for decorative pots and jardinières. Elegantly tapered spirals, cones, and pyramids are simple shapes that can be formed from straight rooted cuttings or bushy plants of rosemary, santolina, lemon verbena or

scented geraniums, while lavender and sweet bay, with their more open growth, make handsome mop head standards and mushroom-shaped plants.

Positive support is essential to reinforce strict upright growth, so from the start, use a straight bamboo cane and firmly anchor it into the compost, and tie the plant's leading shoot to this at frequent intervals with raffia or thin, soft twine. Nurse this leader until it reaches the height of your choice and then remove its tip.

Sideshoots fill out the body of the topiary. Shorten any that disrupt the intended outline, but leave the rest to grow freely, especially those near the base, unless your design depends on a bare stem. Once the shape starts to emerge, you can sculpt a more precise outline with scissors or small shears, using the rim of the pot as a guide for circular forms. Spirals are trained by twisting the flexible leader round its support, mirroring the shape of a stick of barley sugar. Trim frequently and cleanly, for the basis of all topiary is a crisp and symmetrical outline. Proceed cautiously, for it is safer to cut off too little and have to go over the piece again, than to have to wait for regrowth to restore the results of overenthusiasm. Two or three

seasons will see the topiary finished and probably pot-bound; moving it on to a larger container will boost further unwanted growth, so repot into the same size annually, trimming off some of the outer roots to make way for fresh compost.

PRUNING

KEEPING LAVENDER IN TRIM Even if you do not gather spikes of lavender blooms to perfume your fresh linen, the spent flowers should be cut off, together with the tips of shoots, to discourage the straggly bad habits of most varieties. An annual trim can maintain a low hemline on lavender bushes and hedges, at least for many years, but sooner or later their lower stems become bare and the time arrives for sterner treatment. Unfortunately lavender is one of the species that resents hard pruning, and cutting into old wood often leads to the death of a stem rather than to its rejuvenation.

You can root sideshoots as semi-ripe cuttings from now onwards, but it is sometimes possible with lavender hedges to bend branches low enough to root them as layers, reclothing the base of the hedge with minimal upheaval and risk because layers continue to be sustained by the parent plant until they are cut off as self-sufficient plants. A special type of layering called dropping is a more wholesale way to salvage old woody plants such as lavender, hyssop or erica. The complete plant is dug up in spring with a good rootball and replanted in a deeper hole, either in the same place or in a nursery bed, so that the bare stems are covered with moist fertile soil in which they will root after a year or so. Either leave the plants at their new level or carefully excavate around the stems, cutting off those that have rooted and transplanting them elsewhere.

UNDER GLASS

COLOUR IN THE CONSERVATORY Stocking a conservatory must not to be undertaken lightly, despite irresistible visions of a tropical tangle of *Lotus berthelotii*, bougainvilleas, passion flowers and other tender exotica. Good glasshouse management depends upon skill and experience, and it is best to make a modest beginning. Any houseplant, especially the larger evergreens sold by chain stores and garden centres, will rejoice in the enhanced light and warmth of a conservatory, and you can start your collection with these.

For a flamboyant and foolproof display of indoor colour in early spring make sowings now of classic annuals such as

Above Bays trained as mop head standards are impressive sentinels in the open border. Lavender, too, can be transformed into interesting topiary but is more commonly used as a fragrant evergreen hedge (right)

schizanthus, salpiglossis, larkspur and sweet scabious, and grow them lavishly in 15-20cm (6-8in) pots of good compost. Pot up nerines for winter flowering, planting them in the same way as hippeastrums, with the upper half of the bulbs exposed. Grow arum lilies, especially snow-white *Zantedeschia aethiopica*; ignore funereal connotations, for this arum is handsome and easily grown, with enormous flowers like reflexed trumpets appearing in spring and early summer.

Lilies grow happily indoors, and on grand estates it was once customary for gardeners to pot up hundreds of sweetly scented kinds such as *Lilium regale* and the immaculate Madonna lily, *L. candidum*. An advantage of growing lilies in containers was that they could be easily moved, and when in

bloom, they would be gathered in strategic groups in passage-ways, or perhaps arranged to line a staircase, where their heady perfume could spread throughout the house. Lilies grown in pots can be more closely supervised, which is especially desirable where garden soils are far from ideal. Some kinds, such as *L. auratum* and *L. speciosum rubrum*, resent a lot of lime, and where the ground is chalky it would be prudent to indulge these fussy but glorious species with containers of lime-free compost. Free drainage is also critical for good health, and it is usually easier to add extra grit to potting compost than it is to naturally heavy clay. Where possible, use a loam-based compost with an additional 20% grit. For single bulbs a 20cm (8in) pot is adequate, while three or four will fit comfortably into a 30cm (12in) container. Check a catalogue or handbook for individual preferences about planting depths – most lilies succeed if planted with their base 7.5-10cm (3-4in) from the top of the compost, but some (such as *L. auratum* and *L. henryi*) are stem rooting and should be planted 5cm (2in) deeper, whereas Madonna lilies like to be fairly near the surface.

Pot up bulbs in early autumn, water in and then keep barely moist for the rest of the winter. Stand pots in a cool but frost-free place, such as a shed or under the greenhouse staging, and do not disturb until growth appears in spring, when they can be moved into full light indoors. For early blooms, bring pots into warmth in mid-winter and start watering as growth commences. After flowering all potted lilies are best planted in the open ground, once frosts are past, but if they have been fed conscientiously every week during growth they can be repotted in autumn for a further season in containers.

NEW PLANTS FROM OLD

AERIAL LAYERING When a potted rubber plant grows inexorably near to the ceiling or an ornamental tree is difficult to propagate from cuttings, it is time to try your hand at aerial layering, a cunning professional method of multiplication that seldom fails. Summer is the best time to layer houseplants such as crotons, dieffenbachia and ficus species; any time from spring to late summer is suitable for rhododendrons, pieris, medlars and other reluctant trees or shrubs.

Make an upward cut half-way into a stem or branch, about 30cm (12in) or so from its tip and wedge the wound open with a piece of matchstick or a pad of moist sphagnum moss. Pack plenty of moss around the cut as a fat bandage and enclose this with a length of clear polythene tied firmly at top and bottom with raffia. When white roots become visible beneath the plastic (after a few weeks for houseplants, a year or more for outdoor subjects) unwrap the rooted tip, cut it off and pot up. New shoots may be produced by the donor from its truncated stem, and you can use these as further aerial cuttings or leave them to make bushy growth.

THE GARDEN SURGERY

VIRUSES   Like gardeners themselves, few plants are immune
to attacks by viruses, a large and widespread group of
pathogens whose behaviour is only partly understood.
Diagnosis is often unreliable, for common symptoms such as
leaf mottling and spotting, distortion of the young shoots,
flower discolouration ('breaking') and unthrifty growth, can
also be the result of other ailments such as mineral deficiency
or simply the normal ageing process.

Treatment, too, is difficult and is usually limited to the
victim's destruction. Viruses are highly transmittable, and are
chiefly passed on by handling or by the migration of insect
pests; even where only a part of a plant is obviously infected,
the only sure remedy is to pull it up and burn it. More often
than we realize many garden fruit trees and bushes are probably infected, their yields dwindling imperceptibly until compared with those of healthy stocks; plants such as tulips,
cucumbers, courgettes and tomatoes on the other hand can be
totally disabled, so it is soon obvious when they have been
attacked. The picture is further complicated by species that
tolerate viruses. Some raspberry varieties, for example, can be
infected and will show little or no ill-effects, but remain infec-
tious to other more susceptible kinds. Virus symptoms are even
welcome in certain instances where they produce attractive
colouration: feathering on the petals of 'broken' tulips and the
gold-mottled leaves of *Abutilon pictum* 'Thompsonii' are both
due to dormant viruses.

There are useful precautions that can be taken to prevent
infection. If you suspect that a virus is present, pull the plant
up straightaway, then burn it, and watch its neighbours for
symptoms. Never propagate from affected plants, as special
techniques are needed to ensure complete good health. You
can buy plants certified virus-free, but these are always vulnerable to fresh infection; virus-resistant stocks are more dependable, especially in ground where soil-borne viruses have
occurred. It is essential to sterilize greenhouses and containers
between susceptible crops, use fresh compost, and always burn
affected leaves and other plant debris.

LOOKING AHEAD

MINIATURE NARCISSI   There is nothing brash or blousy about
any of the daffodil species. Their charm and daintiness
matches the soft colours of an early spring, and because few of
the miniature kinds have felt the plant-breeder's heavy hand,
they look like wild flowers and therefore blend more easily
among the snowdrops, primroses and other stars of the spring
garden. Although more expensive to buy than larger daffodils,
most kinds soon multiply in the garden from a few initial
groups. Order some now to start a lifetime collection.

**Opposite White varieties of lilies, camellias, stephanotis
and other conservatory plants remain unblemished when
grown under cover. Above Narcissus 'Peeping Tom' on the
other hand is totally weather resistant**

Rare and elusive species apart, these miniatures range in
height from the diminutive *Narcissus asturiensis* (syn *minimus*),
only 5-7.5cm (2-3in) tall and a bantam version of the typical
yellow trumpet daffodil, to the 30-35cm (12-14in) stems of
'February Gold' or 'Peeping Tom', both cyclamineus hybrids.
Their dam, *N. cyclamineus*, is a 15-20in (6-8in) high wilding,
with bright yellow flowers, whose petals sweep back like the
ears of a frightened horse. Outdoors it blooms in late winter
and is therefore ideal for early-flowering in pans.

Plant the taller miniatures between border perennials or
through ground-cover plants, and naturalize them in grass left
uncut until mid-summer. Some of the best for this purpose are
N. pseudo-narcissus, the Lent lily or wild daffodil eulogized by
Wordsworth, and any of the sweet-scented poet's narcissi such
as *N. albus plenus odoratus* (double white) or *N. recurvus*, the
renowned pheasant's eye and one of the latest to flower.

In short turf or mossy areas try any of the various forms of
N. bulbocodium, the curious moisture-loving hoop petticoats,
with flowers like inflated funnels. At the base of deciduous
hedges or around small shrubs, plant single and double jonquils
to perfume the air and add a touch of medieval elegance; dark
evergreens are an effective contrasting background for pale
varieties such as 'Thalia', with several white chalice-cups to
each stem, and multi-headed 'Silver Chimes', cream with a
pale yellow corona. In these semi-shaded positions, make sure
all varieties receive at least half a day's sunshine.

Early AUTUMN

Early AUTUMN CAN BE LOVELY, WITH THE SOFTER SUN-
LIGHT FLATTERING THE COLOURS OF FLOWERS, AND LENGTHENING
SHADOWS MAKING CRISP CONTRASTS BETWEEN PLANT PROFILES.

It cannot be denied that mature gardens look irresistibly gorgeous in their gentle decline, as late roses, fuchsias and bedding
plants overlap with autumn stalwarts such as sedums, nerines,
chrysanthemums and Michaelmas daisies. Humid evenings and
perceptibly shortening days coax enough runner beans from
the vines to satisfy even the keenest of appetites. Yet everyone
that I have gardened for has greeted the onset of autumn with
a sense of foreboding, regarding it only as a season of mists and
melancholy, and they have been quite unable to understand
my elation. The view from the potting shed is much more optimistic, with the imminence of a lighter workload and the
prospect of finally clearing away a year's mistakes and unful-
filled schemes. The kitchen garden war on weeds can be
relaxed at last: any that grow now are unlikely to seed themselves and can be left in places as protective winter ground-
cover. Topdressed with dried blood (approximately 33.8g per
sq metre/1oz per sq yard) in early spring and then dug in, they
rapidly decay into valuable humus.

Above all, autumn is the climax, when a primitive squirrel
instinct drives us to spend what little free time that we have
gathering in every available root and berry. Spend the
evenings harvesting the hedgerows, collecting all the hips,
haws, sloes, blackberries and elderberries to make hedgerow
wine – 0.5kg (1lb) of each fruit mixed with 1.5kg (3lb) sugar
makes a rich, portly 4.5 litres (1 gallon). The same amount of
fruit plus 1kg (2lb) apples, preferably crab, will make hedgerow
jelly (use a standard jelly method and add 0.5kg (1lb sugar) to
every 0.5 litres (1 pint) of liquor).

WHAT TO WATCH FOR THIS MONTH

Crab apples STUDDING THE TREES WITH COLOUR AND THE PROMISE OF FLAVOURSOME PRESERVES

THE CURIOUS *physostegia* FLOWER TO TOUCH AND DISCOVER WHY IT IS CALLED THE OBEDIENT PLANT

RIPE *figs* AND EARLY *apples* TO ENJOY AFTER PICKING STRAIGHT FROM THE TREE

TENDER *shrubs in pots* READY FOR RE-HOUSING AFTER THEIR SUMMER BREAK OUTDOORS

A few secret places even conceal hazelnuts – if another kind of squirrel has not found them first – and wild hops; we have propagated both for the garden. The hops have a dual-purpose – firstly as a climber when their extravagant foliage will wreathe old-fashioned roses on poles and arches and secondly, the great trusses of papery cones that follow can be harvested to flavour beer or to use in aromatic herb pillows, solace for anyone with autumn blues.

PLANNING

EMBELLISHING THE AUTUMN GARDEN Berries and other fruits, whether edible or ornamental, are a vital part of autumn's glory. Even raspberries and strawberries, essentially summer crops, persist in our garden until the first frosts – pure self-indulgence, of course, but easy to arrange with the right varieties. 'Aromel', a perpetual strawberry as fragrantly toothsome as 'Royal Sovereign', first crops in spring if protected in a polytunnel. Outdoor berries follow in mid-summer, with later fruit on the runners; if the first flush of bloom is picked off, the crop will come late and prolifically, continuing well into autumn if covered with cloches.

Late-fruiting raspberries such as 'Heritage' and 'Zeva' are a gamble, especially in more exposed areas where the berries are regularly spoilt by rain and early frosts. However, the relative newcomer 'Autumn Bliss' is more dependable, as it starts ripening earlier than other kinds. Yellow raspberries are an epicurean delight: 'Fallgold' is an autumn-fruiting variety and should be grown in a sheltered sunny spot, its mellow vinous flavour compensating for shy yields. Remember these late raspberries fruit on the current year's canes; unlike summer varieties, they need cutting right to the ground in winter.

Crab apples make an inspired choice for the autumn garden, combining edible fruit with flamboyant colours. Perhaps the best variety for culinary use is 'John Downie' and its bright orange-red fruits are among the largest of the crabs. The trusses of small, brilliant yellow fruits of 'Golden Hornet' often keep throughout the winter, and it excels as an efficient pollinator for other domestic apple trees.

Although there are numerous berried shrubs and trees for the ornamental garden, attempts to explore beyond the more familiar cotoneasters, berberis, rowan and rugosa roses sometimes results in disappointment. One reason is that species may need both male and female plants for cross-pollination. *Viburnum davidii*, for example, is best planted in groups to ensure plenty of turquoise-blue berries. If you plant a female *Skimmia japonica* 'Foremanii' with the male clone 'Rubella' it will bear

Right Fruits of the 'quick' or blackthorn, sloes are a popular hedgerow crop for wines and preserves

Right When grown in the right soil rhododendrons provide colour both in spring and autumn. Below The male form 'Rubella' (right) is an essential companion if the female *Skimmia japonica* (left) is to carry many berries

vivid red fruits in large bunches. Hollies are notorious for refusing to berry unless near a male, the most handsome of which is the variegated and inaptly named 'Golden Queen'.

Autumn leaf tints are not so easy to guarantee. Although many species perform well in any soil, there is evidence that acidity affects the intensity of their colours. Some of the most spectacular plants insist on lime-free soil, and if given such conditions you can expect glorious ruby, purple and orange tints from *Rhododendron luteum* (deciduous azalea), or an autumn riot of gold and crimson foliage on enkianthus bushes, especially *Enkianthus campanulatus* and *E. perulatus*.

Weather conditions also affect the intensity of autumn tints. Colour changes depend upon a succession of cold nights, which suppress growth and trigger subtle chemical reactions in leaf and stem physiology, followed by bright sunshine which accelerates the decay of green chlorophyll and encourages sugars to accumulate in the leaves. It takes the perfect balance between warm sunny days and sharply frosty nights to stage the most memorable displays. Protection from damaging winds is essential for sustained brilliance. If you have a sunny sheltered site arrange your autumn panorama there and should there be room for only one specimen, choose a Japanese maple such as *Acer japonicum* and *A. palmatum*, some of which turn to crimson and others to yellow. There is a cultivar for every size of niche, always graceful in leaf but notably supreme in autumn.

UNDER GLASS

FORCING SPRING FLOWERS Daffodils, especially the more slender or fragile miniature species, are happy growing in pots for their first year. Keep them outdoors or in a cold frame until their buds are visible and then bring them indoors to flower.

An alternative is to plunge the pots in a window box until they have flowered, when they can be replaced with other plants. Their scale and ease of cultivation make them ideal contents for decorative containers, crock kettles and small urns; planted this month, a potful of pale fragrant 'Hawera' or the wispy rush-leaved daffodil, *Narcissus juncifolius*, with its many small-cupped yellow blooms, would make a novel and enduring gift, flowering a few weeks earlier than it would do outdoors.

A good proprietary bulb fibre will suit them for a single season. Plant the bulbs in the moistened fibre, covering them with an amount of compost twice their own depth and leaving a distance equal to their width between adjacent bulbs. Keep in a cool and dark situation until several centimetres of top growth can be seen, and then bring gradually into gentle warmth. For permanent cultivation in pots or deep pans use a soil-based compost with a generous layer of broken pots or gravel covering the drainage hole. Take care not to over-water, but continue watering and feeding until leaves die down naturally. Repot every three to four years.

Sweet violets are unusual subjects for pots, tubs and window boxes, especially if combined with small early-flowering bulbs such as bright yellow winter aconites, the dainty narcissi 'February Silver' and 'Tête-à-Tête', or crocus 'Golden Bunch'.

Healthy plants are transferred now to containers filled with a rich loam-based compost such as John Innes No 3, and can be left in place after flowering or transplanted to the garden to make way for summer bedding plants.

One of the most detested duties of a garden boy in private service used to be that of weeding violet frames in the frozen depths of winter. Forcing violets in cold frames was a regular practice on large estates in order to provide uninterrupted cutting from mid-autumn until early spring, when the outdoor crop took over. In less favoured or exposed gardens, flowering violets under glass is the best way to guarantee perfect blooms, and it is the only certain method for gardeners who want to grow the slightly tender but very fragrant Parma violets. Plants are dug from the garden in early autumn and set 23-30cm (9-12in) apart each way in prepared soil, either in cold frames or in the soil border of a greenhouse glazed to ground level. Remember the violet's appetite for fat living – if you have leaf mould, old manure or good garden compost, work plenty of this into the soil, or use spent potting compost mixed with a little fertilizer to topdress the bed. Water well after planting, moderately thereafter. In warm weather give the plants full ventilation but in a cold spell be prepared to cover them with newspaper if frost threatens. In cool conditions plants will flower a few weeks earlier than outdoors, but in a temperature of 7-10°C (45-50°F) they may bloom all winter. After flowering transfer plants outdoors once more.

POTATOES – LATE EARLIES First early potatoes are valuable not only for their fast growth to maturity but also for their ability to be forced out of season. The best for home use are those with neat, compact haulm, as they will require little space. Keep a few 'new' potato tubers, bought or home-grown, choosing those about the size of a bantam's egg. Reserve some for a spring crop under glass, and store them in cool and dark conditions until you are ready to plant them.

For winter use plant some now in pots, with a diameter of 38-45cm (15-18in), large buckets (about 18 litres (4 gallon) capacity) or small half-barrels. Make sure the containers have drainage holes; cover these with pebbles or coarse peat, and quarter-fill them with moist potting compost, preferably a rich soil-based mixture such as John Innes No 3. Firm gently, space three or four tubers on the surface, and cover with about 10cm (4in) of compost. Stand the pots outdoors in a warm position, and water regularly. When the plants are about 15cm (6in) tall, add a further 10cm (4in) of compost, repeating this until the soil surface is just below the rim. Bring the pots under cover if frost threatens. The tubers can be harvested when the plants flower, although they will keep in good condition until winter if top growth is cut off after flowering; the pots should then be stored in a dark frost-free place until the tubers are needed.

PLANT HIGHLIGHTS OF THE MONTH

Saffron **A stunning sight by the fieldful in autumn, *Crocus sativus* is a handsome species with enormous rosy-purple flowers and vivid red stigmata, which are collected for the preparation of saffron. Slightly elusive in cool gardens, the bulbs need planting during mid-summer in a warm sheltered position in full sun. Since they enjoy a rich living, grow them in the kitchen garden around the base of well-fed fruit trees, and divide successful clumps every few years to maintain prolific flowering.**

Elderberry **Children hollow its stems for blowpipes, country women gather its fragrant flowers and great trusses of berries for wines or preserves, and tradition regards it as guardian over all wild herbs. Yet the common elderberry (*Sambucus nigra*) is seldom seen in gardens, even in its several ornamental forms: fern-leaved *laciniata*, golden 'Aurea' or creamy-berried 'Fructu-Luteo' that makes a unique white elderberry wine. Trials are evaluating further decorative forms, that are all robust and well-mannered, especially if they are grown on chalky soils.**

Physostegia **Years ago cottage gardens depended on charming, old-fashioned perennials such as Chinese lanterns, soldiers and sailors, Georgius the Fifth and late-flowering physostegia, better known as the obedient plant. Push any of the frilly-lipped tubular flowers, stacked neatly in erect spires, to one side and they will remain there for some time. Despite this sensitivity, physostegia is doggedly robust, its white or rosy pink flowers never failing to glow brightly throughout the autumn months.**

For very early crops, start in mid-winter, following the same method but keeping containers in a warm place in full daylight. Alternatively, if you have a soil border in a frost-free greenhouse or conservatory, the tubers can be planted there, 10cm (4in) deep and 23cm (9in) apart. There is no need to earth up the plants, but it is a good idea to mulch them with garden compost or well-rotted manure; this will be turned in as the potatoes are dug, leaving the soil ready for planting greenhouse tomatoes or cucumbers in late spring.

TRAINING

FRUITFUL CLIMBERS Perhaps the most satisfying use for a garden or conservatory wall is as support for training fruit. The resulting produce is usually superior to that from trees growing freely, but improved quality is not the sole motive for this practice. The resulting visual effect is also very pleasing, as French gardeners realized last century when they perfected a number of ornate styles for training fruit, most of them sadly neglected in modern gardens. In addition to simple cordons, fans and multi-tiered espaliers, they evolved designs based on lattices and arcures that were clearly influenced by needlework techniques. Lattices are made by training branches sideways at 45 degrees so that each plant assumes the shape of the letter 'V', or a vertical series of these; branches of adjacent plants are interwoven to create an open lattice or trellis work of stems. Training an arcure, on the other hand, involves arching a single main stem to one side to form a semi-circle. From the top of this a sideshoot is then curved the following season in the opposite direction and this sequence is repeated as the tree gains height; a row of finished arcures resembles several tiers of symmetrical arches, each studded with buds that are pruned to form fruiting spurs. These methods can be applied to wall-trained apples, pears, gooseberries, and white and red currants.

Since aspect determines the amount of light and heat received, fruits from warmer climates (gages, kumquats, figs

erected 1-1.2m (3-4ft) apart over a pathway, join them with horizontal wires about 38cm (15in) apart and then allow some of the cordon sideshoots to grow along these to form a simple fruiting tunnel. Most varieties can be used in this way, although tip-bearing apples should be avoided as they are considerably more difficult to train.

As a change from traditional topfruit, try growing thornless forms of blackberries and hybrid berries on arches and pillars, where their rich autumn colours will be seen to an advantage. The most decorative of all is the 'Oregon Thornless' blackberry, noted for its deeply cut 'parsley-leaf' foliage and sharp tasting berries. Crops are light, however, and if yield is the main priority a better choice might be 'Black Satin', thornless and high yielding but more conventional in appearance. The Japanese wineberry, *Rubus phoenicolasius*, has soft reddish bristles and large leaves, white-felted beneath, and makes a colourful display with its elegant racemes of pink flowers and large crimson edible berries.

FRAMEWORK

HYBRID BERRIES Compare any two blackberries growing wild in a hedgerow, and you will probably find distinct differences between them, in the colour of their flowers, perhaps, in their leaf shapes or in the size of their berries. Botanists cannot make up their minds about the wild bramble, *Rubus fruticosus*, some classifying its variations into more than 2000 sub-species, while others maintain they are all one and the same. Over the years the best of them have been brought into cultivation, together with related brambles such as the thornless, cut-leaved and white-fruited blackberries. Their natural mutability, combined with a tendency to cross-fertilize easily with raspberries, American dewberries and other cousins in the genus, led to the enthusiastic breeding of a number of hybrid berries. Many are available today, although they are seldom seen. The Veitchberry, King's Acre berry and boysenberry all had their day, but modern palates find them too acidic, and they need cooking to bring out their strong rich flavour.

Judge Logan of California carried out numerous experiments in cross-fertilization, and is still remembered for his loganberry and lowberry, the latter a back-cross (a cross between a hybrid and one of its parents) between a loganberry and blackberry. Modern plant-breeders have introduced a new

and peaches, for example) are best trained on sun-facing walls, saving shadier ones for the more cold-tolerant currants, berries and acid cherries. A single fruit variety will ripen at different times according to the direction it faces; thus red currants trained on the warmest walls produce the earliest fruit, while those with their backs to the sun crop last, often several weeks later. With a little cunning, a long succession of fruits can be produced on the four walls of an enclosed garden, each kind trained as decoratively as any flowering plant.

Many kinds of fruit make attractive climbing plants elsewhere in the garden. Apples and pears, suitably trained, have always been favourites for arches and tunnels, as well as for walls. In 1911 the agricultural writer Dr F H King reported that the Japanese grew their best pears on pergolas, where the fruit hung within easy reach and was protected from birds by the overhead canopy of foliage.

Try planting cordon apples or pears on dwarf rootstocks, one on each side of an arch, and train their stems up to meet overhead in the middle. Where two or more arches can be

Opposite Where space is short topfruit such as apples or pears can be trained as arches over a path without casting too much shade. Left Hybrid berries too, such as the Japanese wineberry, are adaptable for clothing an arch or training on fences and walls, as are pears (top)

generation of hybrid berries – the tummelberry, jostaberry, tayberry and sunberry, for example – and all these have their devotees. Although casually grouped together as 'hybrid berries', and sharing similarities in growth habit and cultivation, each is a distinct fruit with its own characteristic flavour. A few are admittedly more useful as ornamental plants and their fruits are best treated as an occasional small bonus. One such is the curious strawberry-raspberry, *Rubus illecebrosus*, another the Japanese wineberry (*R. phoenicolasius*) which produces highly aromatic, bright orange fruits and thin red hairy spines throughout the winter.

Every now and then another hybrid has a brief period of popularity. The marionberry, for example, appeared in garden centres for a few years before lapsing into obscurity. Bred in 1956 from two named forms of the American West Coast dewberry, 'Chehalem' and 'Olallie', it has large black berries with a delicious tangy flavour, held clear of the foliage over a long season from mid-summer to mid-autumn. Like most hybrids, it is a manageable bramble for small gardens, producing a fairly sparse number of long thick, slightly thorny canes.

Train any of the hybrids like blackberries, arching the stems on wires or fences; more decorative thornless kinds are useful for growing up pillars and over arches. Unlike many brambles, hybrids usually continue to bear fruit on old stems for more than one season, and it is not so important to replace fruited wood with new canes annually.

Once you have planted a hybrid or located a plant growing elsewhere, producing more is simple. As with blackberries, any new cane will develop roots wherever its tip touches moist soil. In early autumn choose a strong cane that has not yet borne fruit, dig a hole and then bury the last 7.5-10cm (3-4in) of it in the ground, replace the soil and press it down firmly, or simply anchor the end to the soil with a brick. The following spring, a shoot will appear at this point; when this is growing strongly, the rooted tip can be severed from the cane (which will still fruit as usual) and transplanted to a new position.

DOWN TO EARTH

LIVING WITH YOUR SOIL Mulches of compost, bark, lawn-mowings or manure can help bind the soil particles together and so protect its surface from rapid change; ground-cover plants are equally valuable in this respect and will also add colour and help prevent weeds. In the vegetable garden, for example, sow hardy cover crops such as grazing rye or winter tares as ground becomes vacant in autumn, and then dig these in as green manure in spring just before sowing starts. Surplus flower and vegetable seeds can be sown in an empty patch for turning in any time before the resulting plants bloom. Remember always to sprinkle green manures with dried blood before cultivating, as this accelerates their decomposition.

In time you can ameliorate your soil's worst characteristics, but no amount of improvement can transform clay into sand or vice versa, and certain plants will always be unhappy in particular conditions. However, every soil has its natural flora that has learnt to adapt and succeed in it, and you will find that this will flourish with the least effort. Enrich sandy soil with organic matter and then grow alstroemeria, arctotis, dierama, epilobium, lupins, incarvillea, nicotiana, pinks, tulips, violas and the best carrots in the district. Use dung and mulch clay for crinum lilies, anemones, daffodils and hyacinths, bergamot, camassia, paeonies, polemonium, roses and luxuriant brassicas. Chalky soils are thin and hot: work them full of humus and green manures to make ideal conditions for acanthus and asphodeline, border carnations and evening primrose, eschscholzia, erigeron, lavender, thyme and periwinkle. Wet soils can be drained or planted with astilbes, crocosmia, dicentra, fritillaries, day lilies, arum lilies, hostas and Asiatic primulas. If your ground is acid, specialize in ericaceous plants: erythroniums and rhododendrons, lewisias and lithospermum, meconopsis, pieris and *Trillium grandiflorum*.

FOCUS ON FOOD

FILLING THE STORE In the fruit and vegetable gardens this month is very much harvest time. There are many ways to preserve produce other than deep-freezing, and while we may not have root cellars, smoking ovens, or even salting crocks for beans now that block salt is a mere memory, there is still no reason to waste any kitchen garden produce.

Chop herbs and freeze in ice-cubes or small plastic bags: alternatively you can still gather and dry most of them. Keep surplus tomatoes on a cool shelf, or liquidize and freeze them for winter soups; many other vegetables (even asparagus) can be frozen in this way. Store potatoes in paper sacks, or boxes lined with newspaper, in a frost-free dark shed, and pack other roots in sand or peat in wooden boxes. Topfruit needs special treatment. Early apples and pears do not keep, but any fruits you do not eat can be cut up and frozen, or dried slowly in rings. Later crops may be kept under the bed, as is traditional, but are much better spread on racks, or packed in boxes or perforated plastic bags, and then stored in a cool shed. Ventilate for the first week after picking, as many kinds 'sweat'. Check crops regularly, a critical routine with pears that is especially important because they finish ripening when in store and may be at their best for only a few days.

Opposite A cool, dry and well-ventilated shed is ideal for storing long-keeping varieties of fruit and vegetables, for drying herbs and heads of decorative seeds such as honesty. Crops like marrows and white cabbage are best suspended in nets

NEW FROM OLD

INCREASING LILIES Lilies can be increased by division of clumps, and by seed (which may take from two to seven years to reach flowering size), but the simplest method is to root the scales. These are the pointed fleshy plates joined at their base that overlap to form the typical lily bulb. Most kinds of bulbs can be easily propagated in the following way. They can be dug up this month, and their outer scales gently detached from the outside and inserted tip upwards, in a potful of cutting compost in a greenhouse. The original bulb can then immediately be replanted in the soil. Anyone buying lilies, especially the more expensive kinds, should examine carefully the bag in which they arrive, for very often bulbs shed a few scales in transit and these are easily overlooked among the packaging.

An alternative method which is usually very successful, is to bury the scales in a moist 50:50 mixture of peat and sand in a polythene bag; tie this up tightly and hang in a warm place such as a kitchen or airing cupboard. Check the contents every few weeks and pot up any scales that have formed roots and a growing tip. Most lilies will take two to four years to form a flowering bulb from scales. *Lilium tigrinum*, the robust and exotic Tiger lily, is noted for forming numbers of small black bulblets at the base of its leaves, and these can be detached for planting on the surface of a potful of compost.

INSPIRATION

IVY HEDGES A wire-netting or chain-link fence can be transformed over three to four seasons into what is known as a 'fedge', using ivy varieties such as 'Dentata Variegata', 'Deltoidea' or 'Sulphur Heart' to develop a dense evergreen cover. Space the ivies 45cm (18in) apart and tie their shoots horizontally or at an angle to the wires, or lace them through the netting. Once the fence is nearly covered, plant rambler roses, thornless loganberries or the parsley-leaved blackberry at 1.8m (6ft) intervals, training their growth along the face of the fedge. Trim the ivy with shears whenever the companion climbers are detached for pruning.

To create a low edging to beds and borders, bend strips of 30cm-(12in) wide wire netting to form low tunnels and arrange them end to end over small-leaved ivy plants, whose stems will grow up through the netting and can then be clipped to form a neat low hedge. A taller and more robust hedge is made with 'tree' ivy; a fine example of this, made from the 'tree' form of 'Hibernica', surrounds the Palm House Terrace at Kew Gardens, London.

When ivy reaches the top of a wall or tree, its growth habit changes with increased exposure to light, the plant maturing from its juvenile climbing state into the adult form known as tree ivy. The head of the plant then tends to bush

Top Tiger lilies can be propagated conventionally from scales and also from bulbils at the base of their leaves. Above Ivy is similarly versatile, almost all parts of the plant rooting freely in contact with moist soil

out, producing plain oval leaves and clusters of greenish yellow flowers in autumn, followed by small black (occasionally yellow) berries. Plants grown from tree ivy cuttings retain the adult characteristics of simple leaves and stiff woody growth.

Cuttings may be taken any time during autumn. Cut 15cm (6in) pieces of the previous season's growth, trim each just below a leaf joint, and remove the lowest leaf or two. Insert them vertically around the edge of pots filled with a cutting compost or a home-made mixture of two parts peat to one part sharp sand or perlite, and stand them in a cold frame or cool greenhouse. The following spring pot them up individually and grow on until well-rooted and growing strongly, at which point they are ready to plant out. For hedging, space the plants 30-45cm (12-18in) apart and clip to shape when large enough. Individual tree ivies can be trained into small standard trees by confining growth to a single stem tied initially to a strong cane; when the shoot is 60-90cm (2-3ft) high, pinch out the tip to produce a bushy head of foliage. The more decorative younger growth of ivies can be trained into standards in the same way, using several shoots tied together, but these are less rigid and therefore need permanent support. Take cuttings of young growth as for tree ivy; alternatively make softwood cuttings in summer, pinching out the tip of each, or allow some stems to trail on the ground where they will root as layers; these can then be cut off for transplanting to a nursery bed for training.

LOOKING AHEAD

WINTER POT CARE Containers too large or heavy to be brought under cover need outdoor insulation against the winter weather. Strong, cold winds dehydrate and 'scorch' the foliage of evergreen shrubs and trees, even though these might be hardy in all other respects. Provide shelter, especially when they are young, by surrounding them with a screen of loosely woven material (plastic windbreak mesh, fine netting or hessian sacking), arranged about 15cm (6in) away from the foliage and supported by stakes or canes to just above the height of the plant. Pack leaves inside the enclosure all round the rootball to prevent freezing. Except in very severe winters, hardy deciduous plants usually survive if you protect their roots from the elements; this incidentally will also prolong the life of the pots themselves. Wherever possible gather several pots together, and encircle the group with a ring of netting. Cover the enclosed ground with dry leaves, bracken, pine needles, straw, shredded bark or conifer trimmings. Put a thick layer of the same material over the tops of the pots, holding it in place with a piece of netting.

Tender shrubs and climbers need total insulation outdoors. This is more neatly done if you can assemble the plants against a wall or fence. Stretch a panel of fine plastic netting, chicken wire or woven mesh across the plants and their pots, attach it to a framework of bamboo canes which will prevent the netting from touching the plants, and then secure it on each side to wires, nails or battens on the wall. Attach another piece of netting outside the first one, and then stuff the space between the two panels with straw, bracken, leaves or fibreglass insulation to make a protective quilt.

Individual containers that cannot be moved must be wrapped snugly where they stand. Enclose them with old carpets, layers of 'bubble' polythene, or large plastic bags stuffed with paper or similar dry insulating materials, and tie firmly in place with string. Top growth is wrapped up in the same way, while long clear stems such as the trunks of standard bay trees can be insulated with moulded foam or polystyrene pipe lagging. In a long or severe season the insulating jacket can be extended over the soil surface and around any stems, but if the plants die down in the autumn or are grown for winter decoration, give them a thick mulch of chopped bark instead.

AUTUMN SOWING AND PLANTING Seasoned gardeners sow and plant in autumn as well as spring, partly to relieve the pressure in the new year, but also to take advantage of warm soils and likely rainfall before winter sets in. Planting hardy trees and shrubs now will reduce the need to nurse them if the following summer is dry. Start preparing planting positions now by deeply forking and cleaning 0.8 sq metres (1 sq yard) or so of ground for each plant. Add a little compost if the soil is poor, although firm planting, shelter, plenty of water and freedom from competition are more crucial than increased fertility for healthy early growth.

When planting woody subjects in autumn, always start with evergreens, moving on to deciduous plants later, once their leaves have fallen. Many gardeners prefer to order hardy trees and shrubs from nurseries in districts that are colder than their own gardens, on the assumption that the plants have tougher, and therefore healthier, constitutions. This sensible though unproven precaution is worth taking in extremely cold or exposed gardens, but be particularly careful when choosing edible fruits, for in their case, variety is just as important as origin: late-flowering and early ripening are vital qualities where the growing season is short. Make sure, too, that fruit trees are grafted on identified rootstocks, not simply labelled 'bush' or 'half standard'.

Check that virus-susceptible plants such as rhubarb and strawberries have been certified healthy. Order unusual soft fruit specimens for summer desserts: varieties for connoisseurs include the purple raspberry 'Glencoe', the yellow raspberry 'Golden Everest', marionberry, the sharp flavoured thornless boysenberry and dewberry. There is still time to sow lettuces, 'Little Gem' in a cold frame, 'Novita' in the greenhouse, and '(Winter) Density' outdoors for spring hearts. Unless your winters are savage, it is worth planting garlic cloves now, as a period of exposure to low temperatures improves later growth. Autumn onion sets, too, will make just enough leaf to over-winter safely for a head start next season.

Mid AUTUMN

If dead leaves GATHER IN YOUR GARDEN, SAVE THEM — LIKE GRASS CLIPPINGS, WEEDS AND OTHER WASTE MATERIALS, THEY ARE A PRECIOUS RESOURCE TO RETURN TO THE SOIL: REMEMBER THAT FOREST TREES MANURE THEMSELVES IN THIS WAY.

Stack leaves in a pile to make leaf mould, heap them over frost-sensitive perennials as a protection from the cold, chew them up with a rotary mower and then use for mulching, or mix them with lawn-mowings to make compost.

Trees of course, can also sustain themselves without digging. Whether to dig the soil is a contentious matter, and much depends upon your own inclination and what you intend to grow. Root vegetables, peas and beans need open soil, which is only achieved by digging, though not necessarily every year if you avoid walking on crop beds. Sites for fruit, shrubs and trees need digging initially, but the lavish preparation once customary is now being questioned. Except on infertile or poorly drained ground, digging deeply and adding manure are less important aids to rapid establishment than is the suppression of competition from weeds and other plants in the first few years. Vacant areas of heavy clay benefit from rough digging in autumn to expose a large surface to frost. Any improvement in friability is temporary, whereas permanent relief from the worst features of clay comes from working in lime or a mixture of dolomite and gypsum, and then protecting the soil from the elements with a generous mulch.

Digging light ground at this time of year is not a good idea. Left exposed to winter rains, surfaces usually slump into hard, sandy crusts beneath which little can grow or live. Unless you are sowing or planting, leave light soils undisturbed until spring. In clear areas of the garden, you can spray weeds (their roots will remain to bind the soil together), while large areas of open ground may be suitable for sowing a hardy green

Hanging baskets THAT CAN BE BROUGHT INDOORS TO PROVIDE COLOUR FOR ANOTHER MONTH OR TWO

Early frosts TINTING LEAVES TO ARRANGE IN VASES OR TURN INTO LACY SKELETONS

Fairy rings ON LAWNS: ENJOY THEIR FANCIFUL ASSOCIATIONS OR SPRAY WITH FUNGICIDE

Ripening grapes UNDER GLASS WHOSE FLAVOUR CAN BE ENHANCED WITH A LITTLE HEAT

manure crop such as forage peas to dig in next spring; alternatively in well-planted areas cover the bare surface with a mulch. This protective cover is especially important after having dug deeply into the soil, when harvesting roots or digging up dahlias, for example. The insulating properties of a mulch were obvious one winter after I lifted our 'Bishop of Llandaff' dahlias. Left to dry in a shed, the whole precious collection was killed by a sudden vicious and penetrating frost, whereas overlooked portions survived in the ground beneath a heavy mulch of compost to reappear the following summer. Instead of replacing the venerable Bishop (a useful if unclerical carrot-red), I sowed various dahlia seeds that produced a gloriously diverse selection of large-flowering plants. Several we tagged and dug-up in autumn for saving, while the others were left in to take their chance, for plants are as easy to raise from seed as they are to store. A few outstanding plants, though not perfect, were worth multiplying to replace our lost stock; after all, no bishop is indispensable, and in any case this is a non-conformist garden in many respects.

DOWN TO EARTH

MAKING LEAF MOULD Tucked among mature deciduous trees, our garden is annually buried in autumn leaves, a signal to shed our inhibitions and blithely toss or kick the accumulated drifts around when nobody is looking. With childhood delights revived and duly exhausted, there follows the more serious business of sweeping and raking the leaves together into a huge stack – not for burning, though, as that would send precious humus up in smoke. Leaves have a number of essential uses around the garden. In cold areas they are excellent protection against frost when heaped over the crowns of tender plants and held in place with a piece of netting weighted down with stones. Hedgehogs, too, appreciate their insulating properties and they have been known to pass much of the winter tucked beneath a heap of leaves, so don't be too conscientious when tidying the garden for winter.

In the ground, leaves play a mechanical role by improving soil structure. Although they have little or no food value, they decompose into first-class durable humus for any type of soil. Ours is very light and thirsty, for example, and in the autumn I save as many leaves as I can, even gathering them from the roadsides. As the soil warms in spring, spread them in a thick layer when the ground is moist and leave them as a mulch for the rest of the season. Holes are easily made through the leaves for planting, or they can be

drawn aside for sowing; later routine cultivation gradually incorporates them into the soil. On clay the same method protects the surface from turning into concrete in summer, and putty after winter rains.

Older gardeners used to transplant seedlings into leaf mould instead of using modern peat composts. It takes at least two years in the stack to make the best leaf mould, dark and crumbly like peat, but superior to it in every respect, not least because it is free but it also helps save over-exploited peat bogs that have become endangered habitats. Decay is hastened if the leaves are first chopped into small fragments; this is best done with a rotary mower pushed once or twice over leaves that have collected on the lawn, together with any others you like to tip there en route to the leaf mould bin. This need be no more than a simple enclosure made from wire or plastic netting. Even a plastic dustbin liner will do for small quantities, or you can use any of the widely available compost bins, but don't add garden refuse to the leaves, for they are best stored on their own. Pile the leaves in the container, treading them down firmly as you go. Soak the heap using a hosepipe or watering can if it dries out, for damp leaves are less likely to blow away as you gather them, and they are easier to compress into a solid stack. There is no point in adding a chemical compost activator, but if you are really in a hurry you can mix the leaves with grass clippings (either now or in the spring), since these heat up and hasten decomposition, sometimes making the leaf mould ready to use within only six months. The leaves also add roughage to the mowings.

The resulting leaf mould can be used wherever you would normally use peat. Passed through a coarse riddle or sieve, it is a valuable medium in trays for growing on seedlings, and can be mixed with well-broken garden soil to make an all-purpose compost. Be prepared for a few weed seedlings to emerge; leaf mould must never be sterilized, since this destroys some of its structure and may release injurious chemicals. Used straight from the stack, it is a substitute for garden compost, peat, or shredded bark, wherever these are recommended when planting or improving the soil. Even simply spreading a thick layer around garden trees and shrubs is less wasteful than burning it, and imitates the way every wood and forest sustains itself.

NEW FROM OLD

SAVING SEEDS Anyone who saves ripe seeds from hardy annual flowers will find that many edible plants can be propagated in the same way, provided only the best specimens are selected as donors, for there is no point in perpetuating inferior plants. In cold gardens nominally hardy varieties of broccoli, broad beans and other winter vegetables may succumb to frost, but by saving seed from survivors you can establish your own reliable strain. It is not worth collecting from F_1 hybrids: these

Top Ripe seed heads of *Allium christophii* and nigella.

Above If housed in good time, before frost can damage them, tender perennials will continue to flower for another month

are deliberately bred from very distinct parents, to which home-produced seeds are likely to revert, often with disappointing results. However, seeds from non-hybrid or 'open-pollinated' varieties, can be saved from one year to the next, and with care quality can be maintained, or even improved as the strain becomes adjusted to the particular soil and locality.

Some of the easiest vegetables to perpetuate are root crops, many of which are biennial, growing a usable root one season and flowering the next. Parsnips are the most spectacular of these plants. When clearing the remains of a crop in late winter, transfer two or three of the best roots to the back of a flower border. There they will soon revive and by mid-summer produce several flowering stems, whose fern-like leaves and 1.8-2.4m (6-8ft) stature rival the magnificence of angelica or fennel. Ripe seeds can be gathered in early autumn for storage until the following spring, when they will often germinate faster and more evenly than bought seed.

Salsify and scorzonera both merit leaving for seed; some gardeners in fact prefer their bright flowers (purple and yellow respectively) to the subtle flavour of their roots. Forced chicory belongs firmly among the flowers, especially wild borders, where its clear sky-blue daisies feed honey-bees foraging in mid-summer. Like scorzonera, it is a perennial and can be left permanently in place to cheerfully seed itself.

UNDER GLASS

OVERWINTERING PERENNIALS Geraniums (otherwise known as zonal pelargoniums) are remarkably resilient, usually surviving from one year to the next after being dug up, whether they are then potted up for the windowsill or suspended in paper bags from a frost-free garage roof. Try packing half a dozen geraniums with good rootballs in a deep plastic mushroom basket, or a similarly capacious container, and keep moist under glass until early winter. Resist watering from then until early spring, when they will start growing again to produce cuttings or substantial bedding plants.

As well as making the usual preparations for housing tender perennials, try reviving the tradition of overwintering indoors other bedding plants that are normally discarded. True annuals seldom survive, but many grown as such in our summer gardens are in fact tender perennials, and will survive under glass to produce shoots in spring that will make useful cuttings. Suitable subjects include *Begonia semperflorens*, lobelia, petunias, impatiens, verbena, ageratum and even mesembryanthemums (Livingstone daisies). Either pot up the best as stock plants for a warm windowsill or conservatory, or if space is limited strike 7.5-10cm (3-4in) cuttings now and place them in pots and boxes.

Hanging baskets filled with trailing geraniums and other bedding plants can be transferred indoors to continue flowering for a further month or two. You can leave their contents undisturbed as stock plants for spring cuttings, a novel way to save space on the greenhouse staging. Remember, before bringing any of these plants under glass, they will need plenty of light and at least frost-free conditions; check all heating equipment, wash off greenhouse shading, and spray plants with insecticide before housing.

GREENHOUSE GRAPES The easiest way to grow dessert grapes is to plant a vine in a greenhouse or conservatory soil border, training it on horizontal wires on one side of the house, and up under the roof, so as to expose it to as much sunlight as possible. In lean-to houses always grow the vine on the side opposite the wall and up the sloping roof, saving the back wall for other fruit such as apricots or peaches.

For maximum crops this method demands close and regular attention to pruning, but a vine will still yield good grapes if grown as an ornamental climber, perhaps combined with morning glory or a passion flower such as the fragrant

PLANT HIGHLIGHTS OF THE MONTH

Schizostylis River lilies, as they are known in South Africa, are very colourful and deserve room in all but the coldest gardens on heavy clay. Good drainage and full sun foster prolific flowering, which will start earlier than normal in wet seasons and may continue into winter. With broad grassy foliage and 60-90cm (2-3ft) stems, their crocus-like flowers come in lustrous shades of white, pink and red. In warm moist soils, clumps may need periodic division; elsewhere remember their origins, and overwinter under a mulch of leaves.

Elm Despite the ravages of Dutch elm disease, suckers from infected English elms (*Ulmus procera*) survive in hedgerows as replacements for future generations. The genus includes many very attractive small garden trees with varying resistance to the disease, such as *U. x hollandica* 'Wredei' which is noted for its yellow foliage, but all elms assume golden tints in autumn, including the more desirable Chinese elm, *U. parvifolia*, and the weeping forms *U. glabra* 'Pendula' and x *hollandica* 'Smithii'.

Cobaea scandens Sometimes called the cup-and-saucer vine, this climber is often at its best in mid-autumn, when it is growing on warm sheltered walls where the dense scrambling stems bear numerous large white or opulent purple blooms, like Canterbury bells. Though often grown as a tender annual, its thick fleshy roots are perennial in mild gardens or under glass, where vines will romp up to the roof with tropical boisterousness. Cut to the ground in late autumn and mulch the roots, thickly if outdoors, to protect them from the cold and damaging effects of frost.

Passiflora quadrangularis. Merely pinch out the tips of any fruiting shoot, two leaves beyond its bunch of grapes, and allow other stems to grow freely. Where there is no soil border, plant the vine outside, feeding its stem in through a hole low down in the wall. Alternatively, grow the vine in a decorative box or half barrel, filling the container with a strong soil-based compost such as John Innes No 3 and replacing the top 5-7.5cm (2-3in) of soil with fresh compost each spring. Some varieties can be kept in 30cm (12in) pots, using a similar mixture and confining the crop to four to six bunches. Either tie the main stem to a single 1.5m (5ft) cane like a standard fuchsia and allow a head of sideshoots to develop, or arrange three canes at the edge of the pot and train the main stem around them in a spiral. Feed potted vines regularly while in growth, and stand them outdoors after fruiting, housing them again in late winter to re-start growth.

Victorian gardeners such as William Thompson, the Duke of Buccleuch's fruit expert, used to grow grapes in small pots, which were then presented at table as part of the floral decorations. While some would dismiss this as a typical 19th century conceit, it demonstrates that essential panache modern gardening has lost. The secret lies in keeping a stock vine in a large container, and in spring feeding shoots through the base of a smaller one set on top of the first. By the time the grapes are ripe the vine will have rooted into the smaller pot, which can then be detached for the table.

Remember all indoor vines need pollination. Either draw your hand gently down each truss of blooms once or twice, or sharply tap the flowering branches with a cane to distribute the pollen. A heavy set of dessert grapes should be thinned to allow room for berries to swell; when they are the size of hazelnuts, carefully cut out enough berries to leave the remainder a finger-space apart, and cook the thinnings like gooseberries in a pie. When ripe, cut surplus bunches, each with 30cm (12in) of main stem. Insert the lower end of the stem into a milk bottle half-filled with water and wedged at an angle on a shelf, so that the grapes hang freely; in a cool place they will keep sound for two to three months.

PLANNING

REWORKING BORDERS Most of us are too conformist when it comes to gardening, following established methods and routines, and missing the opportunities for creative adventure, experiment and inspiration that a private garden can offer.

The herbaceous border, for example, is still a sacred institution in some quarters. In the golden age of private service, owners expected their borders to be immaculate and orderly at all times. The only way head gardeners could ensure perfection was to overhaul entire borders every few years, a daunting upheaval relished by no-one involved in the operation at spade-level. Plants had to be labelled, dug up and packed together on a path nearby, covered with leaf mould or similarly protected if frost threatened. Bulbs were retrieved and sorted, and the empty border was deeply dug and manured before being replanted with young healthy portions of the original herbaceous perennials.

Experience in gardening teaches many lessons, perhaps the most valuable of which is how much you can get away with. Perennials inevitably mature and invade each other, thereby providing the orthodox excuse for a complete overhaul. However, border rebels prefer a subtler, evolutionary form of maintenance, periodically ripping out locally unwanted growth and working in new plants or pieces of old ones wherever space permits.

Now is the time for re-ordering old borders, but if you prefer a merry muddle, you shouldn't feel compelled to dismantle them purely for the sake of convention. Simply cut down plants that have finished growth and tuck them up for the winter. Lightly prick over exposed soil, fetching out weeds as you go, and then mulch with a 5-7.5cm (2-3in) layer of anything juicy and nutritious: thoroughly decayed manure, garden compost, or grass clippings mixed with autumn leaves. Research confirms that naturalized bulbs will accept deeper burial than is usually recommended, so if you do happen to disturb spring bulbs in the border, replant them in groups below spade depth for their future safety.

SHRUBS FOR WINTER To some gardeners, depending on stems and leaves for winter colour is like cheating, but in fact used sparingly these have undeniable value in providing both shelter for smaller plants and a background for delicate winter blossom. They are also, of course, trusty reinforcements in severe weather when all else remains sensibly dormant.

Acer palmatum 'Senkaki' is a glorious small tree with brilliant red shoots in winter, much like those of the variegated dogwood, *Cornus alba* 'Elegantissima', which must be cut hard in spring to renew its brightest stems. There are many other equally useful coloured dogwood varieties that should be treated in the same way: *C. a.* 'Spaethii' (dark red) and 'Westonbirt' (scarlet), and *C. stolonifera* 'Flaviramea' (yellow).

Right Most kinds of acer are noted for their spectacular autumn colour provided the foliage is primed by a succession of frosty nights and warm, sunny days

For evergreen foliage combined with winter blossom, *Viburnum* x *tinus* is indispensable. The pale yellow-edged form 'Variegatum' is colourful but must be sheltered from cold winds, while the cultivar 'Eve Price' is more compact and has prettier flowers than the species. The evergreen mahonias are tough and shade-tolerant: *Mahonia japonica* (formerly called *M. bealei*) flowers in late winter with pendulous sprays like pale yellow lily-of-the- valley, a little later than the various cultivars of M. x *media*, whose handsome and floriferous culti-var 'Charity' is probably the best.

Left *Cornus alba* 'Westonbirt' is one of the most brilliant dogwoods, as dependable winter highlight as the fragrant yellow flowers of *Mahonia* x *media* 'Charity' (below). **Opposite** The fruiting bodies of the fairy ring mushroom *Marasmius oreades*. The brighter green area of grass is fed lavishly by nutrients released by the mycelium

Use these hardy shrubs as windbreaks, grouping them to create sheltered alcoves for less resilient plants. Note where the earliest flowers tend to appear (often at the foot of a hedge or beneath the protection of an arching shrub) and recreate these conditions in your winter garden. Make full use of winter sunshine, arranging plants so that they catch as much of it as possible. Not only does this give them extra warmth, but light is a precious commodity in the darker months and will enliven the colours of strategically placed foliage and flowers.

No-one likes chilled feet, least of all plants that cannot escape from cold waterlogged ground, and a single season in such conditions might prove terminal. On heavy soil, dig in everything you can lay your hands on to lighten it and improve the drainage: coarse sand, fibrous garden compost, partly decayed leaves, gritty sweepings from paths, and anything else that will open its texture and help remove surplus water.

FOCUS ON FOOD

A QUESTION OF HARDINESS Whether or not to sow vegeta-bles in autumn depends largely upon where you live and the severity of the weather during the forthcoming winter. If there is one lesson to be learnt from a lifetime's gardening, it is that no two districts or years are alike, and that success one season in a particular garden may not necessarily be repeated else-where or in subsequent years.

In harsher climates few vegetables survive the winter out-doors. However, gardening books regularly advise sowing peas and broad beans in autumn for the earliest crops next year. I recall an elderly gardener at a Yorkshire nursery in north-east England, displaying a handful of 'Meteor' peas early one spring, picked from overwintered plants. We were impressed, until he admitted they were the total crop from a whole row.

If you live in a region of mild winters, then by all means sow round-seeded peas in a warm sheltered bed – 'Meteor' or 'Pilot' are best – and a hardy variety of broad bean such as 'Aquadulce' or 'Express'. Be prepared to protect them with some form of cover, such as cloches, plastic film or fleece in hard weather, and don't expect all the plants to survive: soil pests and persistent wet weather are as much of a threat as frost. As an insurance you can sow them in a cold frame where all-round protection is feasible, but these are probably more usefully planted with spring cabbage and winter lettuce because autumn sowings seldom mature more than a week or two before the earliest spring crops. Nor are the hardiest varieties always the tastiest. Choicer wrinkle-seeded peas and longpod beans can be sown under glass in late winter, in pots or boxes, for transplanting in early spring. They need minimal heat, yield more heavily and seldom disappoint expectations in the same way as overwintered crops outdoors do.

THE ANCIENT ART OF CLAMPING　The easiest way to store winter carrots and beetroot is to dig up the whole crop, leave them on the surface to dry for a few hours, and then pack them (minus their tops) between layers of sand or peat in large boxes. Potatoes can be kept in either paper sacks or in boxes that are lined with newspaper.

Failing this, you might try reviving the art of clamping. Large field clamps used to be constructed to house carrots, turnips and potatoes, even apples in some places, their contents remaining good for many months without developing the shrivelling characteristic of warmer storage indoors. For garden yields miniature clamps are

perfectly feasible and make decorative novelties. All they require is a bale or two of wheat straw, a raised or well-drained piece of ground and a little spade work; the rest is well within the realms of the pottery enthusiast or amateur sculptor.

Lay a 7.5cm (3in) bed of straw in a circle on the ground and start arranging your produce, sound samples only, in neat layers separated from each other by several centimetres of straw. Decrease the circumference as you build, until a steep conical heap is the result. Clad the outside of this with several centimetres of straw and leave a tightly twisted tuft at the apex for ventilation. Finally dig a trench around the clamp to aid rapid drainage of water, and use the excavated soil to make an even, firm and smooth layer to cover the straw sides, right up to the terminal tuft. Use the produce as required, starting at the top and always replacing the coats of straw and soil afterwards; keep the basic conical shape as the contents dwindle, together with the all-important ventilation tuft.

GARDEN SURGERY

FAIRY RINGS　The familiar circles of toadstools on lawns, together with the rings of lush turf and dead brown grass that characterize them at other times of the year, have accumulated all kinds of magical connotations. Essentially, though, fairy rings are a prosaic problem of lawns and other grassed areas, caused by various fungi that live on organic matter in the soil,

in this case the roots of the grass. There are three kinds, two of them relatively harmless and producing nothing worse than a ring of toadstools or dark green grass.

The most serious type is the fairy ring mushroom *Marasmius oreades*, which produces two concentric rings of rich green that enclose a circle of dead turf. The fungus releases waste nitrogen which stimulates the grass nearby into lush growth, the characteristic dark green fairy rings. However, where the fungus has exhausted available nutrients it dies out. Its rotting tissues smother the grass, which dies of drought, leaving a parched brown ring on the lawn. Live areas of fungus meanwhile advance outwards to infect fresh grass, hence the steady growth of the rings, which can continue to spread for a century or more at a rate of 30cm (12in) per year.

Identification is easier than treatment. Professional gardeners use a fungicide based on oxycarboxin, but this is unlikely to be available for home use. If the disfigurement is serious, the only remedy is to dig out the infected area, removing grass and soil to a spade's depth and disposing of this well away from the lawn. Sterilize the exposed area with tar oil wash (eg 'Clean-up' or 'Mortegg'), refill with clean soil and finally re-seed. A simpler though less reliable method is to spike the affected area with a garden fork and then saturate it with a similar solution.

INSPIRATION

HERB LAWNS Perhaps the most familiar lawn species used instead of turf is Roman or lawn chamomile (*Anthemis nobilis* or sometimes *Chamaemelum nobile*), not to be confused with the medicinal true chamomile which is an annual herb, *Matricaria recutita*. Roman chamomile has been used for centuries to make lawns, especially on drier soils where in a drought it remains green longer than grass, although never achieving the close texture of turf. The bright green leaves, resembling those of feverfew, perfume the air when crushed, but the plants cannot tolerate heavy traffic, and where a lawn must be crossed frequently, include stepping stones to avoid undue wear. Another problem is the constant need for hand weeding among plants, and most chamomile lawns need to be remade every few years after cleaning the soil of weeds.

'Treneague' is the best variety, naturally compact and slow to flower. This is usually planted in spring on a weed-free site, with the soil well-broken and levelled. Space the plants 10cm (4in) apart each way, watering and weeding as necessary until they are established and growing strongly. Clip with shears occasionally, or mow with a rotary mower set high. When remaking a lawn, the original plants can be pulled to pieces to make fresh stock. Plant surplus pieces near any sick or unthrifty plants, for chamomile has a reputation of being a tonic and a reviving companion plant.

Other prostrate herbs, with woody stems and often lower maintenance needs than chamomile, are sometimes used for ground-cover and decorative lawns. At Sissinghurst, in south-east England, Vita Sackville-West made a thyme lawn, using *Thymus coccinea* and its creeping relative *T. serpyllum*; the ordinary wild thyme is equally adaptable, as are many dwarf heathers, especially forms of *Erica carnea*, which have pink or white flowers from mid-winter to mid-spring. These are all planted 10-15cm (4-6in) apart and will succeed in almost any type of well-drained soil, although a light peat is preferable. Clip with shears after flowering.

For small ornamental lawns that are seldom trodden on, soft stemmed creeping plants may be used. Try pennyroyal, which is the prostrate mint, *Mentha pulegium*; mats of Corsican mint, *M. requienii*, or of thrift, *Armeria maritima*; or tiniest of all, *Sagina glabra*, the Irish moss or pearlwort. All of these thrive in partial shade, and prefer moist sandy soils in which they can spread freely. Plant 5-7.5cm (2-3in) apart, either in drifts or between paving stones.

Various kinds of trefoil, too, make durable evergreen lawns that need no feeding, for clover forms its own nitrogen

Opposite Sissinghurst's thyme lawn is a well-known example of an alternative to grass. **Below** In moist fertile soils sweet peas are rampant climbers given any hint of support; on a formal frame such as a lattice pyramid (right) they are easy to train for garden decoration and frequent cutting for button holes

in tiny root nodules. Clover was popular for lawns in early Persian gardens, a custom that was taken across Asia by the 16th-century Mogul emperor Babur, who conquered Afghanistan and northern India, creating gardens with trefoil lawns wherever he paused en route. It is possible for modern gardeners to recreate this effect by sowing wild white clover (*Trifolium repens*) in the same way as for a grass lawn. The equally resilient shamrock (black medick or *Medicago lupulina*) is also sometimes used for this purpose.

LOOKING AHEAD

CLASSIC SWEET PEAS Enthusiasts sow their sweet pea seeds singly in deep pots now or in mid-winter. Seedlings from either of these sowings will make sturdier plants and flowers than those sown in spring, when all energy is devoted to rapid growth. The secret of growing large blooms, with long stems and all-round splendour, lies in this early sowing, together with the practice of pinching out to force the emergence of sidestems, and cordon training on a similar cane structure to that used for runner beans. Grown thus they require dedicated attention, often as frequently as every other day, but the routine is gentle, straightforward and suitably relaxing for sunny afternoons in spring and summer.

When sweet pea seedlings have made two pairs of leaves, pinch out the tip to stimulate sideshoots. As soon as the sideshoots are long enough to compare, pinch off all but the strongest; this will produce a sturdier vine than the original seedling. Thoroughly harden off the seedlings before planting them out during mid-spring. Plant one sweet pea to each cane and secure it with a loop of raffia or a wire pea ring, available from garden centres. Continue to tie in the vine as it grows, nipping off any tendrils and sideshoots that develop, so that the plant is kept to a single stem.

Cut the flowers regularly when two or three blooms are fully open, the others just unfurling. Never leave any to fade or set seed, otherwise the plant's vigour may be impaired. When vines reach the top of the canes, untie them and either coil around the base of their supports or, if grown in rows, lay them along the ground at the foot of the canes, in each case securing the tips once more to the nearest support to continue vertical growth. Feed them at this stage with Growmore or a specialist sweet pea fertilizer, and water if necessary.

Late AUTUMN

Sir Thomas Browne's 'pleasing Quince, the stomach's comforter', is packed full of flavour and a perfume so powerful and contagious that most people know, at least by repute, that quinces must be isolated from other fruits in store, even in a large attic. Few, however, might recognize the pleasantly gnarled and downy-leaved tree, Cydonia oblonga, from which this classic fruit is gathered.

Rarely exceeding 3.6m (12ft) tall in average garden soils, a quince makes an intriguing ornamental accent in a sunny sheltered corner. It is not particularly fruitful in exposed gardens, but trees are hardy down to about -23°C (-10°F) and will still flower handsomely after a cold winter. The wide delicate blooms, white with a pink blush like a single wild rose, appear in late spring and therefore usually escape frost damage.

Trees are self-fertile, and a single specimen often sets a heavy crop of large apple- or pear-shaped fruits. These are left to ripen until mid- to late autumn unless severe frost threatens, hence the need for a warm sunny site. In Mediterranean countries where quinces grow wild, crops ripen outdoors, but there are few gardens in colder climates where fruits do not have to finish maturing in store.

As quinces grow fairly slowly, a young tree will thrive for many years in a large container which, if portable, can be moved under cover for the fruit to mature on the tree. Alternatively, plant against a warm wall, arrange the branches like those of a fan-trained pear and simply remove any shoots that grow away from the wall, cutting each back to a sideways-facing bud. There the reflected warmth of the autumn sun will help to colour the richly golden fruits.

Bought quince trees are already pruned to a basic open shape, but home-raised trees must be trained by shortening the growing stem by a third from late autumn onwards, doing the same the following year to the branches that are then produced. Keep the main stem clear of shoots and also shorten any weak sideshoots on the main branches to two or three

WHAT TO WATCH FOR THIS MONTH

Quinces TO PICK AS SOON AS FULLY COLOURED AND STORE FOR FRAGRANT PRESERVES

Leaves falling IN DRIFTS; STACK THEM TO DECAY INTO HOME-GROWN HUMUS

SUMMER *begonias* GOING TO REST; REPLACE WITH THEIR WINTER-FLOWERING COUSINS FOR OUT-OF-SEASON COLOUR

STEMS FOR *hardwood cuttings*, THE EASIEST WAY TO MULTIPLY YOUR FAVOURITE SHRUB

DOWN TO EARTH

buds. Thereafter little pruning will be necessary, apart from thinning out untidy or overcrowded branches. Mulch trees with well-rotted manure every spring, especially in dry areas, since quinces prefer moist growing conditions.

Pick the fruit as late as possible. Although looking ripe, they will still be hard and astringent in autumn, and need to be kept stored in boxes for a further month or two to develop their flavour. The characteristic and penetrating scent will increase as fruits ripen, so much so that Roman gentry used to arrange quinces on their statues to perfume the room. They are then ready for use. In one of Edward Lear's nonsense poems, the owl and the pussycat ate slices of quince with a runcible spoon after their marriage, not such a fanciful idea because fruits were considered tokens of love and were traditionally served at weddings. A single slice was often included in apple pies for additional flavour, and this, together with quince jelly, are perhaps the most familiar roles for quinces today.

Over its long history, however, the fruit was treated more imaginatively and gave rise to numerous culinary delights. It was baked, pickled, turned into quince candy (cotignac), or the moulded quince dessert the Spanish call *dulce de membrillo*, and with its lavish pectin content made a range of distinctive preserves – 'marmalade' comes from 'marmalo', the Portuguese name for the fruit. Two dozen quinces with 1.5kg (3lb) of sugar, 2 lemons and yeast makes 4.5 litres (1 gallon) of potent and fragrant wine by the time the next season's crop is ready. In fact, enterprising cooks can find any number of reasons to plant a quince tree in the garden.

MAJOR MOVEMENTS In many gardens this is a season of great earthworks. Later the ground will be frozen or too wet, whereas now most soils are manageable, their temperature congenial for helping new roots to settle in. Except on cold sticky soils, autumn is the ideal time to plant new trees and shrubs, and also to move existing plants around the garden. Sometimes inspiration nods or ideas change, and it becomes obvious that certain plants are in the wrong place. When that happens, don't be afraid to move them. Prudent rearrangement can revive a tired area, especially if you seize the opportunity to work in a little extra fertility during the process. When care and assistance are given where necessary, even established shrubs and small trees can be moved, although older plants will need more post-operative care with watering and support.

Success depends upon keeping plants as comfortable as possible. Whereas small herbaceous plants can be sprung from the soil with a fork, shrubs must be moved

Right Though primarily grown for its fruit, a mature quince deserves prominence as a specimen tree

with a generous undisturbed rootball 60-90cm (2-3ft) across, or more, according to the plant's size. Bundle up arching foliage with loops of string, and then cut a circle around the main stem with a spade. Gradually dig underneath the plant to produce a hemi-spherical rootball.

Tuck a square of sacking right under the rootball, which you should try to keep intact. Wrap the material right round the ball if the plant is to be lifted and carried; alternatively, drag the plant on its mat of sacking to the new site. Make sure the hole is large enough for the rootball, and turn the plant until you are satisfied with its position before backfilling and firming the excavated soil. Until self-supporting, use strong cord to tie top-heavy plants to stakes driven in outside the rootball.

Above Hoar frost, the decorative result of high humidity in cold weather, will harm plants less than a dry air or ground frost, providing plants have been hardened by decreasing temperatures

NEW PLANTS FROM OLD

ADVENTURES WITH CUTTINGS Once when I was ambling through the greenhouses during one of our annual open days, I was stopped by a visitor who praised our luxuriant busy lizzies. We had a number of choice plants, selected and propagated over the years from various sources. In full bloom they made dense, magnificent mounds of vibrant colour, growing to more than 60cm (2ft) across in 20cm (8in) pans. One or two in particular caught our visitor's eye and I promptly offered some cuttings, much to her evident consternation, as she admitted to having already slipped a few into her capacious handbag. All keen gardeners are covetous and often ruthless opportunists, quite incapable of resisting a tempting cutting or ripe seed capsule. It is of course socially unacceptable to steal cuttings, even from plants that lean within tantalizing reach over front garden walls, but who has not acquired a tamarisk, daphne or crimson aubretia by unpremeditated theft?

Ethics of plunder aside, this dubious practice does raise the question of when is the best time to take cuttings. While handbooks recommend the ideal moment, many plants propagate successfully at unorthodox times of year. If you see a suitable shoot, try rooting it by your favourite method – some gardeners thrust stems into the ground beside the parent plant, others

96

stand them in water on a windowsill or strike them conventionally in a pot of cuttings compost.

Even this late in the year, most shrubs are worth attempting from hardwood cuttings: buddleia, spiraea, jasmine and soft fruit are all likely to grow. When you cut back roses after planting, trim a few promising stems into cuttings and bury their lower two-thirds in the soil. Sturdy pieces from pansies or sweet williams will root in pots indoors.

Experiment at any time of year. Tomato sideshoots root quickly, as do the tips of raspberry canes. Cut flowers and foliage such as hydrangeas, pussy willow, chrysanthemums and flowering currant develop their roots in vases. Remember that when catalogues describe plants as annuals, this may only be practical advice for cool climates: try potting up scarlet salvias and 'annual' pinks in late summer for cuttings next year. When a cinerarea finishes flowering in spring, prune it back to the main stem and pull off the resulting sideshoots to root as new houseplants.

All cuttings are live things, full of vitality and an instinct to grow. Even a clothes-post, freshly hewn from the hedgerow and driven deep into the soil, will root and start to branch into a new tree. This is the countryman's way of extending his streamside willows, and a traditional ploy to save time when propagating a mulberry, which will fruit several years earlier if started as a cut branch or 'trungeon'. Some trees don't grow from cuttings, but on the whole the gamble is worth taking – most species have a better than evens chance.

FOCUS ON FOOD

CROPS IN POTS The year that we grew potatoes in buckets, runner beans in 25cm (10in) pots and gathered a winter's supply of lettuce from a boxful of saladini, demonstrated to us the possibilities of the small-scale harvest. Although self-sufficiency in fruit and vegetables may require anything up to an acre of ground, depending upon the crops grown, few of us have such an area at our disposal. An allotment will supply an average family for much of the year, while part of a small town garden can yield a steady supply of salads and small fresh vegetables of superior quality to shop produce. Where there is no soil at all, worthwhile crops can still be grown in various containers, such as pots, troughs and window boxes. That much is familiar to resourceful town gardeners. However, many fail by trying to translate open garden techniques to the specialized field of growing in containers.

Not all vegetables or fruit will succeed, for example: a 20cm (8in) pot might just support a single Brussels sprout plant, but it is hardly worth the effort when bought supplies are so good. On the other hand, herbs, salads, small carrots, spring onions, summer cabbages, peas, beans, strawberries and most dwarf kinds of fruit trees are ideal for growing in pots of

PLANT HIGHLIGHTS OF THE MONTH

Tomatoes **With a little heat and considerable skill, you might still have ripe tomatoes in late autumn. The real importance of this month, though, is that tomato plants are grown commercially for eleven months of the year, starting now. If you can maintain 15°C (60°F) under glass, at least during germination, sowing a cold-tolerant variety such as 'Counter' to start cropping in early spring could be worth the gamble. Otherwise wait until late winter before sowing a normal variety on a warm windowsill or beside the stove.**

Russets **These are the aristocrats among apple varieties: crisp, rough-skinned fruits that may be either round or conical, bronzed, green or crimson-flushed, but all sharing an aromatic and juicy nuttiness that complements elderberry port and fireside ease. They need careful picking and storage for a few months until they reach perfection in mid-winter. Search out Rosemary Russet, Orleans Reinette, Norfolk Royal Russet and Adam's Pearmain, the perfect birthday gift for a child of that name.**

Winter begonias **Flamboyant summer begonias are dormant now, leaving the stage for their refined cousins, *Begonia* x *chiemantha* and *B.* x *hiemalis* (formerly *B.* x *elatior*). The classic chiemantha is 'Gloire de Lorraine', large and bushy with a froth of pale pink flowers; 'Love Me'**

is a compact modern version to grow from seed. Hiemalis hybrids, available in bloom about now, are stouter, with large orange, red or white flowers in autumn and winter. Keep moist and moderately warm; after flowering take leaf or tip cuttings and discard old plants.

various sizes. Most of these, furthermore, are decorative plants, an important virtue where space counts.

When choosing crops, consider their aesthetics and try to exploit their ornamental value. Marrows and outdoor cucumbers are excellent screening plants on panels of trellis work, as are runner beans which can be grown up canes arranged as a summer porch over a doorway. Ruby chard makes a brilliant crimson centre piece for a tub of bedding plants, while bushy tomatoes, asparagus or peas combined with trailing lobelia are all you need for spectacular hanging baskets.

One year I assembled a tripod of canes in a 38cm (15in) pot and grew the pink and white runner bean 'Painted Lady'. Among their stems the crimson sweet pea *Lathyrus tingitanus* scrambled up above a carpet of white petunias and bushy 'Red Alert' tomatoes, to make an exotic and fruitful combination until exhaustion set in during the autumn. Most vegetables will adapt to pots or small tubs, and when combined with one or two flowering plants, never look too agricultural for the patio. Try growing blue morning glories blended with golden podded climbing French beans, or asparagus edged with red leaf lettuce and trailing lobelia.

Mobility is an essential virtue of all but the heaviest containers; plants can be moved into the sun where necessary or brought under cover when frost threatens. Growing mints and tarragon in pots not only restrains their invasive urges, but also prolongs their useful season if they are moved indoors in

the autumn. Greek housewives keep huge bushes of basil in pots outside their doors all year round, but in cooler climates it is best to treat many Mediterranean herbs as nomads, for they need full sunshine in summer and indoor warmth in winter. Indulged in this way, the native American lemon verbena, *Lippia citriodora* (also known as *Aloysia triphylla*) can be grown into a large spreading bush, or trained as an informal standard in an ornate pot or urn. Its slender pastel-green leaves are highly aromatic, and when dried preserve their lemon scent from one year to the next. Another tender classic pot herb that is seldom seen today is *Westringia fruticosa*, or Victorian rosemary, with whorls of narrow blue-green leaves, silvery beneath, and white flowers in mid-summer. Plants are sufficiently dense and bushy to be clipped into simple topiary shapes such as mop head standards, spirals and cones; planted in a decorative jardinière, this herbal topiary would add Italianate distinction to the potted garden.

PLANNING

CREATIVE EDGES The era of municipal symmetry, when flowerbeds were inevitably framed with precise rows of lobelia and 'Little Dorrit', is past. Gardeners are more sophisticated these days, prepared to question old assumptions and experiment with more adventurous designs. Not that the old bedding plants merit disdain: sweet alyssum still has a place, grouped in generous mats to concentrate its honeyed perfume, while lobelia is too obliging and richly coloured to be abandoned altogether. Try growing trailing lobelias, especially white-eyed blue 'Sapphire' interplanted with tightly curled parsley, as an informal edging to summer bedding.

Parsley is not the only culinary plant worth growing in flowerbeds. Dainty chervil's light green ferny leaves blend prettily with dwarf annuals such as that childhood favourite linaria (toadflax), intense gentian blue *Phacelia campanularia*, or shorter forms of *Phlox drummondii* (eg 'Twinkle Star', only 15cm (6in) high). Red lettuces , for example 'Lollo Rossa' and 'Red Sails', are stunning as edging plants, although their harvest will leave gaps in a row; grow loose-leaf 'Salad Bowl' instead, both red and green kinds, for these will last all season.

The veined and cut leaves of strawberries are so attractive that I once used surplus 'Royal Sovereign' plantlets to edge our asparagus beds, and regretted it for several seasons thereafter.

Left At this stage red mountain spinach (Atriplex) is compact, but it needs pinching back to limit its naturally tall growth. Opposite left As edging plants flower, their new growth spills onto the path and softens its outline. Opposite right A pond makes a still centre amid a riot of marginal flowers

So fertile were the beds that they rapidly became a dense mat of runners and overlooked survivors from a ruthless slaughter still pop up here and there. Runner-less alpine strawberries are far more restrained, and are easily raised from seed sown indoors now. Several red (and one or two yellow) varieties are available to fruit over a long season, or you can sow the classic scarlet, crimson and golden mixture 'Fraises des Bois' as a delicious perennial edging.

To create an informal effect, or to relieve the stern lines of a path, plant rugs of prostrate flowers to billow over the edges. In warm sunny positions, hardier forms of osteospermum (Star of the Veldt, also known as dimorphotheca) are unsurpassed for brilliance and continuity of flower. Pinks of all pedigrees are attractive both in and out of bloom, especially the old-fashioned laced varieties and the auricula-eyed maiden pink

Dianthus deltoides 'Microchip'. Thrift (armeria) makes tough and rounded mats of dense foliage, improved varieties such as *Armeria hybrida formosa* and 'Seaspray Mixed' bearing large rose or white flowers in summer.

DESIGNING A WATER GARDEN Most of us, at some time or other, have been tempted to include water as a feature in our gardens. It can be used as a mysterious reflective pond, an animated chattering stream and as a place in which to grow a new range of plants. Water is a living element that never fails to seduce and captivate visitors and seasoned gardeners alike.

Introducing it to the garden, however, might seem at first an alarming undertaking, one that has no doubt deterred many people who visualize complex hydraulics, levelling pegs and concrete mixers as essential preconditions to sitting beside a little rippling water on a hot summer's day. If you crave cascades and fountains or cool tanks and canals, this is undoubtedly true, but few have the room or resources for water on such a scale. Nor would such grand designs necessarily be apt.

Water has quite a profound effect on its setting, and a little can go a long way. Large areas of still water may dominate or overwhelm a whole landscape, whereas a tiny pond strategically placed in the corner of a garden can add an atmosphere of serenity out of all proportion to its size. The sound of the smallest waterfall might be intrusive on a quiet day, compared with the soft murmur of an artificial spring bubbling from a hole in a stone. Exploit the vivacity of the simplest fountain by siting it so that the water falls between you and the sun in order to get the maximum sparkle.

Running water usually blends more easily than ponds into an existing garden layout, simply because it follows a linear route, rather like a narrow unobtrusive path, but its planning needs careful assessment of changing levels, as water must run downhill. This could entail laborious spadework, unless there is already a ditch or stream course. Remember, fast flowing water discourages marginal plant growth because of continuous scouring along the banks; if you want streamside plants, carve out quiet eddies and backwaters where there is less agitation.

Most gardeners will settle for a pond, which may be formal or natural in appearance according to its surroundings. A formal pond is often the easiest to construct and tends to look best as a simple feature in a level open space. Keep the shape clean and crisp, defining its edge with hard materials such as stone, bricks or tiles. To save labour, consider building the pond above ground level, using concrete or a pre-formed liner supported within a retaining wall, low enough for you to sit and trail your fingers in the water. The inner surface can be studded with designs in coloured pebbles, or painted black for a moody reflective surface.

If you want a less formal pond, use nature as a guide. Choose a depression or low part of the garden, perhaps where water naturally lies, and make your pond here, using a flexible liner and cunningly softening its margins by relaying turf over the edges of the pond and down below the surface. Keep the water topped up so that a little seeps into the adjacent grass. This encourages moisture-loving species which, together with aquatic plantings around the pond's edge, will soon create a naturalized habitat and quickly attract frogs, dragonflies and other wildlife to populate the garden.

NATURALIZED TULIPS Whereas daffodils are among the first spring bulbs to be planted, tulips can wait until last without harm. Late autumn is the time to get them in, after spring bedding has been transplanted and herbaceous borders tidied for the winter. Scatter candytuft seeds over the area as it will flower in spring as the bulb foliage dies down.

Some gardeners experience difficulty in deciding where to grow tulips, such is the formality and intense colouring of many cultivars. If you think these look brash and unyielding among other plants, explore some of the species, which often bloom with more grace and poise than their large-flowered relatives, and blend easily into the spring garden.

A few species can even be naturalized in the same way as daffodils, snakes-head fritillaries, *Iris reticulata* and crocuses such as 'Cream Beauty', ie by planting them in short turf. The problem with most tulips is that they come from regions with hot dry summers; if left in the ground where the climate is wetter and colder, they may decline after a few seasons. To prevent this from happening, dig up the bulbs some weeks after flowering and then store in a dry place until the autumn. With care they should then last for many seasons without deterioration. This applies to most large-flowered cultivars, which would in any case be out of place in a wild setting. But a few species or 'botanical' tulips have been found to survive and multiply when naturalized. They are not fussy about the soil, provided it is free-draining. Choose a position that is not overhung by trees and gets plenty of warm sunshine; where the ground is cold or heavy, it would be wise to lift all tulips for dry storage over the summer.

The best candidate for naturalizing is the wild European tulip, *Tulipa sylvestris*, with its charming yellow flowers, narrowly oval-shaped petals and a welcome tendency to spread freely by underground runners. If this thrives, also try the bright red and white Lady tulip, *T. clusiana*, which spreads in the same way, or shade-tolerant *T. sprengeri*, a late species with rich red blooms at spring's end. These must be planted at least 15-20cm (6-8in) deep, although experiments suggest that their natural depth of 25-30cm (10-12in) might be preferable. As with daffodils, scatter the bulbs and plant them where they fall, or dig out a square of turf, evenly space a handful of bulbs at the bottom of the hole and then cover with the turf. Always wait until after mid-summer before mowing, to allow the tulip foliage to wither naturally.

UNDER GLASS

EXOTIC BULBS One morning as I entered the nursery stove house, closed the doors and reluctantly breathed in steam, an irresistible fragrance led me to ghostly white 'daffodils' that

Tulips flowering en masse – 'Pinocchio' (opposite) and (above) the water lily varieties 'West Point', 'China Pink' and red 'Aladdin'. These are growing in a border, but would be worth naturalizing in a well-drained lawn

peeped shyly from a tangle of creeping figs. They were Amazon lilies (*Eucharis grandiflora*), tropical bulbs that flower three times a year in high temperatures, filling the house with their intoxicating perfume. You occasionally find Amazon lilies for sale in garden centres, together with a number of other tender bulbs, few of which need the tropical conditions in which I first met them. Sweet-scented Peruvian daffodils (variously listed as *Ismene*, *Hymenocallis* or *Pancratium*), the golden lily-flowered *Chlidanthus fragrans* and the bizarre *Cypella herbertii* can all be grown in pots in a greenhouse or conservatory for flowering on a windowsill indoors.

Compared with Victorian gardeners, we are timid about trying unusual bulb species as pot plants. Apart from the annual rash of monstrous hippeastrum blooms on windowsills, few of us now grow clivias, gloriosas, the renowned Scarborough lily (*Vallota speciosa*) or other tender bulbs, although all of them are easy to bring into flower and to keep from year to year. They have few demands other than protection from frost and in some cases an annual period of dry rest.

Some tropical species prefer glasshouse humidity throughout the season, and it would be imprudent to try flowering eucharis or ismene bulbs outdoors. Since the majority of these have evergreen leaves, their appearance out of flower would certainly not disgrace a conservatory arrangement; quite the contrary, their strap-like leaves would add a bold foliar ingredient to groupings.

Most, however, are deciduous and need dry storage while dormant, usually in their pots, which can be laid on their sides beneath greenhouse staging. At the end of this period some are repotted in fresh compost, although a few such as zephyranthes and haemanthus flower best when pot-bound. Once growth resumes and spring frosts are past, there is no reason why containers should not be moved outdoors in the same way that citrus and other tender shrubs are released from the protection of orangeries in summer.

They are ideal complements for summer bedding in tubs and baskets. When grown in a decorative pot, an established clump of flowering clivias, with their spherical-heads of pink to red, or occasionally white flowers, will enhance any patio corner (but beware, do not jeopardize your most precious Mediterranean containers, for congested clivia roots can burst even the strongest pot). Pineapple lilies (*Eucomis comosa*), nerines and the flamboyant climbing *Gloriosa rothschildiana* all flourish in a warm sheltered niche outdoors.

In cold gardens, start slightly tender bulbs such as sparaxis, acidanthera and ixia in pots under glass and transfer outdoors once the weather conditions are safe. Gather them in groups on the ground and at the edge of steps, or bury them, still in

Summer flowering bulbous plants for a warm greenhouse —
***Vallota speciosa*, the vivid Scarborough lily (right); the bizarre**
climber *Gloriosa rothschildiana* (far right); and luminous white
***Eucharis grandiflora* (below)**

their pots, among other plants in tubs or in the open ground.
By keeping a reserve of growing bulbs in a greenhouse or cold
frame, a sequence of colour could be maintained in window
boxes, large indoor containers or staged groups outside as
respective species come into bloom.

Whichever bulbs you choose to grow in pots, make sure
that you are familiar with their individual requirements. Arum
lilies, for example, make the most spectacular centrepieces in
30cm (12in) pots and come in several colours; the white variety (*Zantedeschia aethiopica*) grows all year, whereas pink and
yellow kinds (*Z. rehmanii* and *Z. elliottiana* respectively) should
be dried off after flowering. Although most bulbs are buried at
planting time in the normal way, a few such as nerines are left
partly exposed. When their blooms fade, water and feed regularly if they are to do well the following year.

GARDEN SURGERY

ROSES ON LIGHT SOIL   If your soil is light and hungry, the opposite in fact of the classic 'rose soil' preferred by modern cultivars, do not despair of growing roses successfully, for many older kinds will tolerate spartan conditions if fed with manure annually and kept well-watered.

On one estate, with the sandiest conceivable soil, we assembled a small collection of irresistible classic varieties. 'Nevada', although one of the great shrub roses, were grown around a courtyard as climbers, their strong arching stems fanned across the face of 3.6m (12ft) high walls that disappeared early every summer beneath a froth of creamy white blossom. The effect was stunning, especially when complemented by the heady perfume lingering in the yard, not from the lightly scented 'Nevada' but from enormous bushes of the hybrid musk 'Penelope' nearby.

There were already several comfortable specimens of easy-going *Rosa rugosa* and its countless varieties: luxuriant stalwarts such as 'Blanc Double de Coubert' and 'Sarah van Fleet', sumptuous crimson 'Mrs Anthony Waterer' and daintily fringed 'Fimbriata'. To these we added the medieval alba roses, all of them white or pastel pinks with soft grey-green foliage but, for all their delicacy, hardy and self-sufficient even in that ill-favoured garden. Celebrities such as 'Maiden's Blush' and the fragrant Jacobite rose ('Alba Maxima'), the languid camellia-flowered 'Mme Legras de St Germain' and the majestic 'Queen of Denmark' combined to prove that true aristocrats are undeterred by a little poverty.

BITTER PIT   Ripe apples, perfectly sound in every other respect, are sometimes disfigured by a rash of dirty brown, sunken speckles that extend well into the flesh and spoil their flavour with a metallic bitterness, although some varieties are more susceptible than others. These are classic symptoms of bitter pit, a curious physiological disorder caused by lack of calcium. All fruits need some calcium if they are to develop perfectly, but plants only absorb minerals and nutrients when dissolved in water. Lack of calcium in the soil or an irregular supply of water interrupts the circulation of essential chemicals to a plant's extremities, with various results, such as blossom end rot in tomatoes – in which the nose of the fruit darkens and eventually shrivels – and bitter pit in apples.

Professional growers spray apples with soluble calcium, but the real problem occurs at soil level. Apples like a pH of 6.5, and if a soil test reveals a lower reading, garden lime should be applied to adjust this. Calcified seaweed can be used as a regular soil conditioner, at a rate of 60g/sq metre (2oz/sq yard). Substituting organic manures for chemical fertilizers may also make a difference as the latter tend to leave potash and phosphate residues which block the uptake of calcium.

New trees are most commonly affected, mainly because their precocious vigour, which often fuels rapid growth, cannot be matched by the uptake of minerals. In excessively wet or dry seasons, depressed root activity is also a contributory factor. Although beyond the gardener's control, it is reassuring to know that immaturity and unfavourable weather are both transient, and that there is no need to discard affected trees, since their susceptibility is only temporary.

INSPIRATION

FRUITING HEDGES   One of my son's friends marvelled at our apparently eccentric hunter-gatherer activities: 'your family's great,' he enthused, 'they find a hedge, and then they eat it.' Hedges used to be a dependable source of food and timber and many remain a cornucopia of produce. Modern versions, however, planted only to demarcate boundaries and exclude intruders, usually consist of a single fast-growing species, but you can revive the hedgerow as a productive feature by planting a diverse collection of cropping species, or by introducing a few to an existing hedge.

Gooseberries are a traditional summer fruit and can be clipped to a formal outline; blend with rugosa roses for an impenetrable and decorative barrier. *Prunus cerasifera*, the cherry plum, makes a fine hedging shrub on chalky soil; blueberries thrive in acid conditions. Try growing blackberries and hybrid berries on fences and wire netting, together with hazelnuts or mulberries, both of which respond to espalier training.

Instead of maintaining a level top, relieve the uniformity of a hedge by planting within it small trees spaced approximately 3-3.6m (10-12ft) apart to form a second, higher tier. Half-standard apples or pears on semi-dwarfing rootstocks are ideal, together with damsons, quinces, bullaces and almonds. Medlars are often grafted on hawthorn rootstocks, offering the possibility of ornamenting an established thorn hedge. Crab apples and damsons, both easy to raise from seed, make sound hedge rootstocks for grafted apple and plum varieties.

Choose one or two small trees which in the past were put to good use in the following ways: The spindle tree, *Euonymus europaeus*, supplied cottagers with spindles, skewers and knitting needles. *Sorbus aucuparia*, the rowan with its harvest of edible berries and tough wood was used for making tool handles; its close relative, the service tree (*S. torminalis*), is still used in France to make wine-press screws. The wood of *Robinia pseudoacacia* or locust tree is as hard and as attractive as oak for cabinet work, whereas the tiny wayfaring tree, *Viburnum lantana*, has tough young twigs, so pliable that they were once used to edge shrimping nets, and would now make an acceptable substitute for garden twine. With just a few of these survivors from a more enterprising age, an uninteresting hedge can be transformed into a whimsically economic asset.

Early WINTER

At this time OF YEAR THE WILDER MARGINS OF OUR GARDEN, AS WELL AS THE SURROUNDING WARWICK-SHIRE HEDGEROWS, ARE RICH SOURCES OF EVERGREENS, MUCH OF IT IDEAL FOR MAKING SEASONAL GARLANDS AND THE TRADITIONAL KISSING BOUGH.

The kissing bough is a far more impressive creation than a few sprigs of Christmas mistletoe pinned to a door lintel. It is a hoop or ball of bent wire, covered with interwoven branches of ivy, sweet bay or rosemary, and then decorated with ripe apples suspended from bright ribbons. Mistletoe is tied beneath as its final raison d'être.

If your ivy is home-grown, you can collect ample supplies for decoration when pruning annual growth back to old wood, to keep plants within bounds. Stout stems carrying berries, pushed into the ground like softwood cuttings, will root as 'tree ivy', and keep their woody habit, so they can be trained for flowering standards or shrubs. Save bushy serpentine ivy stems, especially variegated ones, for garlands and festoons. One year I helped make thick garlands of greenery and flowers to decorate the royal box in a nearby theatre, and every winter since I've been pressed into weaving a home-spun version to place around our fireplace. The basis of the garland is a loosely draped rope, which is then sheathed with all kinds of evergreen, bound in place with thin wire. The royal original had sported thousands of spray chrysanthemum heads, but more durable and appropriate substitutes at this time of year are apples, cones, dried flowers and seed heads. To add the finishing touches use ribbons and large, bright tree decorations. Basic greenery for the garland is ivy, holly, Portugal laurel and conifer foliage, especially Christmas tree prunings.

In our family, the decision of whether or not to have a real tree requires an annual conference, which arouses all kinds of environmental passions. However, in the end, since

Bare branches REVEALED AND INVITING ARTISTIC PRUNING TO IMPROVE THEIR SILHOUETTES

THE EARLIEST WINTER *aconites* AS THEY COINCIDE WITH THE LAST OF THE ROSE BLOOMS

Frost THAT DECORATES AS IT DESTROYS TENDER PLANTS YOU FORGOT TO MULCH

PATCHES OF DAINTY HARDY *cyclamen,* WHICH WILL INSPIRE YOU TO PLANT MORE

Christmas trees are deliberately planted like any other crop, the argument that their harvest can hardly amount to vandalism usually wins, and every year an otherwise undistinguished conifer comes indoors for its magical fortnight in centre-stage. You can, of course, grow your own Christmas tree, either from seed or from a bought potted tree, planted outside after Twelfth Night and dug up annually for as long as it remains manageable. Although the species usually bought for this purpose is the Norway spruce, *Picea abies*, discerning buyers look for attractive alternatives such as Serbian spruce, *P. omorika*, and various silver firs, the best of which are *Abies procera* or noble fir, and the Caucasian fir, *A. nordmanniana*. Fresh seeds can be found between the scales of dry cones in early autumn. Store the seeds in polythene bags, in a cool place, until sown outdoors in spring, although noble fir seeds need to be sown immediately, and be exposed to frost. When three to four years old, a young tree will be large enough to make its debut indoors, with several more seasons to follow before it grows too big for a 38cm (15in) pot. Groom for the occasion by lightly pruning to shape wherever necessary, and replant outside in a moist site between festive seasons.

NEW PLANTS FROM OLD

MISTLETOE Wassailers, from the English county of Somerset, fire shotgun volleys through their apple trees, ostensibly to guarantee good future crops in their orchards, although the explosive custom might simply be an inevitable result of too much sloe gin and scrumpy cider. The only shooting party I have ever joined took place during preparations for Christmas one year, as we gathered quantities of greenery for distribution to the estate workers. The majestic lime trees growing beside every road and lane were festooned with swags of mistletoe, but all were well beyond the reach of the tallest ladder. Amassing enough for the gardeners and farmworkers was strictly the gamekeeper's responsibility, because the only realistic way to collect it was to blast clumps down with a shotgun. Busy and elusive like all conscientious gamekeepers, ours came only when he was ready, even though tradition insists that mistletoe must be gathered on the sixth day of the moon's waning if it is to have any mystical powers.

In the northern hemisphere modern druids try growing domestic supplies on branches of garden apple trees, another favourite host for the semi-parasitic plant,

Right The Serbian spruce, *Picea omorika*, is a graceful conifer for gardens and makes a hardy windbreak

Above An apple tree unharmed by semi-parasitic clumps of mistletoe that are many years old. **Below** The pretty flowers of the single snowdrop are unrivalled for their simplicity

by squeezing the contents of Christmas mistletoe berries into cracks in the bark. Frequent failure is blamed on the assumption that in order for seeds to germinate, they must first pass through a bird's digestive system, but this is apocryphal because birds only eat the flesh of the berries, not the seeds themselves. A more likely explanation is the fact that a lot of mistletoe on sale in shops is imported, and while botanists are still not sure if plants are host-specific (ie growing only on a particular species), it is thought to be a likely cause of failure in germination; for example, mistletoe from Normandy poplars might not relish growing on English apple trees. But the greatest obstacle to success is that the berries, although appearing towards the end of autumn, are not in fact ripe until spring, sometimes quite late in the season.

If you want to grow your own, ignore the Christmas kissing boughs and instead collect berries from early spring onwards, from plants growing on the same type of tree as the proposed host. Gently lift a flap of bark on the underside of a branch and squeeze the berries inside, where the sticky flesh will bind the seeds in place. After one to two years, a short stem bearing two

leaves should appear. This is as far as any mistletoe branch extends in a season, each stem dividing annually to produce two such shoots. But remember that you need more than one plant to guarantee berries, because male and female flowers are borne separately. Even then it will be at least five years before any appear, so you might prefer to leave the plant as a wild opportunist, to harvest when required.

PLANNING

'PUSHING AHEAD' During my days as a trainee I cherished a musty old gardener's handbook. It was illustrated with dark engravings of lantern-jawed men in waistcoats and enormous boots, grimly inspecting the well-ordered potting shed, or bent double over immaculate trenches as they triple-dug rods, poles or perches of kitchen garden. Every month had its catalogue of essential tasks which I resolved to follow to the letter once in charge of a garden of my own. After the shortest day of the year I would industriously start to blanch seakale and rhubarb, force French beans and turnips on hotbeds, damp down the orchid house and syringe the vinery, prepare mushroom beds and 'push ahead with trenching, pathmaking and erecting pergolas, arcades &c.'

As far as 'pushing ahead' is concerned, there is always new work which needs to be done during the winter days, whether it be reclaiming neglected areas of the garden and extending into new ground, or replacing rotting rose pillars and erecting new ones for climbing roses and the new orchard of trained fruit. But the start of winter usually finds us here at The Lodge still raking up autumn leaves that should have been cleared well before now. Fortunately the lawns require less attention during this season, especially if they are wet or frosted, when walking on them might cause damage. Only in mild weather will they need the occasional light cut. Nor is it the time to do much digging. Heavy soils are best turned in autumn to give frost an opportunity to pulverize clods into a crumbly tilth,

whereas digging thin sandy ground such as ours would expose it to winter rains, which batter the surface into a hard crust, and so we postpone major cultivation until early spring.

Digging seems to be the favourite winter standby of gardening manuals, old or new, and of the supervisors who study them. 'Nothing like a spot of vigorous digging to work off a weekend's inertia,' the foreman used to declare cheerily on a Monday morning as he led us youngsters to the kitchen garden. His parting shot was always 'looks grand when it's all turned over nice and rough', but we were never really sure whether all that ritual spade-work was kindly therapy, essential husbandry or merely a cosmetic exercise.

Certainly freshly turned earth can be visually satisfying, for bare ground makes subtle but insistent demands, as though rebuking us for mismanagement. Soil can be protected with ground-cover plants and over-all mulches, both of which make aesthetic as well as practical common-sense, suggesting that everything is snugly wrapped up and only temporarily dormant, until spring returns. The problem of empty patches seldom arises in a small garden, where fitting in all the plants you want to grow is a greater challenge than camouflaging the spaces in between them. On a larger scale, though, bare ground is an inevitable stage in the annual cycle of a herbaceous border or a successful kitchen garden, and whether you plant, hoe or dig, something must be done to show that the emptiness is not due to idleness or lack of vision.

You might need a certain amount of heroism to venture out in winter with a spade or hoe, but strategic ground-work now does reap dividends later, by reinforcing humus levels and allowing the soil to breathe. Start by lightly pricking over bulb beds with a fork, and by dressing the surface with a general fertilizer to encourage early growth. Watch out for opportunist weeds in a mild season and eliminate them while they are still tiny. Remaining drifts of autumn leaves can be spread between shrubs, together with lawn clippings, if you have to trim the grass during a dry spell.

While a little steady cultivation does wonders for the spirits and for the circulation on a sullen day, always stop work before your enthusiasm wanes. Relax instead by walking round the garden, partly to check such things as plants heaved from the soil by frost, but also to spot the earliest aconites, snowdrops and *Iris unguicularis*, which may bloom for weeks before being noticed. If the weather is too severe, you can settle back indoors with the seed catalogues, to plan ahead in the light of last year's experience, satisfied that you have done your honest share of 'pushing ahead'.

FIRST PRIORITIES It is always worth pausing to assess the merits and successes of your garden, to remind yourself of the vision that lies behind its evolution and also to reconsider its purpose. When confronted by a new garden, this period of

PLANT HIGHLIGHTS OF THE MONTH

Camellia Camellias can be difficult to site outdoors, because of their preference for shelter and acid soils, but small kinds make ideal fragrant pot plants for cool conservatories. Choose prolific *Camellia* x *williamsii* hybrids such as 'Anticipation' or 'J C Williams', or forms of *C. sasanqua*. They need lime-free compost and watering with rainwater. Repot after flowering, and feed in spring and summer. Shade from bright sunlight, ventilate freely, and stand outdoors during the summer.

Hardy cyclamen All species are charming, perennial candidates for autumn, winter or early spring flowering in many unlikely sites outdoors. On well-drained soil they will colonize chalk, hedge bottoms and shaded ground beneath deciduous trees, as well as rock gardens, joints in crazy paving and grassy areas in wild gardens. Plant in groups 7.5cm (3in) deep and allow them to sow themselves, or search out seed capsules on their coiled stems and scatter the ripe seeds further afield. Mulch while dormant with fine decayed leaves or grass mowings.

Hippeastrum Sometimes mistakenly called amaryllis, hippeastrums are obliging bulbs. Simply wait until old bulbs resume growth now and they will bloom in early spring, but if heated in autumn – four weeks at 18°C (65°F), followed by four weeks at 24°C (75°F) – and then potted up, bulbs will flower after only a few weeks; unlike many bulbs no initial period of darkness is needed. Keep flowering plants cool to prolong their display, and continue feeding and watering until early autumn, when plants are dried off in their pots. Replace the top layer of compost when reviving dormant bulbs.

reflection is even more important, giving you the opportunity to appraise its assets, deficiencies and potential for change, for making a garden is an intensely personal project, reflecting the aims and personality of its owner.

Soil type and aspect are critical, and plans that ignore these factors are unlikely to succeed; soils can be upgraded gradually, but their essential nature is immutable. Aspect will affect the microclimate within the garden: it might lie in the shadow of trees and buildings or be exposed to strong winds, trap summer heat and sunlight or remain a lethal frost-hollow in winter. In the light of this assessment you will, at an early stage, need to arrange windbreaks or drainage, adjust soil fertility or eliminate unsuitable plants from your plans.

Decide whether the garden is a place to work in or a place for relaxation, or both. Existing lawns might not be suitable for children's games, boundary fences and hedges might be too low or frail for privacy and seclusion, paths barely wide enough to admit a wheelbarrow – these are important considerations that should not be left out of your plans. Remember that gardens evolve and mature: plants die or grow too large, mistakes become obvious or your tastes alter, some experiments fail while others succeed too well.

If gardens are constantly changing, so too are their gardeners. Decide whether you really enjoy the necessary manual

work, and what will happen if your stamina or resources wane; do your plans demand too much time or inclination, both unpredictable factors? Understanding seasonal rhythms and the way plants grow and compete will help ensure the success of your garden plans, but it is also important to respect your own capabilities and to adopt a realistic, measured approach to a long-term commitment that should then prove a creative and exhilarating challenge.

FRAMEWORK

BANKS AND SLOPES Orthodox gardening wisdom generally assumes the ground to be level. Yet many gardens include, or are built on sloping ground, and coping with this requires quite unorthodox techniques.

Small undulations are better levelled if you intend to make a lawn or grow vegetables in rows. You might prefer to even out all gradients for the sake of convenience, but moving a lot of soil from one place to another is strenuous work, and a flat patch of ground, while admittedly easier to cultivate or to walk on, may in fact seem uninspiring compared to the dramatic possibilities that changes of level offer inventive gardeners. The main problem with steeper slopes is erosion, as heavy rains tend to run off instead of soak into the ground, and take

Opposite Frost and snow embellish iron-work alike.

Above Ivy is an efficient and attractive ground-cover plant even when growing in full shade, unlike heather (top) which gives its best colour in full sun

with them any loose top soil. The best way to avoid this is to protect the surface with ground-cover plants, whose roots will bind the soil together. If rows of fruit and vegetables are arranged across a slope rather than up and down it, they will help prevent soil movement downhill, especially if the surface is also covered with a coarse mulch.

Terracing is another solution, particularly effective for grass banks, which may be difficult and dangerous to mow unless the slope is cut into a series of broad, level steps. Turf is easier than grass seed to establish on steep banks, although fine plastic netting laid on the surface helps to stabilize the soil until seeds germinate. Use a fine slow-growing seed mixture and underplant it with naturalized bulbs in order to reduce the frequency of mowing.

Many ground-cover plants need little maintenance, and common subjects such as *Vinca major*, *Polygonum affine* 'Superbum', *Geranium macrorrhizum* or *Ajuga reptans* soon carpet a bank with attractive foliage and flowers; robust invaders like epimedium, lamium and euphorbia may be banished here and allowed to romp freely. Some climbers grow equally well as trailing plants: honeysuckle, Virginia creeper, clematis and ground-cover roses are all ideal for clothing banks. Remember, slopes are usually prominent, so choose flamboyant varieties that justify a conspicuous position.

On steeper ground, plants may need help to get established. Don't disturb the soil more than is necessary. Kill weeds with herbicide so that their roots remain to bind soil particles together, and scoop out small hollows for your new plants – these depressions will retain water and loosened soil where the plants need them. Drainage may be erratic on banks, but you can choose plants that prefer extreme conditions, and thus turn a problem into an attractive feature, such as a dry rock garden or a moist fernery. Add a generous flight of steps in some complementary material to complete the transformation.

LOOKING AHEAD

THE EFFECTS OF FROST Frost is winter's greatest peril for most gardeners, and experience quickly shows where and how much timely insulation, protection, or removal under cover is needed in a particular district. Locality is not the only critical influence on the impact of frost; the weather over a long period, before and after a savagely cold snap, may make all the difference to a plant's prospects of survival. In a normal season the worst frosts usually occur in the second half oí winter, allowing plants several weeks beforehand in which to prepare their defences. Falling temperatures in autumn have the same effect on plant tissues as hardening off; this is the deliberate process of gradual exposure that gardeners use to wean plants from indoor temperatures. Acclimatized in this way, they have a much higher tolerance of cold than untempered plants.

Hard precocious frosts in autumn may catch hardy plants unprepared, and so cause early injury. A heavy fall of snow spreads a protective blanket at ground level, but above its surface heat radiates rapidly, often leading to a dramatic and damaging drop in air temperatures. This, too, can intensify the impact of frost, especially if snow arrives early before plants are ready, or late when they are beginning to recover. Late frosts, even if light, may be the last straw for plants struggling to make replacement growth, which is young and therefore highly vulnerable.

Plants of doubtful hardiness need physical protection, and as further insurance you can take cuttings, or even dig and pot up a specimen to keep under glass. Where you suspect serious injury, don't be too hasty in pulling up plants before they can revive – figs and roses, for example, may die back to graft or ground level and still sprout again, and some shrubs, apparently dead, have been known to start growing again late in the year. Allow a whole season before condemning shrubs and

woody plants, and be sure to give a good tug before digging them up: if the roots resist, reprieve a plant until the following autumn, by which time any possible regrowth will be apparent.

FOCUS ON FOOD

BLANCHING Most people today use the term 'blanching' to describe an important stage in the preparation of vegetables for freezing. Sterilizing vegetables and sealing in their flavour by immersing them briefly in boiling water, far from turning them white, often enhances their colour, with the exception of some red bean varieties, whose unique colour leaches during the process of cooking.

In the garden blanching is a simple way to tenderize and sweeten crops otherwise unpalatably fibrous or bitter. Leeks are blanched for perfection, traditionally by covering their shafts with soil to exclude light. Commercial varieties need no earthing-up, and produce white stems naturally even when grown in full light. Perhaps it is this development of self-blanching strains that has caused the neglect of a traditional gardening skill, together with a significant loss of quality, for no self-blanching variety can equal an earthed-up leek, a tied cos lettuce, or trench celery with soil on its stems.

A determination to save labour has resulted in the neglect of vegetables that need blanching before they are ready for use. Until recent years, few grew cardoons, seakale or endive, once essential to the well-furnished kitchen garden. But a growing sense that tradition and diversity are important has revived the fortunes of these delicious vegetables, and gardeners are trying them once more, sometimes without realizing the need to blanch them in order to produce first-class crops.

Just an ordinary clay pot may be sufficient to transform a tough astringent plant into a delicacy. Dandelion leaves, for example, are often recommended as 'interesting' salad ingredients, but they are inedibly bitter to many palates unless they have been blanched. In spring, while it is growing fast, try covering a plant for two to three weeks with an upturned pot,

Opposite For many the misty atmosphere of a frost bound garden is one of the great joys winter brings. **Above** Colour variance of Swiss chard, is the same today as in this 19th-century lithograph

its drainage hole blocked with a stone or piece of tile; the resulting pale leaves should improve any salad. Many endive varieties and cos lettuce are supposedly self-blanching, producing pale crisp centres without assistance, but unless grown very quickly they may still be disappointing. For the sweetest, crunchiest salads, blanch them as gardeners used to, by folding outer leaves up over the hearts when the plants are almost full size, and tying them in place with a loop of raffia. Leave for a week or two before cutting, a little less in wet weather to prevent the hearts from rotting. Simplest of all, just lay an upturned dinner plate over a head of curly endive for a week, and compare the difference between its blanched heart and the dark outer leaves. For seakale you must use much larger covers, such as chimney pots or the old-fashioned forcing pots, with little lids for easy inspection. Though authentic and ornamental, these pots are expensive to buy, and where appearances are not paramount many gardeners use large buckets, wooden tea-chests and even dustbins to bleach more robust crops.

Soil is an efficient excluder of light, which is why the whitest celery is grown in trenches that are gradually filled in to cover the plants as the plants grow. If leek seedlings are transplanted into dibber holes 15-20cm (6-8in) deep, their stems rapidly fill the available space, and they blanch perfectly, arriving in the kitchen juicy and stringless. Other vegetables, also, blanch successfully: try leaving turnips, chicory or Swiss chard in the ground over winter, 'mulching' the dormant roots with a thick layer of leaves or garden compost. Scrape this aside the following spring and a tempting crop of tasty young leaves will be revealed.

UNDER GLASS

CONCERNING GREENHOUSE FRUIT Gardeners of old used all kinds of professional skills to raise perfect fruit for their employers, often out of season and in conditions that were far from ideal. The Victorians thought nothing of building greenhouses designed specially for fruit crops. These might be heated to high temperatures, as were the hot pine houses

where pineapples were coddled into productivity in outlandish mixtures of beech leaves and deer manure, or, like the traditional orchard houses, merely kept frost-free at blossom time. Whatever fruit they decided to grow, perfection demanded glass protection of some kind.

It is true that even normally hardy fruits benefit from cultivation under glass, especially the choicer, frost-shy varieties: the flavour of figs is enhanced beyond measure when they are grown in a greenhouse, peaches escape the devastating leaf curl when sheltered from wind and rain, while strawberries, if provided with minimal heat, can be forced into fruit in early spring. All these less exotic crops grow readily in a domestic greenhouse or conservatory.

If you have soil beds under cover, fruit trees can be planted in the same way as outdoors, sited 30cm (1ft) or so away from the side or the end of the house, or, in the case of a lean-to building, close to the rear wall. They occupy very little room grown as fans, with branches radiating from a short central stem, or as espaliers, with the fruiting shoots trained sideways from a vertical main stem. Prune and feed as for outdoor crops, but remember that most fruit under glass needs help with fertilization: in fine weather, leave doors and windows open to admit bees and other pollinating insects, or do the job manually by sharply tapping flowering branches daily with a garden cane. Greenhouse fruits will grow vigorously, with warmth, shelter and annual feeding, so resist the temptation to cram several specimens into a small house. A single peach or apricot on a rear wall, together with a grape vine trained up the roof from the opposite side, will be enough; other dwarf kinds of fruit can be grown in pots and moved outdoors in summer if space is precious.

Remember, too, the differing cultivation needs that might make some fruits uneasy companions. A dormant vine is best exposed to low temperatures, whereas figs like warmth all year round; sun-loving crops like peaches and apricots will resent the shade cast by roof-trained grapes or kiwi-fruit. Choose one or two compatible varieties of pear, gage, peach, nectarine, apricot, citrus fruit, grape or fig, and settle for excellence rather than diversity, unless you are prepared to extend the structure of your greenhouse after a few years.

PLANTS FROM PIPS An elderly Carmelite nun in a Yorkshire monastery once buried some apple pips while saying a prayer, and now the community remembers her with joy and pride each autumn, as basketfuls of fruit are gathered from the spreading 'Sister Raphael' tree. Similarly, the first fragrant blossoms unfurling on a potted grapefruit bush will be the cause for celebration when you recall sowing the pips fifteen years previously with a casual 'Let's see if they'll grow'.

Sowing fruit pips and stones is a fascinating pastime, irresistibly compelling as much for the perennial reward of watching a home-grown tree grow from a mere dormant spark of life, as for any prospect of harvesting good fruit. The chances of the latter occurring are at best very slim, and none at all with fruits such as avocados. If you wedge the stone of an avocado in the top of a bottle of water, it will almost certainly sprout into a coarse, swaggering little evergreen tree, whose ultimate size could be 18m (60ft) or more. When a thick single root has developed, transfer the plant into a container, filled with well-draining soil and position it in good light. The tree, however, will rarely flower in captivity and it will certainly never fruit.

Like the avocado, the coconut palm is short-lived in the dry heat of most houses, and it's quite an achievement to grow from a nut one that will survive for three or four years. If you want to attempt it, either use an old sprouting coconut or choose a fresh one with no 'milk' inside it (a sign of immaturity). Bury it on its side in a pot of damp sphagnum moss, leave in a warm place (18°C (65°F) or more) and wait at least six months until one of the eyes eventually produces roots and a shoot. Pot up the nut, still on its side and buried to half its depth, and grow on in a heated conservatory. Spray the foliage regularly to keep up humidity levels.

The date palm, a prickly but ornamental pot plant, which is happy in normal household temperatures, is far easier to grow. You can sow fresh date stones in normal seed compost, but those from dried fruit need soaking in water for 24 hours before being sown. They soon germinate and should then be potted up in soil-based compost, which is essential for providing the good drainage that phoenix palms demand. The date palm, *Phoenix dactylifera*, is content with 7°C (45°F) in winter if the compost is kept barely moist; in summer, water freely and stand in full sun, or move outdoors in a warm season.

Opposite Although they germinate quickly from pips, lemon trees may take years to crop unless grafted with a fruiting variety. Sweet cicely (right), on the other hand, is usable as a sugar substitute the year after sowing

DOWN TO EARTH

CARE FOR NEWLY ACQUIRED HOUSEPLANTS For obvious reasons, retailers would have us believe that even perennial pot plants are short-living, disposable gifts. As if to support this dubious contention, some plants start to wilt the moment they arrive in their new homes, and many fail to thrive for another season. However, a few simple precautions could help them settle in more comfortably, and could improve their chances of long-term survival.

Most pot plants will have been grown in heated greenhouses, often in a warm moist atmosphere. Their transfer from nursery or shop to home, perhaps on a cold winter day, is the first hazard that they face, though it can easily be overcome by wrapping pots snugly and keeping them out of the wind. Acclimatize the plants gradually to the drier home environment by standing them in a cool well-lit room for a few days. Spray lukewarm water over the foliage of evergreens daily for the first week, to help the transition from high humidity to dry conditions. Placing the pot inside an open-topped clear plastic bag will create a more moist atmosphere; progressively lower the bag each day to harden plants to room conditions.

Not all containers have drainage holes, a factor which will affect the frequency of watering. Pot up such plants in the normal way as soon as possible, and in the case of flowering

species, immediately after blooms have faded. It is also important to split collections in bowls before neighbouring plants start jostling for space. Look up the best way to keep each species, for many popular houseplants vary considerably in their preferences: azaleas and cyclamen, for example, need cool humid conditions, whereas kalanchoes and capsicums like warmth and bright light. Water according to need, rather than on an appointed day each week, and distinguish between species such as solanum, which prefer humid air, and chrysanthemum, which are prone to mildew if grown in a damp atmosphere.

INSPIRATION

SUGAR SUBSTITUTES Sucrose, the traditional content of everybody's sugar bowl, is nowadays considered to be a dietary villain, and manufacturers are eager to find an acceptable substitute for it. Considerable interest was aroused a few years ago when an American botanist identified the 'sweet plant', a herb cultivated by Aztecs, as *Lippia dulcis*, a close relative of lemon verbena, *L. citriodora*, whose aromatic leaves are widely used in tisanes. This rediscovered herb contains a potent substance called hernandulcin, which is very much sweeter than sucrose and has therefore been the subject of intensive research as a substitute for the sugar that many of us find addictive.

The popularity of cherry tomatoes such as 'Gardener's Delight' owes a lot to our craving for sweet things, for these varieties are unique in containing sucrose, which is what gives them their apparently greater flavour. Older gardeners recall producing their own sugar in times of austerity by boiling beet until the liquor reduced to a syrup, but the classic alternative to sugar has always been sweet cicely, *Myrrhis odorata*, which was traditionally grown close to cottage backdoors. It is a stout, handsome perennial that eventually reaches the height of 1.5-1.8m (5-6ft). It resembles cow parsley with fern-like, mid-green foliage and fragrant creamy-white flowers in early summer. To grow it, sow the large seeds individually in pots in autumn or early winter, and leave outdoors, exposed to frost. A year later the young plants will be ready for transfer to the open ground, but choose sites carefully because powerful tap roots make plants difficult to move once established. Pick leaves when fully opened; adding several to a pan of acid fruit such as rhubarb or gooseberries will halve the amount of sugar needed in any recipe.

$\mathcal{M}id$ WINTER

Working GARDENERS ARE COMMONLY THOUGHT TO HIDE FROM 'PALE, RUGGED WINTER', HUDDLED AROUND POTTING SHED STOVES, COMFORTABLY ASSESSING THE SEASON'S PERFORMANCE OR SCOURING CATALOGUES FOR NEXT YEAR'S NOVELTIES. REALITY IS NOWHERE NEAR SO COSY.

I can recall that as a trainee I seemed to spend most of the time dabbling in icy cold water, either washing down greenhouses or scrubbing mountains of grubby clay pots. Nowadays, with the responsibility of reviving a large garden, I find the calendar is quite awry and we are never up to date – is anyone who has a garden larger than a patio or pocket handkerchief? At the end of early winter the new season looms increasingly nearer, so that a certain apprehension spurs us outdoors in all but the worst weather.

How much you do outside this season depends on the local climate, of course. If your district freezes solid all winter, or disappears beneath a thick quilt of snow, then there is no alternative other than to spend your gardening hours choosing seeds and sharpening hoes. Mild sunny days, however, should tempt you out, if only for a critical tour, because winter reveals a garden's fundamental assets and weaknesses, hidden during the rest of the year while all is green and growing. On a cold morning look for the sunniest corners. These are death traps for frost-sensitive species, because rapid thawing completes the cruel work of a night's frost, and only your toughest plants should be grown in these areas. A bed that receives afternoon sunlight, on the other hand, or any spot where the thin green haze of winter weeds seems unaffected by frost, is probably the warmest part of the garden, and is therefore ideal for growing hardy salads, winter-flowering shrubs, or even to attempt to overwinter peas and beans.

It is important to note the places where rainwater or thawing snow lies in pools, as these probably suffer from

THE DELICATE BLUE FLOWERS OF *Iris stylosa*, HIDDEN IN THE ARCHING FOLIAGE

FAT BUDS OF *rhubarb crowns* READY TO COVER AND FORCE INTO TENDER GROWTH

LAST YEAR'S *chrysanthemum* STOOLS STIRRING INTO GROWTH FOR EARLY CUTTINGS

DORMANT CLUMPS OF *herbaceous perennials* TO EXPLORE FOR ROOT CUTTINGS

impeded drainage. Digging will often break up compacted ground or a buried soil pan (ie unbroken subsoil made impervious by repeated cultivation at the same depth), but if the problem seems incurable you can always exploit the area by growing bog plants or anything that loves constant moisture.

These are hungry times for garden wildlife, and vandalism starts now. While on your tour round the garden, watch out for signs of pigeons browsing on cabbages, Brussels sprouts and broccoli, or for bullfinches destroying gooseberry buds, and squirrels digging up everything from broad bean seeds to tulips. Slugs and snails love a mild winter, and where they are active surround vulnerable plants with garden lime, soot, fine cinders or slug pellets, which kill by dehydration. If you do find that snails multiply in your garden, reassure yourself that this is a reliable indication of alkaline soils, since they need a calcium-rich diet to build their shells.

PLANNING

WINTER FLOWERS Every year I have looked in vain for even a fraction of the blooms which a list in a comprehensive gardening guide states we can expect from a selection of winter-flowering plants. I came to the conclusion that the author was hopelessly optimistic. Even though mid-winter might be the natural season for many species, there is no guarantee that plants will flower obediently to time. Margery Fish is far more realistic in her guide, *A Flower for Every Day*. Some days, she concedes, there are only a precious few blooms to be found,

and for her winter was a time to 'prowl and peer'. This is not always the case: during early winter for the past three years, the seasons have overlapped in our kitchen garden, and pillar-trained 'Phyllis Bide' and 'Altissimo' roses have still sported a few belated flowers above a promising speckle of crocuses and winter aconites. At other times, though, you must search carefully for that odd brave flower; usually something will be found, even if it is only a solitary spike of daphne or an impetuous spray of Mary and Joseph (pulmonaria or lungwort). That is enough to dispel seasonal gloom. While evergreens and conifers are no doubt more reliable for winter colour, they sometimes seem just as stiff and immutable as dried flowers compared with the fragile vitality of unfurling buds, a handful of which, in the depths of winter, is worth a whole mid-summer border.

Use evergreen shrubs for a winter framework, by all means, but between and beneath these stalwarts plant

Right Welcome for its bright colour on a winter day, *Eranthis hyemalis* is an important bridge between autumn- and spring- flowering bulbs

Top For dependable winter colour, bergenias such as

'Bressingham White' are indispensable border plants, while

crocuses and snowdrops (above) are ideal in grass.

Below A long narrow path benefits from a contrasting feature

the earliest bulbs and herbaceous flowers. For guaranteed winter colour, mix aconites, snowdrops and the first crocuses with
Iris histrioides – solitary, stout, bright blue with a golden ridge
and totally weather-resistant. The form usually sold is 'Major',
which has the largest flowers, in a darker blue violet colour.
The numerous varieties of *I. reticulata* are beautiful and are easily grown, varying in colour from pale blue to deep reddish-
purple. Inexpensive if bought in bulk, they can be planted by
the bagful to reappear from now onwards, year after year.
Either confine named varieties to single-colour groupings, or
plant mixed reticulata seedlings for supreme value and a long
succession in every available hue. *I. unguicularis* (which most
gardeners still prefer to call *I. stylosa*) is equally reliable once
happily settled. Ours is peripatetic, still searching for the ideal
spot at the base of a wall where it can enjoy both winter
warmth and hot summer sun. If grown in the right place, and
dressed with lime every spring, plants will respond from late
autumn to spring with a steady supply of pale flowers ideal for

cutting, as the buds start to unroll. Trim the sprawling foliage
back in early autumn, otherwise clumps will bloom unseen.

Among hellebores, or in between the early bergenias
'Bressingham White' and *Bergenia purpurascens*, plant ordinary
yellow primroses and the related primula 'Wanda' hybrids,
where their colours will be noticeably enriched by the shade of
their neighbours' large leaves. Both, as Shakespeare noted,
come 'in battalions' by spring, though 'single spies' may be discovered now. *Crocus tommasinianus* is irrepressible: one week
you find just the occasional purple or ruby bloom, the next
moment cheerful 'tommies' are everywhere. Plant them under
mats of *Erica carnea*, the winter heath whose countless forms
bloom in almost any soil for much of the winter.

FRAMEWORK

DOWN THE GARDEN PATH It is all too easy to forget the
importance of paths, or to add them as an afterthought. Where
one already exists, it is likely to be merely utilitarian: an
unadorned run of paving slabs or concrete, perhaps, joining the
house to the bottom of the garden by the most direct route.
Yet it takes only a little imagination to transform a simple path
into an attractive feature.

The size and direction of a path can dramatically alter a
garden's overall mood and appearance. A path is a functional
element in any design and must lead somewhere, even if it is
only round the garden and back to the house, but the way it
does so profoundly affects the scenery en route. Straight paths
take you somewhere quickly; you are not intended to linger on
the way. If they are very long and broad, however, they add an
impression of opulence and importance to their destination.
Winding paths, on the other hand, tempt you to pause and
admire plants in passing, but they do need to be designed with
care: too leisurely a meander soon encourages unintended and
ultimately destructive short-cuts.

While the eventual choice of material for making a path may be dictated by expense and availability, its compatibility with the style and appearance of the garden is also important. Natural stone, for example, blends in well with older buildings and walls, but it is essentially formal and could seem too inflexible for a more relaxed garden where coarse bark, logs buried on their ends or wooden sections might be more appropriate (though much less durable, of course).

Crazy paving wears well and is ideal for informal or irregular paths with a cottage garden character. Bricks are a versatile medium for paths of all kinds, but you must make sure that you get the right type, not forgetting to take durability and safety into account. Ordinary house bricks, or flettons, flake and crumble after prolonged exposure to rain and frost; instead, ask for engineering or superior quality bricks, or use clay pavers or sets. The way in which these are laid determines a path's character. The least formal pattern is herringbone, although this involves a lot of cutting at the edges. Bricks laid with their longest sides parallel to the course of the path make it seem long and narrow, an impression softened by using contrasting decorative margins. When laid across its width, on the other hand, bricks will make a narrow path seem more substantial. Where there is enough room, bricks can be arranged in more complex patterns, but on most paths the best material for this is cobbles, perfect for creating intricate mosaics in contrasting colours. They can also be laid on their own to form a plain but decorative path which will prove very durable, though a little uncomfortable underfoot unless broken cobbles are used, and laid flat side uppermost.

Simplest of all are turf paths. Among bulbs or wild flowers naturalized in grass, mow a strip of adequate width and keep this to a consistent height, slightly lower than the surrounding grass and wild flower foliage when this is cut after the flowers have set seed. Try to avoid walking along grass paths when they are wet; if used in all weathers, reduce wear by laying stout plastic netting with a wide mesh along the path (this soon disappears from sight within the turf). Alternatively, inset stepping stones at comfortable distances apart, made from log sections or stone, and laid just below ground level to allow a mower to pass across undamaged.

Bricks, cobbles and crazy paving are normally bedded into concrete or sand, and where weeding is likely to be a problem the same matrix should be worked into cracks and joints. On informal paths, however, leave odd spaces to be filled with soil and planted with a few prostrate flowers. This soon adds charm and an air of long establishment to a path that may be only a couple of seasons old. Most bushy rock garden flowers are suitable – pinks, gentians, saxifrages or thrift for example – together with creeping herbs such as dwarf thymes, marjorams and pennyroyal. Compact wild flowers are equally at home, and small crevices make ideal niches

PLANT HIGHLIGHTS OF THE MONTH

Cineraria **Cineraria is botanically known as** *Senecio* x *hybridus*. **It makes a brilliant houseplant when grown in cool conditions. Keep evenly moist, as over- and under-watering are both lethal. Deadhead after flowering; plants are perennial and produce sideshoots which can**

be used to root as soft cuttings. Sow in spring to bloom now, or in summer for next spring, and propagate the best. Compared with Edwardian greenhouse specimens, which were a metre high and across, modern varieties are diminutive but neat, the boldest ('Charisma') a mere 38-45cm (15-18in) tall.

Onions **Entries for 'largest onion' championships start life now, with the sowing in a warm greenhouse of 'Ailsa Craig', 'Kelsae' and seeds of other exhibition strains. Seedlings need pricking out before they straighten up. Thereafter feed lavishly and they will grow fast, both**

in pots and after planting out in spring; too large for kitchen use, supreme bulbs should be kept and then replanted for seed to refine the strain. Sow any variety now, whether for autumn show entries, or for an early crop of impressive ware bulbs.

Iris unguicularis (I. stylosa) **The Algerian iris often starts flowering in late autumn but really gets under way now, its large blooms nestling deep in the grassy foliage. They are good for vases if their stems are gently pulled from the base. Grow at the front of a**

border or at the foot of a warm wall, and give annual dressings of garden lime after flowering ceases in early spring. The species is lavender blue with yellow markings, but white, purple and other blue cultivars are available.

for *Arenaria balearica*, scarlet pimpernel, germander speedwell and common dog-violets; a long informal path would provide valuable sanctuary for a number of these native flowers, which would appear out of place elsewhere in the garden.

Defining path edges with ornamental stones or strips is a matter of personal choice, but whether edged or not, the stark sides of most new paths are quickly overlapped by adjacent plants. This may be welcome, for mounds of foliage soften the lines of a path and help it to blend in with the surrounding garden. Along the meandering edge of a bed, shrubs strategically planted in the outward bends conceal part of a path's course and so introduce an element of surprise. If a trimmer boundary is preferred, however, consider planting a dwarf hedge of ivy, lavender or box, or for a less disciplined but still tidy appearance, edge with a single prostrate species, such as London Pride, mixed auriculas or blue grass (*Festuca glauca*).

UNDER GLASS

SPECIAL SOWING TECHNIQUES At some point during our gardening careers, most of us are seduced by a particular species or type of plant. This early enchantment sometimes matures into a consuming and acquisitive passion for collecting all the available members of our chosen subject, whether it be show auriculas, potatoes, insectivorous plants or elusive named varieties of coleus. Starting a collection by sowing packets of mixed seeds is simple, inexpensive and rewarding. Many species seed shyly, setting only enough to add to mixtures rather than list separately, so mixed collections often hold surprise treasures which once found can be picked out separately if desired. There are disadvantages, though: resulting plants need to be identified if their botanical names are important, and species can germinate at very different rates, some up to a year or more after others. Mixtures remain popular nevertheless, and if treated cautiously usually provide a sound foundation for a valuable collection. Always sow thinly, so that pricking out early seedlings will not disturb those yet to emerge. Species in a particular genus generally require the same conditions and therefore can be sown together, but remember that to germinate successfully the genus as a whole may need special sowing treatment, such as exposure to cold and heat alternately, or a preliminary soak in water.

Cacti, for example, grow readily from seed (although seedlings of a genus like *Opuntia* can take up to a year to emerge), providing you give them efficient drainage and adequate heat. Sow in an open compost such as John Innes No 1, barely covering larger seeds and simply pressing small ones into the moist surface, and then keeping at 15-21°C (60-70°F) in a propagator or plastic bag to retain humidity.

Ferns, on the other hand, need constant moisture because their spores germinate first into a rudimentary structure called a prothallus. At this stage the compost will be covered by a green film, beneath which free male cells swim to search out and fertilize female egg cells, but this only happens if the compost is kept consistently damp. Successful completion of this sexual phase results in the emergence of miniature fronds from the young ferns, which can then be separated for pricking out when they are large enough to handle.

All this is part of the persuasive fascination of raising plants from seed, but suggests that it is crucial to discover all you can about your chosen subject. You may have the seeds of *Streptosolen jamesonii*, a glorious climber which according to

Opposite Inventive use of contrasting materials adds colour and pattern to a garden path. Right Unlike their larger relatives, Charm and Cascade chrysanthemums flower with unique vitality and profusion

handbooks is always grown from cuttings. If you are unable to find any useful guidance, divide the seeds into equal portions and then try several approaches: sow some conventionally, store others in the freezer for a few weeks in case they need preliminary chilling, keep one batch in a high temperature, and sow another on the surface exposed to light. One of these techniques should work, even if you have to wait many months for the first seedlings to appear.

TRAINING

CHARMING CHRYSANTHEMUMS The prolific Charms and Cascades are two of the easiest and most rewarding groups of chrysanthemum available for home cultivation, with their neat fern-like leaves and wiry stems branching freely to bear thousands of small brilliant daisies from autumn to mid-winter. There are hardy early-flowering kinds for the garden, and later-flowering varieties for growing in pots and containers. Specialist nurseries will supply rooted cuttings for spring delivery, or you can sow now in gentle heat – seedlings vary in quality, but the best resulting plants can be perpetuated from cuttings each year. Prick out seedlings individually into small pots; indoor varieties are potted on regularly as they grow, while hardy kinds are planted out after the last frosts.

Hardy Charms grow into neat mounds about 60cm (2ft) across outdoors, and they usually survive from year to year in the ground. In a 30cm (12in) pot a well-fed Charm can reach a triumphant 1.2m (4ft) or more in diameter, thus forming a

spectacular centre-piece for a table or conservatory staging. To achieve this size, plants need a long season of uninterrupted growth, preferably outdoors in a sunny position, from after the last frosts until mid-autumn. Check for watering daily and feed with a liquid chrysanthemum or rose fertilizer every week. Final potting up is in late spring, in a strong soil-based compost such as John Innes No 3. Transfer the smaller plants to 20-25cm (8-10in) pots, larger specimens to 30cm (12in) ones, and using the handle of a trowel ram the compost until it is very firm. Pinch out the main growing tip when a plant has four or five pairs of leaves, and pinch the sideshoots if they become too long; Charms are naturally bushy, though, and normally need no special attention other than ensuring their steady growth into a dense mass of slender stems. Bring indoors as their buds form (earlier if frost threatens), and keep cool to prolong flowering. When this finishes, cut the branches back and water occasionally to encourage new sideshoots for cuttings in late winter.

Charms first appeared as a 'sport' among Cascade chrysanthemums, a tall, more vigorous strain widely used in China and Japan for ornamental training. This particular type of chrysanthemum forms a long tapering mass of blossom that can be trained to fall in a brilliant tress up to 1.8m (6ft) long; you can also grow them as standards, an equally decorative form, but less demanding on both space and attention, or simply leave them to make dense bushes about 1.2m (4ft) tall and 60-90cm (2-3ft) across. Cascades are grown in the same way as Charms, usually starting with mixed seeds, but again the best specimens can be propagated by cuttings.

To train a Cascade into a tress, confine early growth to a single stem tied to a vertical cane. After final potting in late spring, plants go outside for the summer. Position each pot securely on a shelf, at the top of a wall or at the side of a flight of steps about 1.8m (6ft) above the ground. Fix a cane at a steep angle from the ground to the pot, untie the stem from the original cane and gently refasten it to the sloping one, down which it is trained and tied at frequent intervals with raffia as it grows. Pinch out sideshoots after two or three leaves to encourage bushy growth, continuing until early autumn, when the cascade is left to develop flower buds. A couple of weeks later, release the cascade from its cane and carefully bring it indoors to a shelf or pedestal, where the pot should be securely wedged to allow the foliage to hang freely to the ground. It will then blossom into an extraordinary torrent of colour, remaining in flower for two or more months.

When training a cascade into a standard, cultivation is identical, except that the young plant is confined to a single vertical stem, tied to a sturdy cane, until it reaches a height of 90cm-1.2m (3-4ft), when the tip is pinched out to encourage sideshoots. Stop these after two to three leaves, and keep pinching out any sideshoots until mid-summer, when branches

are left to grow naturally. As the head develops, trim off all foliage from the main stem and also cut out any weak sideshoots from the head, to leave an evenly spaced framework of branches radiating from the top of a clean 'trunk'. These branches will bend gracefully when in flower, like a small weeping tree. Alternatively, a series of concentric wire hoops can be fixed to the cane and the flowering branches tied to these, to form a symmetrical mound of blossom, a variation of the spectacular 'Thousand-headed' style popular with enthusiasts of Japanese gardens.

PRUNING

ESSENTIAL TREE CARE Decisions can be made about pruning deciduous trees, now that their bare framework of branches is visible. Removing a complete bough is often preferable to snipping bits off here and there, as this has the added benefit of letting air and light through the canopy, giving the plants below a healthier environment. Most trees outgrow their sites, and now is the time to identify where a few bold cuts might reduce height and spread to more appropriate dimensions.

Despite its magical beauty, snow can be a serious problem in the garden. As well as clearing essential pathways, make a point of shaking settled layers from the tops of formal hedges. Box hedges especially should be brushed clean before their flexible stems are forced outwards beyond repair; also check other evergreens whose branches may not bear the unaccustomed heavy burden. Conifers are particularly vulnerable to injury from snow and even heavy rain, the weight of which can force vertical branches permanently out of position – Irish yews are regular casualties. Cutting out affected branches leaves glaring gashes in the face of a tree, so it is better to pull them back into place with strong wire attached to the main stem. If mishaps recur, encircle the whole tree with several loops of wire, bound tightly enough to stay in place but without visibly strangling the foliage. While on the subject of conifers, choose cultivars for sinks and rock gardens with great

care, because many nominally dwarf kinds will in time slowly outgrow their sites. Prostrate varieties that might spread to no more than 90cm (3ft) in twenty years are the most reliable. Try *Pinus mugo* 'Corley's Mat', *Abies balsamina* 'Hudsonia', *Juniperus procumbens* 'Nana', and similar genuine miniatures with dilatory growth habits.

Neglected deciduous trees can be reshaped now. Make an honest decision about your ability to manage the work safely, and remember that you have the option of summoning a qualified tree surgeon if in any doubt. Smaller trees, though, may only need the removal of one or two branches to restore their shape. Cut out dead wood first, followed by any obviously misplaced branches; thin congested growth, together with any vertical stems threatening to raise the canopy out of reach. Always wear protective clothing when working in trees, and don't cut out more than is necessary: removing a couple of main branches is more constructive than intricate pruning, and may be all that is required. Remember, when sawing main branches, that an initial shallow upward cut from below will prevent the bark from tearing as the bough falls. Shorten long branches in stages, leaving a final short section to be removed near its base, at the point where it swells; a cut here will heal faster than one flush with the trunk.

GARDEN SURGERY

OLEANDER PROBLEMS While undeniably stunning in flower, an oleander (*Nerium oleander* to give it its full name) is not the easiest plant to grow indoors. Most commercially available varieties, especially doubles, are too temperamental to be successful in the home, whereas the old-fashioned oleander, with its single rose-coloured flowers, is far more vigorous and adaptable, and always provides a more lavish display than sophisti-

Opposite Prostrate tree cultivars make excellent ground-cover, especially conifers such as *Pinus mugo* 'Corley's Mat'. Above Even in winter tall trees provide visual interest whether bare, frosted or snow-clad

cated variants, if given sympathetic treatment. Domestic climates tend to be too warm for most cultivars; plants used to be grown in unheated conservatories and glasshouses, where they flowered consistently with little fuss.

During the summer oleanders can stand outdoors in a sunny spot sheltered from the wind, though they will be content in a window in full sun, provided plenty of fresh air is available. From autumn until early spring they are best kept in a cool greenhouse where temperatures do not drop much below 5°C (40°F) (though a little light frost will do no harm), nor exceed 10°C (50°F) without compensatory ventilation. This cool interlude is the most effective way to ensure plenty of flowers the following season, and it also helps to prevent an early build-up of insect pests.

All oleanders are very thirsty plants, and thrive best in plastic pots with a water-retentive, peat-based compost; on warm days it is even advisable to leave a little water in the drainage saucer. In winter just maintain an evenly moist rootball, and when watering do so from below with very warm water in a saucer or bowl. It was once thought essential to indulge the oleander's winter preference for a cool head and warm feet by keeping it on a foot warmer, but this is excessive coddling. Pruning is usually unnecessary, except to reduce height or thin congested stems – when you do prune, cut boldly to keep a simple structure, and dress the weeping wounds with powdered charcoal or fine ash. Beware when handling torn leaves because the sap is highly irritating.

DOWN TO EARTH

DIFFICULT SOILS Unless you are a perfectionist, it is worth reminding yourself that a garden should be a pleasure, not a penance. In spring and early summer, when everything is brimming with loveliness, reappraisal is rarely necessary. But when the soil and all its shortcomings reappear in winter or during summer droughts, contentment sometimes melts away.

The perfect garden soil is a medium loam – crumbly, free-draining, fortified with moisture-retentive humus, and so elusive that most of us doubt its very existence. Apparent soil deficiencies are often due to our own obstinacy in growing unsuitable plants in a particular soil. You would need a geologist's collection of soil types for lupins, blueberries and cauliflowers to co-exist happily in the same small garden, for each prefers conditions in which the others would perish or at best sulk. If you want to grow certain plants that dislike your garden soil, grow them in tubs or confine them to a special raised bed filled with the ideal blend of compost.

In the open garden there is a straight choice between improving a problem soil or adapting to its particular nature. However, first you must identify its type. Light sandy soils are easily cultivated and warm quickly in spring, but they soon become dust dry in summer and acquire a surface crust after heavy rain. They are both hungry and thirsty, needing annual doses of manure or compost, and a good watering after five or six days without rain. Clay, on the other hand, is potentially very fertile and moisture-retentive, tolerating drought for up to three weeks, but it is difficult to work, and slow to dry or warm up enough for sowing and planting. Most garden soils lie between these extremes, with the legendary medium loam perfectly balancing the virtues of each; you will soon know which kind you have from its texture and workability. Soil acidity (pH), the cause of many plant problems, is not so instantly assessed. Buy a simple and inexpensive kit for testing pH and check several areas of the garden: results will guide your choice of plants and where to grow them; most kits will also suggest ways in which to increase the level of acidity or alkalinity.

All soils benefit from a little attention now, and if you work on it some improvement should be noticeable next season. Good soil evolves slowly and needs annual encouragement to reach and sustain a desired level of quality. Strenuous earthworks are seldom necessary and are often a waste of time.

I once gardened on the stickiest yellow clay imaginable. Over the previous half-century annual trailer-loads of manure

Clay soil

Sandy soil

had been dug in labourously, only to vanish without trace or hint of improvement. After digging and manuring part of it once more, we planted soft fruit and roses, finally covering the area with a thick layer of shredded bark. A year later 5cm (2in) of friable soil had appeared beneath the mulch, a depth that steadily increased without further exertion on our part. Although mulching is fashionable as a weed-suppressor and as cosmetic top-dressing, its most valuable role is as a protective blanket to stabilize soil structure. During the year light soils pulverize or slump, and clay turns to putty or cracked concrete – all of these processes are destructive to your initial hard work in draining, digging and manuring. Traditionalists admire an expanse of freshly dug ground left bare all winter but this is the most transitory of improvements. Cultivate thoroughly and cover the soil with an organic mulch to shield it from the elements, and you are half-way to never having to dig again.

NEW PLANTS FROM OLD

ROOT CUTTINGS When planting or moving dormant herbaceous perennials, you can take the opportunity of multiplying your favourites by dividing them if they are large enough. Taking root cuttings is an alternative method for many species; it does not reduce the size or vigour of the original, and may even be used without disturbing the donor – just scrape a little soil from a hollyhock, oriental poppy or gaillardia to expose some of its larger roots and cut a few off with a sharp knife.

Phlox and other fine-rooted plants propagate as successfully as those with roots as thick as horseradish and seakale for example. In all cases cleanly trim sound roots into straight 5-7.5cm (2-3in) sections. Arrange thin pieces horizontally on the surface of a boxful of compost, and cover with a further shallow layer of soil. Insert stouter roots vertically into the compost. A root fragment has a 'top' and 'bottom' in the same way as a stem cutting: the end of the root that was nearer the original plant is its top, and since the new shoot will grow from this end, it must be uppermost in the compost. To distinguish one end of a root cutting from the other, trim the upper end horizontally and the other at an angle. The oblique end must be pushed into the compost so that the top lies just below the surface. Water thoroughly and stand the boxes in a cold frame or under the greenhouse staging. Roots from hardy plants need no heat, although protecting them from frost will accelerate their growth. Keep them moist, and pot up individually when fine white lateral roots and young leaf shoots are visible.

FOCUS ON FOOD

FORCING Victorian cooks were more familiar with traditional gardening techniques than their current day counterparts. They needed to be: many held regular early morning conferences with the head gardener to discuss the progress of vegetables in the kitchen garden, and to give their orders for the day's menus. Excellence and variety were paramount, and to achieve this in winter meant that many vegetables had to be forced into early production. Part of the gardener's routine, therefore, was to peek daily beneath pots and boxes in dark sheds and under greenhouse staging to check if any covered stems and hearts were sufficiently forward for the table. To pass the cook's scrutiny they had to be tender, juicy and well-flavoured, merits of the perfectly forced vegetable.

These days only rhubarb is deliberately forced by most gardeners, to ensure early supplies and to keep light from causing any woody fibres to develop, hence the melting succulence of those first pale sticks in early spring. The earliest rhubarb can be forced any time during the winter, if it is kept in a heated environment. Sturdy healthy crowns are dug up in late autumn and left on the ground exposed to frost; they will come to no harm there, and it is this pre-chilling that will stimulate more rapid growth when they are transferred to a warm shed or greenhouse. Make sure that plants are very dry before blanching. They must be kept dark during forcing, so curtain off an area under the greenhouse staging, pack the crowns close together, cover with a thin layer of soil, water and keep moist while the sticks are growing. After harvesting these, the crowns are too exhausted for further use, and can be discarded.

Below Traditionally the first fresh fruit of the year, rhubarb is particularly juicy and succulent when forced, either under glass or as here, in situ, under purpose made pots.

Right Many kinds of fungi have been used as a natural resource, as in the preparation of amadou or tinder

Forcing rhubarb outdoors is less wasteful, although crops are ready much later. In mid-winter cover the strongest plants with inverted tubs, large wooden boxes or purpose-made forcing pots. Depending on the weather, sticks will be ready for pulling six to eight weeks later. Once you have gathered these, uncover the crowns, mulch generously with rotted manure, and leave them alone to recover for the rest of the season. Next year you can pull sticks in the normal way, but don't attempt to force them again until the following winter at the earliest.

Good King Henry, mercury or poor man's asparagus, as *Chenopodium bonus-Henricus* is variously known, is a decorative perennial vegetable, easily raised from seed and traditionally forced under pots for its young shoots. Leave some plants uncovered for their spinach-like leaves in spring, and later for their edible flower-buds. Deadhead flowers conscientiously before they can ripen to seed, or you will have plants everywhere.

INSPIRATION

GERMAN TINDER Resourceful gardeners find a use for everything in the garden. Nettles and grass clippings can be used for mulching or heating compost heaps, and tree and hedge prunings for supporting peas and languid flower stems. Old tights and stockings make durable, elastic tree ties; corrugated cardboard rolled into sleeves will blanch leeks; clean, used tin cans be recycled into pots; while jam jars are invaluable for collecting and destroying snails, or for suspending in fruit trees to fertilize the flowers with sprigs of blossom from another variety. Even some fungi have traditional practical value, larger kinds having been used for centuries to make amadou (the name comes from the Latin for 'lover', apparently because of the substance's inflammability). This is also known as German tinder, and it once provided the best touchwood for catching a spark from a flint and iron. Its spongy absorbent texture made it popular as a fishing accessory, mainly used for the delicate task of drying flies.

Amadou can be prepared from any of several fungi distinguished by an open spongy nature – polyporus bracket fungi, found growing on tree trunks, and several kinds of terrestrial boletus are some of the best. To do this the material is simply dried, sometimes after a soak in saltpetre; for a fisherman's purpose drying alone is sufficient. The fungus is cut into strips about 3-5mm (⅛-¼in) thick and laid in a warm place until dry to the touch, but not so dry that the strips crumble into crisp fragments. Provided an eye is kept on the process, the strips can be strung on a stick or skewer and suspended in a cool oven. The tinder can be stored in an airtight tin until needed.

$\mathcal{L}ate$ WINTER

Though EVERY SEASON HAS ITS OWN PECULIAR LOVE-
LINESS SPIRITS MAY BE AT THEIR LOWEST THIS MONTH,
DESPITE THE NOTICEABLE INCREASE IN THE LENGTH OF DAY

Winter often seems eternal, with outdoor temperatures too
low for comfort and a stealthy gloom always lurking to snuff
out any weak ray of sunshine that may happen to appear. But
there is always a dimension of hope; this is a time to hold your
breath, and wait in faith for the first stirrings of thaw and
reawakening life in the hedgerows.

Trees, hedges and wild plants are more reliable indicators
of growing conditions than any weather forecast. There are, of
course, many home-spun ways to test whether soil is warm
enough for the first outdoor sowings. My old foreman used to
thrust a poker in the ground each day and then feel its temperature against his cheek. His timing was infallible, but he could
never explain precisely how he knew when the right moment
to sow had arrived, and I came to the conclusion that his
method probably depended more upon intuition than science.

The modern approach is to take readings every morning
with a soil thermometer; thrust the instrument approximately
7.5-10cm (3-4in) below the surface and if the temperature of
the soil remains above 7°C (45°F) for a week, you may sow
hardy seeds with hope of success. Otherwise wait as gardeners
always used to, until the hedgerow buds visibly fatten and confidently shed their frost-proof cases. Never sow whole packets,
though. Keep some seeds for a later sowing, because even seasoned trees and shrubs make mistakes, or there would be no
blackthorn winters and frosted fruit blossom.

This month is the most capricious of all: one year saw us
shovelling snow, hacking holes in frozen troughs to find water
for our ducks and pigs to drink, and clearing a shoulder-high

barricade of fallen boughs from the main garden path after an exceptionally strong gale. Yet the end of the month brought enough gentle days to enable us to prepare seed beds and plant onion sets. This is a crop that welcomes an early start. Be sure to bury the sets just out of sight of inquisitive birds, but remember to expose them again once well rooted otherwise the bulbs may refuse to fatten.

Beware of mild spells. There is always a danger that you might try to race too far ahead this month, tempted by precocious hints of spring into gambling on frost being over. Be patient: the secret of stress-free maintenance in all but minimal gardens is to pace yourself: adapt cautiously to the weather and disregard the calendar, concentrating instead on how the first few seeds and plants respond to prevailing temperatures before speculating with others.

PLANNING

THE SMALL-SCALE HARVEST A progressive farmer I once worked for occasionally employed overseas students, with the idea of teaching them the principles of modern farming. One or two dismayed him by their conclusion that it was in fact we who needed enlightening about good husbandry.

According to one of his most testing pupils we wasted most of our resources, especially land. He told us that back home in Holland the farmers would never leave strips or verges of ground uncultivated. Even the tiniest corner that no tractor could reach was dug by the farmer's wife and planted with a few potatoes, marrows or cabbages. No patch of soil, he insisted, was too small to raise something to eat. Whereas to my boss 'economies of scale' implied saving money by using the largest areas and quantities possible, in Holland the same expression meant getting the most from the smallest resources. It was a lesson I took to heart, for it applies to gardening no less than farming. For years domestic vegetable crops were planned in terms of the 30ft (9m) row. This was the width of a full size allotment that has little relevance for modern gardens and their small scale harvest.

The secret of growing crops in confined places is to give them the best of everything. Keep fertility high; this is easily achieved where areas of soil are small, by adding spent mushroom compost or one of the proprietary dried manures that are pleasant to handle. Feed little and often with a liquid fertilizer or topdress with dried manure. Crops in pots are best grown in a strong compost – John Innes No 3, or a less nourishing kind fortified

Right Vegetables, such as tomatoes, lettuces and beans mingle happily with summer annuals as companion plants

with manure – and then fed regularly after a month or two.

Plants must have room to grow, but some need less space than others. Choose small, compact varieties of vegetables, and only sow a few at a time; maintain continuity by sowing radishes, carrots, lettuce and salad onions every three weeks from spring to early autumn. Crop them when young and then plant more. Keep replacements growing in a nursery bed to fill gaps as they appear. Sow in pots or cell-trays for uninterrupted growth and easy planting out; repeat this sowing when the first seedlings are up, and again when you finally transplant them.

Avoid growing in long rows as this wastes ground and may not give maximum yields, unless you also raise catch crops in the intervening spaces. To develop properly every plant must be able to spread comfortably in all directions, and for this it is better to sow in patches or squares, and then thin the seedlings to a symmetrical close pattern of plants, an arrangement that also suppresses weeds more effectively than row cultivation.

Finally, plan the season carefully. Decide the vegetables you like most and concentrate on these. Become familiar with their habits, which will help you keep up supplies; once you know radishes take eight weeks to mature, for example, you can plan the next sowing to follow without a break. Mix vegetables together, or with flowers to make maximum use of space, and plant seedlings between older crops nearing maturity. Eventually you will develop a cunning and intricate growing plan that will astonish you with its productivity.

THE NEGLECTED GARDEN As we burn more and more tropical rainforests, rare plant species are becoming extinct before we can either name or rescue them. Similarly, who knows what treasures have been obliterated with equal finality in our impatience to reclaim overgrown gardens? It is fashionable to be

Above After only a year of neglect, a garden can begin to look overgrown and dishevelled. Below First sowings of the new season are made in pots, under cover

dynamic, but overall clearance of neglected beds or shrubberies, before taking stock of their hidden contents and merits is vandalism, not restoration.

Before making any dramatic changes, wait a season, especially if it is winter, or better still a whole year to see what surprises lie dormant in the soil. Identify each plant as it emerges or flowers, for it may be a rarity or one of numerous classic varieties thought lost to cultivation. Assess its health by checking for obvious signs of disease: fungal growth, extensive die-back, weak stems and discoloured or misshapen leaves. Unmanaged fruit trees and bushes are particularly susceptible to disorders of this kind. Lack of vigour is sometimes due to age or starvation, however, and feeding or pruning might be all that is needed. Hard pruning and thinning will remedy a lot of neglect. Most hedges and trees will respond well if they are cut back hard over two to three seasons, and fed to stimulate young growth. Healthy herbaceous plants can be moved, divided or propagated from cuttings.

126

If you tidy obviously dishevelled areas and gently modify others during the first season, the character and qualities of the garden will gradually become apparent and this will probably lead you to adjust your first dramatic plans. Transferring a number of plants, re-aligning a path, cutting back an overhanging branch or two, and reviving the lawn may often be enough to make a neglected garden look well cared for.

FOCUS ON FOOD

AN EARLY START Despite instructions on seed packets, it is too early in many districts to start outdoor sowings. If you live in milder regions and have a sheltered, sunny garden on very light soil, then you might gamble with a sowing of parsnips, peas, lettuces and hardy annuals in a warm bed. For most of us, however, it would be more prudent to wait until temperatures rise next month, or even the month after in the case of parsnips which will then germinate faster and often get less root canker than batches planted earlier in the season.

Set glass or plastic cloches in place now, to dry and warm the soil for a few weeks, and then turn your attention to indoor sowings, which ought to be well under way by the third week in the month. If you can maintain 10°C (50°F) or more in a greenhouse, conservatory or heated propagator, it will be safe to sow most seeds there; otherwise use an airing cupboard or warm windowsill. Start tomatoes now for planting in a warm greenhouse in late spring, but delay sowing until next month for crops that are to be raised in an unheated situation.

For earliest pickings, we make small sowings this month of leeks ('The Lyon'), Brussels sprouts ('Peer Gynt' and the delicious red 'Rubine') and celery ('Brydon Prize White') for pricking out next month. Broad beans started now in boxes will crop as early as outdoor autumn sowings: try the longpod 'Express' and crimson-seeded 'Red Epicure'. In a greenhouse border or cold frame there is still time to sow a radish such as 'Robino' and lettuce 'Novita', both of them cold-tolerant varieties, and therefore ideal for forcing.

Only work soil outdoors when it is dry enough to stand on without its sticking to your shoes. When this is not possible, spend a few congenial hours tidying fruit and other perennials. Autumn-fruiting raspberries are pruned now by cutting back every stem right to the ground. American gardeners often leave fruited stems to give a second picking in summer, after which they are cut out to make way for new canes that crop late in the season. We tried this with 'Heritage', a valuable autumn variety with a pronounced old-fashioned flavour less acid than most, but with its summer yield lower here than normal maincrop kinds, because of our colder weather conditions, dual-season experiments seem only worthwhile if space limits you to a single variety.

PLANT HIGHLIGHTS OF THE MONTH

Achimenes Any of the colourful achimenes (hot water plant) varieties make charming and durable houseplants. Old cottage windowsill favourites, they dislike draughts and direct sunshine but need good light to flower well. Tepid water is best for the plants, which die down for a dry rest every autumn. Start the tiny tubercles into growth now, planting several in each potful of ericaceous compost. Multiply by snapping larger tubercles into a few small segments.

Hazelnuts This month is their moment of glory, when their slender bare branches are laden with heavy catkins or tiny flame-red female flowers. Grow as ornamental shrubs with soft green, red or purple leaves, as deciduous hedging or for home-grown peasticks. Fruits are cobnuts (round, exposed nuts) or filberts, with nuts hidden in a tapering fringed husk. Keep bushes compact by shortening branches bearing catkins, and fill vases with the prunings. 'Cosford' is the best cob, and 'Kentish Cob' ('Lambert's Filbert') the most prolific filbert.

Azara Whereas many evergreen shrubs are grown to provide substance in the winter garden, the elegant Chilean azaras are more than mere make-weights. With branches like graceful fans bearing tiny glossy leaves, all except *Azara serrata* will stop you in your tracks on a sunny day in late winter, when their minute yellow flowers perfume the air with the intoxicating scent similar to that of old-fashioned vanilla ice-cream at the seaside. *A. microphylla* is the hardiest – down to -15°C (5°F) – its pretty cream/green form 'Variegata' is less hardy and for the best results grow on a warm wall.

NUT TREES To produce a regular heavy crop almonds need a garden with a warm climate, but in a good year mature trees can yield a surprisingly large harvest. They are close relatives of peaches and should be grown and pruned in the same way, ideally as decorative fans trained against a warm sunny wall. They are among the most beautiful flowering trees, and the nuts are perhaps best accepted as an occasional bonus. Make sure you grow the right variety though, the sweet almond, *Prunus dulcis*, and not *P. amygdulus* var *amara*, or bitter almond, which contains a glucoside that changes into poisonous prussic acid if eaten; for safety avoid any almonds that taste even slightly bitter.

Most walnuts available these days grow slowly into very large trees. In France, however, dwarf kinds that fruit early in their lives are widely grown, and if you happen to find one when you are there, it is worth bringing back a few nuts to sow at home. A great many choice varieties were once offered by nurserymen but most have disappeared; they urgently need rediscovery, and many gardeners would be keen to locate specimens of 'Excelsior of Taynton', 'Northdown Clawnut', 'Patching Secret' and 'Stutton Seedling' among others.

The walnut is a handsome tree for larger gardens, but very often bears nothing. One reason is that male and female flowers (produced on the same tree) often bloom at different times, and to be sure of getting nuts more than one tree should be grown. Another reason is their extreme sensitivity to low temperatures, just a few degrees of frost being sufficient to injure the leaves and female flowers. They are wisely among the last trees to break into leaf, but even so, unusually warm weather in spring may entice them into producing early growth, which may then fall victim to a later frost. It is therefore a good idea, when planting in colder gardens, to choose a position sheltered from spring frosts, or at least from chilling winds.

When you do get a crop of nuts, they can be left on the ground until the husks rot away, provided the squirrels do not get to them first. Otherwise gather them as they fall and peel off the husks, wearing gloves to prevent staining your hands. Scrub the nuts to scour off remaining fibres and then lay them out on newspaper for a few days. When their shells are quite dry, pack the nuts in large jars or wooden boxes, spreading them between layers of salt mixed with an equal amount of dry sand. Store them in a cool dry place and they should keep sweet for several months. Walnuts for pickling should be picked in the summer before the hulls and shells harden.

If your walnut persists in remaining barren, you could always try making a sugar syrup from its sap, a practice recommended for self-sufficiency during the last world war. Anyone who has pruned a walnut will know that saw cuts can 'bleed' for several weeks. Turn this to advantage by cutting off a small patch of bark in the autumn, taking care not to go deeper than the cambium layer underneath this. Collect the sap that oozes from the wound and boil until it forms a thick syrup.

DOWN TO EARTH

PLANT WELFARE As well as warmth and water, plants need adequate light and air for positive health. The old smallholders understood the importance of light, and in limited spaces pruned fruit trees to simple, open structures to prevent them from shading crops planted right up to their trunks. For consistent density, hedges need good light on all sides, as heavy shadows result in sparse long shoots and threadbare patches.

When siting any plant, check whether it needs full sunlight, tolerates some shade or actually prefers to be out of the sun. Flowering, fruiting and leaf colour are all affected by light levels, most obviously in the case of houseplants, many of which must be moved from one room to the next until the

ideal position is found. Leaf variegation is most pronounced in good light, whereas shade stimulates a greener colouration to sustain photosynthesis. Light affects the impact of flower colours outdoors, as a critical stroll around the garden as dusk approaches will reveal. All those reds that look rich and vibrant in full sun become invisible as shadows lengthen, whereas white flowers, comparatively insignificant by day, catch the dwindling light of evening and gleam until dark. If you want to relieve a gloomy corner, plant white, yellow and bright orange flowers for impact – some seedsmen offer colour co-ordinated seed blends which are ideal for the purpose.

A good circulation of air is also essential for all-round development, and helps keep diseases at bay. Although not the sole cause, still air near walls, fences and under trees favours mildew. Michaelmas daisies are susceptible and gooseberry bushes regularly suffer from it if you don't hard prune excess growth each year to open up their centres. The problems some gardeners have when raising antirrhinums from seed indoors often stem from poor ventilation and sowing too thickly, leading to the collapse of promising seedlings from lethal damping-off disease. Chrysanthemums are notoriously prone to sickness in a stagnant atmosphere, and many growers keep huge fans revolving lazily above their cut flowers. Always watch for the first signs of fungal disease on indoor crops, remove affected leaves promptly and spray with fungicide. This applies to seedlings, mature chrysanthemums in pots, and even overwintered early-flowering kinds now that they are starting to revive and produce soft sideshoots for cuttings.

FRAMEWORK

FOUNDATIONS FOR A LAWN Making a new lawn, whether from turf or seed, involves the same careful groundwork as preparing a seedbed. In many cases the soil will be infested with perennial and very persistent weeds – perhaps it will even be overgrown with nettles, thistles, brambles or worse. To transform it into a site fit for the perfect stretch of grass will take most of a growing season.

Assuming the proposed area is a wilderness, start by clearing all growth to ground level using shears or sickle, or with a powerful rotary mower if you are satisfied that there are no hidden obstacles such as bricks or bedsteads. When the weeds are actively growing again, spray the whole area with glyphosate ('Tumbleweed' or similar); this should kill most weeds completely, although some may need a second application. If you do not want to use a herbicide, you will have to fork out the weeds manually, taking care to remove as many root fragments as possible.

Provided there are no drainage or subsoil problems to be seen to first, the patch can be dug or rotavated during the summer to a spade's depth. Rake the ground until it is roughly

level, removing stones and other intrusive debris, and then tread the surface firmly to compact soft areas. Rake once more and leave fallow for surviving weeds to appear, when they can be forked out or 'spot' sprayed with glyphosate. In early autumn or late winter, according to when you propose to make the lawn, spread a dressing of lawn fertilizer and rake the ground to a final level tilth.

Whether to sow grass seed or to use turf depends on many factors. Turf can be laid at any time of year, but may cost five to twenty times more than seed, especially if it is laid for you. Cheaper turf is often lifted from farm pastures, and you should always check that samples are free from stones and weeds, and that they have an even texture. Different types of seed mixture are available to match the intended use and site. Seeds are normally sown at a rate of 60g per sq metre (2oz per sq yard) in early autumn to encourage good establishment before the winter, or in mid-spring for faster growth (but remember you must irrigate during the first summer if the weather is dry).

TRAINING

VERSATILE IVY As a houseplant, ivy is an established favourite. Virtually indestructible and tolerant of cool or shaded positions where little else thrives, it comes in a wide range of attractive green and variegated forms. Most of these are hardy, yet many gardeners think of ivy growing outdoors only in the form of the wild species, *Hedera helix*, which is to be seen everywhere, clothing old walls or scrambling up trees. This kind of ivy is so common that we take it for granted. Yet it is one of the most reliable of hardy evergreens, sufficiently versatile to be planted for hedging, topiary and ground-cover, in addition to its more familiar use as a self-supporting climber on house and garden walls. Arguments continue over the wisdom of allowing it to cover walls, some gardeners regarding it as a potentially destructive menace whose roots penetrate and loosen mortar joints, eventually threatening the stability of the wall. In fact the ivy's aerial roots merely attach climbing stems to the face of its support, the plant deriving all its sustenance from the soil below. Provided they are structurally sound, walls clad with ivy are dry and warm, so much so that some householders in Germany are positively encouraged to grow it on their house walls as insulation to conserve heat.

When planting ivy to cover a large area of wall, choose a vigorous hardy variety – avoid forms of *Hedera canariensis*, for example, most of which are too tender for all but sheltered sites. Brightly variegated ivies such as 'Goldheart' and 'Buttercup' are valuable for enlivening gloomy walls or shady situations, whereas the best kinds for sunny aspects are those with rich green foliage in interesting shapes: 'Emerald Gem', for example, or 'Woeneri'. Space plants 45cm (18in) apart along the base of the wall, and spread the stems to each side

Above With the discreet support of a simple framework, many topiary species such as green and purple beech are trained into ornamental features. **Opposite** Frost enhances the impact of evergreen foliage and decorative bark

on the ground, pegging or weighting them down with stones if necessary. After a year (during which time the plants are settling in), numerous climbing shoots will grow from these stems to quickly cover the intended area.

An established covering of ivy can be trimmed with secateurs into a simple decorative silhouette. This is best done in spring, taking care when cutting away growth not to sever a main stem. Fortunately plants usually recover quickly from such injuries because congested stems tend to graft on to each other where they cross, thus allowing branches of one plant to draw nutrients from their neighbours. A shaped picture needs trimming several times a year to keep its outline sharp; a plain overall covering of ivy on a wall or fence, on the other hand, requires only one annual trim with shears in early spring.

While yew and box are standard topiary media in European gardens, across the Atlantic ivy is commonly trained over wire skeletons of animals or birds, or into a simple geometrical shape such as a spiral, to make three-dimensional topiary in the open garden or in large pots. Bend stout fencing wire into a basic outline, or make a hollow replica of an animal with wire netting, and then stuff it with damp sphagnum moss. Plant a branching small-leaved ivy ('Emerald Globe' or 'Telecurl') wherever the frame touches the soil, training stems up and around the topiary, and if necessary tying some of the growth into place and pinching out protruding shoots to encourage branching. When the model is completely covered, trim with shears whenever the outline begins to look shaggy. Both moss and compost of pot-grown specimens need watering with diluted fertilizer every few weeks.

improved that the crops began to dwindle. Apricots like poor soil with good drainage, plenty of lime and copious water, all of which the Aynho trees enjoyed, but when owners fitted guttering to the roofs and fertilized their front garden beds, the trees began to ail. Worst of all, the trees lacked the firm pruning they were used to. Protected on a warm wall, apricot blossom often escapes spring frost injury and sets heavily, while the naturally vigorous trees produce far too much new wood.

The gardener in Shakespeare's *Richard II* appreciated the need for a firm hand when he advised 'Go bind thou up those dangling apricocks'. When the branches begin to bend and look overladen, thin the masses of tiny apricots to individual fruits 7.5-10cm (3-4in) apart. The best fruit grows on young horizontal shoots, so while immature pinch out all other new growth, and also remove fruited stems over two years old to keep the framework constantly rejuvenated. Combine restraint with generous watering and liming, and your apricots should grow to honeyed perfection.

UNDER GLASS

CONSERVATORY CLEMATIS Collecting pot plants to keep on the floor or staging is only part of the challenge of growing under glass. There is the vertical dimension too – the walls and glazing bars that will support climbers of all kinds, and the roof to fill with aerial foliage and flowers. Some of the most colourful and exuberant plants are tender climbers, ideal subjects for furnishing a new conservatory. Blue or red passion flowers and fragrant white *Mandevilla suaveolens*, the waxy red bells of *Lapageria rosea* and soft blue *Plumbago capensis* are only a few of the many choices available.

Make sure you match plants to the temperature you can maintain, for some are steamily tropical while others are almost hardy. Some of the choicest climbers for a cool conservatory are the tender clematis species, such as *Clematis indivisa* from New Zealand. Sometimes listed as *C. paniculata*, this evergreen is smothered each spring in starry white flowers with conspicuous golden stamens. *C. napaulensis* has long, creamy flowers, while the fern-leaved clematis (*C. cirrhosa balearica*, formerly *C. calycina*) has daintily divided leaves and speckled yellow blooms. Both are semi-evergreen and doubtfully hardy, except in very mild districts, but under glass they flower in winter with gay abandon. Grow them as you would outdoors, with their roots cool and shaded in a tub or soil border under the staging, and only prune to limit their spread.

PRUNING

APRICOT TREE PRUNING By the time they reach the greengrocer, ripe apricots tend to be woolly, dry and insipid – only sweetcorn deteriorates faster after picking, so they are prime candidates for growing in the garden and eating while still warm from the sun. Hardier than the peach, apricot trees will fruit even in the chilly weather of the English Midlands, and the village of Aynho in this region, for example, was once called 'Apricot Village' because every house sported a trained tree on its walls for the benefit of the estate.

It was only when the houses were sold and consequently

Above For quality fruit, apricots need thinning as well as training into place. **Opposite** Vigorous conservatory climbers such as *Plumbago capensis* (top) and its white variant 'Alba' (below) also need frequent routine tying in

GARDEN SURGERY

DEGREES OF POISON We are all familiar with the dangers of chewing laburnum seeds or handling monkshood. So many other plants, however, can cause some kind of allergic reaction, that it seems the medieval physician Paracelsus was near the truth when he announced that 'all things are poison and nothing is without poison.'

Plants contain all kinds of substances, some of them potentially lethal. We are regularly urged to be beware of fool's parsley, bryony, datura, hemlock, foxglove, lily of the valley, yew and several of the nightshades, for example, as the toxins they produce can cause particularly violent reactions, but there are many other plants that contain milder poisons which affect only the unfortunate few. Handling the hairy leaves of parsnips, primulas and some aromatic herbs may produce blisters, rashes and other skin irritations, and anything with a milky sap should be handled with care.

Children in particular are at risk, as they are more inclined to handle, taste or eat parts of plants, and will often react to a relatively small dosage. The best way to guard against misadventure is to identify every plant in the garden and discover whether it is harmful or not. Warn children not to sample plants unknown to them, especially temptingly

Classical medicinal plants that may be poisonous if misused, include the common Foxglove (far left) by J le Moyne de Morgues (c.1568), and Laburnum (left) from William Curtis' *Botanical Magazine* (1792)

coloured fruits – only certain juniper berries, for example, can be used in the kitchen, while others are poisonous even in small quantities. The onus is on us to treat plants with respect, for ironically some of the most toxic plants are widely used medicinally; as Paracelsus added, 'the dose alone decides that a thing is not poisonous.'

INSPIRATION

DON'T FORGET THE VIOLETS The box hedges that fringe our vegetable beds are not always neat and manicured like those of disciplined Victorian gardens. Once every summer, when we have time, they are clipped to shape, but other plants have invaded their soil over the years and now their strict lines are softened by volunteer columbines, campanulas, polyanthus and stray alpine strawberries. In early spring the hedges bulge with fat mounds of primroses, but earliest of all are the violets, their first fragile blooms peeping through the shapely foliage from late winter onwards.

Violets have been grown and revered since ancient times; in classical Greece, for example, they were sold in street markets. They have remained a popular cut flower to this day. Raising them was considered a fine art, especially when they were grown for cutting out of season, and their cultivation attracted many enthusiasts, among them the irascible Victorian poet and critic, Walter Savage Landor. In a high dudgeon one day, he is said to have flung his cook out of the window; after a moment's horrified reflection, he rushed over to look out, crying 'Good God, I forgot the violets!'

Such is the devotion these little purple, red or white flowers inspire. They are easy to grow in the garden, although to attain perfection their few specific needs must be indulged. At the turn of the century, the Allen-Brown sisters ran a violet nursery in the south-east of England. Setting off at five each morning, they tended their several thousand charges with 'unremitting attention', feeding and watering, collecting countless slugs, spraying plants twice daily and shading the blooms with muslin, all to ensure that the best violets on the market were those that they had grown.

In the garden this extreme dedication is unnecessary. Plants have a preference for rich, slightly heavy soil, and for this reason they used to be grown in kitchen gardens where the ground was hearty and regularly manured. Light soils need fortifying with a little manure, while decayed leaves are best for opening up clay. The ideal site is well-drained and sheltered from hot summer sunshine; violets make an excellent edging at the foot of a cool wall or hedge, for example, and revel in the dappled shade beneath fruit trees, but avoid gloomy or permanently damp positions where they might rot.

Plant in early spring, setting the crowns about 23cm (9in) apart, or sow seeds of superior varieties now, either in pots in a cool greenhouse or in a cold frame, pricking out the seedlings and keeping them frost-free. Once planted out they will need plenty of water in dry weather, and it is best to cut off runners as they appear, because these absorb the energy needed to build up reserves for prolific flowering the following spring. Plants are good for about three years, after which they should be dug up and divided in spring, splitting the crowns into rooted pieces with two or three shoots each, and then replanting them in fresh sites to avoid 'pansy sickness' (ie failure to grow where violets were previously planted).

For a stunning mound of blossom, indoors or in a conservatory, bring in a few young plants now to revive the Victorian conceit of growing them in pots arranged as terraces. Start with a large bowl 45cm (18in) across and half fill it with compost. In the centre of this firmly set a 30cm (12in) half-pot; similarly part fill this and then insert a 20cm (8in) half-pot, repeating the process and finishing the structure with a 10cm (4in) pot. Once all the containers are in place, top them up with compost and plant young violets, spaced evenly around each exposed ring, with one in the centre of the uppermost pot. When the violets have finished flowering, the structure can be transformed into a cascade of summer blossom with trailing lobelia, petunias or miniature ivy-leaf geraniums.

LOOKING AHEAD

BACK IN THE POTTING SHED At the end of a year in the garden, take a little time to recall the season's highlights and reappraise any failures or disappointments. There are no real gardening experts, for every year reveals a few more insights into the mysterious workings of the community of plants whose care gives us so curious a blend of pleasure and pain.

This sense of community is important if we are to appreciate the living nature of a garden. Plants from all over the world grow happily together, so that even tubs and window boxes can be home to a cosmopolitan collection. Each species, though, is programmed to strive and succeed – to grow, flower and reproduce itself, very often at the expense of its neighbours. Competition is a botanical fact of life, and the art of gardening, like that of managing human society, depends on judiciously encouraging some species while restraining others, so that all can thrive happily. Wild gardens as much as formal schemes need this sensitive interference.

How we organize the plants in our care and arrange their orderly co-existence is a matter for personal choice. Each of us knows the kind of garden we would like, and only we can judge whether the result is truly 'a thing of beauty'. But achieving this means knowing the fundamental rules, being aware of plants and how they live; 'green fingers' is not a magic quality but an ability to understand plant personalities and meet their changing needs. With contented plants we are halfway to a successful garden.

This cannot be achieved overnight, as owners of new gardens soon discover. Whereas the basic design and construction can be completed on the ground in only a matter of weeks, a living garden, on the other hand, takes much longer to grow and mature, and much of the fascination of gardening comes from being a partner in this gradual evolution, albeit a hardworking partner. When our boots are heavy with mud and frost carries off the hebes it is easy to lose sight of this relationship. But time after time we are drawn back by the fact that a garden needs a hand if it is to flourish.

Sometimes, too, we forget that this participation is voluntary. If the garden becomes a chore, we are unlikely to give our plants the care they deserve, and it is time then to re-assess its demands on our time and energy. Gardeners have rights as well as responsibilities, and one of these is the liberty to decide just how much we want to be involved in the life of a garden. Get the balance right, and we are almost certain to discover the peculiar contentment that seduces so many people back into the garden at the first hint of spring.

In sheltered little nooks a hint of spring is already apparent –

primroses (top) and wood dog violets (left)

A YEAR IN THE GARDEN

At a glance

When I gardenened in the south of England, I followed my neighbours' example and sowed runner beans in pots in mid-spring for planting out one month later, a routine that subsequently proved disastrous here in Warwickshire, where late frosts and lethal cold winds regularly delay planting.

Any gardening calender must allow for regional differences in weather, soil type, altitude, and other factors that make precision impossible. It is more sensible to sow courgettes a month before you would normally expect frosts to end, or to delay pruning a shrub until it finishes flowering, than to act on a particular date in the month. Gardening strictly according to the calender causes unnecessary anxiety and often poor results.

For these reasons our guide is divided, like the book itself, into twelve approximate seasons which should be interpreted according to local conditions. Similarly, any list of tasks to be done is inevitably selective, and those that follow are meant to be helpful rather than exhaustive. Activities mentioned in the text are included, together with many other suggestions based on the work usually carried out during a year in this garden.

Early SPRING

A very fine morning; a man, eighty-two years of age, just beginning to mow the short-grass in the garden: I thought it, even when I was young, the hardest work that man had to do. To look on, this work seems nothing; but it tries every sinew in your frame if you go upright and do your work well. This old man never knew how to do it well, and he stoops, and he hangs his scythe wrong! but with all this, it must be a surprising man to mow short-grass as well as he does at eighty. I wish I may be able to mow short-grass at eighty! That's all I have to say of the matter.

from Rural Rides: William Cobbett

WEATHER
One of the busiest months of the year, and an unpredictable one, when frost and chilly winds scorch the magnolia blossom and rain can keep soils too wet to cultivate. Gardeners pray for a dry start to the season but even when conditions are ideal, outdoor sowing remains a gamble unless the soil has been warmed by cloches and frames. It is a good time to plant and transplant herbaceous perennials, though, and there is always plenty to do under glass on bleaker days.

THE FLOWER GARDEN
● resume cutting lawns with the mower blades set high
● start planting gladioli and other summer-flowering bulbs (p.17)
● finish planting bare-root deciduous trees, shrubs and hedging
● lay turf for new lawns, and repair edges or bare patches
● scarify mossy areas of lawns with a wire rake, and spread general lawn fertilizer. Keep the moss, and use later for lining hanging baskets

● prune caryopteris, *Clematis jackmanii*, hardy fuchsias and similar late-flowering shrubs
● start pruning roses towards the end of the month
● clip deciduous hedges to shape, using a taut line for a guide
● prepare patches of soil for hardy annuals and sow at the end of the month
● divide vigorous perennials such as rudbeckias and Michaelmas daisies
● treat paths with a residual weedkiller to keep them clear all season
● hard prune eucalyptus if you want a supply of young foliage
● plant out autumn-sown sweet peas in rich soil
● bed out wallflowers and other spring plants left over from last autumn
● look for clumps of daffodils and narcissi that are not flowering; to dig up, split and replant

THE KITCHEN GARDEN
● check blackcurrants for big bud and spray with insecticide (p.15)
● plant first early potatoes in a warm position (p.17)

● prepare a seedbed and warm with cloches or a sheet of clear polythene for a fortnight before sowing
● plant onion sets in firm fertile ground
● plant new asparagus and finish tidying existing beds (p.18)
● weed and clean up strawberry beds, and plant new perpetual varieties
● sow parsley and make the first successional sowings of carrots, spring onions, radishes and other salads
● if frost threatens, protect early blossom on wall-trained fruit such as peaches and apricots
● sow spinach, beetroot and early turnips late in the month
● feed fruit trees and bushes with a general fertilizer
● finish pruning soft fruit such as gooseberries
● cover a row of strawberries with cloches to force an early crop

UNDER GLASS
● sow hardy annuals in frames for an early show and continue sowing half-hardy bedding
● pack dahlia tubers in boxes of soil and start into growth in a

cold frame
● sow lettuces, summer cabbage, early leeks and autumn brassicas
● water tender perennials such as geraniums and fuchsias to revive growth
● sow primulas and keep moist during germination (p.14)
● give potted cacti a little water to stimulate new root growth
● tie in young shoots on grape vines and tap the rods to pollinate the flowers as they open
● sow basil and other tender annual herbs in warmth (p.18)
● repot or topdress pot plants as growth revives (p.19)
● take soft cuttings of dahlias started in boxes, together with coleus, geraniums and winter-flowering begonias
● pot on rooted cuttings and prick out early seedlings
● continue watering and feeding azaleas, bulbs and other spring pot plants after flowering
● start begonias and gloxinias into growth in cool greenhouses
● sow tomatoes, cucumbers and melons to grow in unheated houses
● harden off early vegetables and hardy annuals sown indoors

Mid SPRING

Nothing is so beautiful as spring -
When weeds, in wheels, shoot long and lovely and lush;
Thrush's eggs look little low heavens, and thrush
Through the echoing timber does so rinse and wring
The ear, it strikes like lightnings to hear him sing;
The glassy peartree leaves and blooms, they brush
The descending blue; that blue is all in a rush
With richness; the racing lambs too have fair their fling.

What is all this juice and all this joy?
A strain of the earth's sweet being in the beginning
In Eden garden.

from Spring: Gerard Manley Hopkins

WEATHER
A month when the garden brims with vitality and colour, and almost anything can happen: storms, gales, frosts and premature heat-waves. Soil temperatures are rising and you can sow whenever the soil surface is dry enough; plant out during showery weather, but keep some kind of cover nearby in case of sudden cold snaps. Be especially wary under glass, where bright sunlight and wildly fluctuating temperatures can parch tender seedlings or scorch foliage plants.

THE FLOWER GARDEN
● deadhead spring bulbs as flowers fade, unless you want to save seeds
● watch out for aphids on lupins and other soft herbaceous plants
● continue pruning started last month, including chaenomeles, most roses and any shrubs or hedges that need hard cutting back (p.20)
● there is still time early in the month to plant new shrubs and climbers such as grape vines (p.20)
● sow grass seed on new lawn

sites prepared like a seedbed
● continue sowing hardy annuals, keeping a few in pots to plug gaps later (p.24)
● start spring-cleaning ponds, removing dead leaves and surplus oxygenating plants
● festoon polyanthus flowers with black cotton to deter birds
● split violets and plant the divisions in a moist shady border for the summer
● clean up garden furniture, and repaint or treat with preservative (p.27)
● clip lavender hedges to shape but avoid cutting into old wood
● feed lilacs and prune immediately after flowering (p.28)
● train in the soft young stems of clematis and other climbers as they grow

THE KITCHEN GARDEN
● sow red cabbages in a frame for transplanting in mid-summer
● prepare fine seedbeds for root vegetables (p.23), main crops of which are sown next month
● sow calabrese in firm soil: a fast-maturing hybrid will succeed even where clubroot disables other brassicas

● repeat earlier sowings of peas (p.23), turnips (p.23), lettuce, short carrots (p.24), kohl rabi, radishes and other successional crops (p.44)
● earth up early potato haulm, especially if frost is forecast
● plant second early and main-crop varieties
● sow Brussels sprouts, sprouting broccoli and winter brassicas in a seedbed, and transplant seedlings already with 2-3 leaves
● dig and manure trenches for celery, and sow lettuce on the ridges of soil
● make a last sowing of broad beans for eating or freezing in the autumn
● feed spring cabbage and sprouting broccoli with dried blood for a spring tonic
● start thinning fruitlets on wall-trained peaches, and rub off young unwanted shoots

UNDER GLASS
● gradually decrease watering once cyclamen have finished flowering
● towards the end of the month sow the first runner beans in pots, together with French beans

for growing under glass (p.23)
● prune fuchsias now they are growing again, and keep the best prunings for cuttings
● repot or topdress trees and shrubs growing in containers (p.26)
● sow Tibetan poppies (meconopsis) - keep pots for 2 weeks in 21°C (70°F), then 2 weeks in the fridge for best germination
● watch out for mealy bugs on cacti and other houseplants, and dab with methylated spirits on a cotton-bud
● start sowing in trays batches of hardy perennials such as gaillardias (p.23), or wait until next month and sow outdoors
● finish taking cuttings from over-wintered chrysanthemums, and pot up those already rooted
● pollinate fruit growing in pots and greenhouse borders (p.26)
● press on with hardening plants in cold frames, leaving the lids open on mild nights (p.27)
● sow winter-flowering pansies for early colour next year
● plant young tomatoes, melons (p.23) and cucumbers in heated glass; there's still time to sow these crops for a cool house

Late SPRING

There is an old Sawe to this purpose:
In Gard'ning never this Rule forget,
To Sow dry, and Set wet.
What is sown, as Seeds, are Plants compacted in a very little Space: and if they are too soon gorged with Moisture, that is faster than they can spend it upon their fibrous Root or Tendrils with which they lay hold on the Earth, they are apt to discompose their inward Parts, and, in plain English, burst. But what is sett, namely, Plants (for Beans, Pease, etc., ought not to be sett too wet, any more than other seeds) have already Moisture in them, and their Texture is already expanded, and in its Shape: these require immediate strong Food, as being out of the Womb: and if their Nurse be dry, instead of getting from her, she sucks the little Moisture they have from them.

from Tusser Redivivus: Hillman. 1710

WEATHER

Frost still lurks in wait for tender plants set out too early, but hardy kinds can be planted safely if fully hardened off. Drought may be a problem on dry soils by the end of the month, so be ready to mulch and water where necessary. Growth accelerates as temperatures soar, especially under cloches and in frames: open to the air whenever possible and paint glass with shading to reduce injury from heat. This is the most hazardous month for greenhouse plants, with ventilation, shading, damping down and frequent watering all necessary to maintain good health.

THE FLOWER GARDEN

● this is the favourite month for planting, transplanting and clipping evergreen shrubs and hedges such as box (pp.32, 35)
● prune forsythia and other spring shrubs as flowers fade
● start introducing hardy aquatic plants to ponds
● plant out early-flowering chrysanthemums over-wintered under glass

● clip aubretia and other prostrate spring plants after flowering
● mow lawns more frequently and apply a broad-leaf herbicide
● compost the next 2-3 batches of clippings (p.10)
● watch out for the first signs of fireblight on members of the Rosaceae family (p.36)
● sow wallflowers, polyanthus and forget-me-nots (p.33) for a bedding display next spring
● stake tall perennials before their stems are distorted by winds
● clear spring flowers as they fade, moving perennials such as polyanthus to their summer quarters; heel in bulbs elsewhere to ripen
● towards the end of the month start planting out the hardiest bedding in prepared ground (p.30)

THE KITCHEN GARDEN

● sow marrows, courgettes and other squashes in frames, or outdoors under cloches
● cut down young canes on summer raspberries if these are normally unmanageable (p.33)
● tuck straw around strawberry plants to keep fruit clean

● sow sweet corn, French and runner beans outdoors after the middle of the month
● there are many reasons why fruit fails to set, among them pollination problems (p.36)
● spray or mulch the base of new fruit trees to keep them weed-free, and check their supports and ties (p.37)
● make further sowings of peas and salad crops for succession (p.44)
● inspect gooseberry bushes for mildew and treat promptly (p.38)
● finish sowing winter brassicas, leeks and sprouting broccoli;
● transplant earlier batches and sow fast catch crops in between
● hoe regularly to keep down weed seedlings
● sow chicory to force for winter salads; sow a little extra for the flower border
● plant out celery, celeriac and bean seedlings at the end of the month (p.31)

UNDER GLASS

● start planting hanging baskets for full establishment by bedding time
● propagate clematis by cuttings as soon as flowering ceases, or layer outdoors (p.39)

● pinch out tips of geraniums, fuchsias and other perennials to encourage bushy growth
● train cordon tomatoes as they grow, and remove all sideshoots (p.57)
● prick out seedlings when large enough, pot up rooted cuttings and pot on vigorous young plants before they become rootbound
● sow primulas, cinerarias and calceolarias for winter and early spring colour under glass
● pinch the tips of chrysanthemum stems unless grown for single large blooms
● feed regal pelargoniums as they start flowering, and deadhead promptly to encourage autumn blooms
● stop vine shoots one leaf beyond flower trusses, and pollinate by tapping the rods
● move exhausted spring bulbs to the coldframe or plant out intact potfuls in the flower garden
● water and feed azaleas regularly, and move outdoors to a shady place for the summer
● continue hardening off early vegetables and bedding, and feed if planting out is delayed
● give glass a light coat of shading paint

Early SUMMER

Soon will the high Midsummer pomps come on,
Soon will the musk carnations break and swell,
Soon shall we have gold-dusted snapdragon,
Sweet-William with its homely cottage-smell,
And stocks in fragrant blow;
Roses that down the alleys shine afar,
And open, jasmine-muffled lattices,
And groups under the dreaming garden-trees,
And the full moon, and the white evening star.

Matthew Arnold

WEATHER

With the longest day this month, the sun is at its strongest and often combines with dry winds to evaporate soil moisture and transform a seedbed tilth into barren dust within hours of rainfall. Under glass, too, the dangers of hot, bright sunshine are at their greatest. Air temperatures are still variable, though, with the possibility of chilly nights remaining a threat to tender plants. Enjoy the genial summer warmth, without relaxing your guard against mischievous late frosts.

THE FLOWER GARDEN

● plant out summer bedding (p.41) but hold back the tenderest plants until the chance of frost is past; water with a dilute liquid feed for quick establishment
● tie in strong replacement stems on rambler roses and cut out any that are surplus
● plant up pots, window boxes and containers with summer bedding
● deadhead rhododendrons, without damaging the new shoots underneath
● there is still time to sow

columbines (p.43) and other perennials in a seedbed
● prune brooms, philadelphus, deutzias and other shrubs that have finished flowering
● finish adding aquatic plants to garden ponds, but avoid overcrowding (p.41)
● deadhead roses, cutting back to a strong new bud
● mow areas of lawns planted with spring bulbs, and dress with a general fertilizer
● cut down old hellebore stems to expose young basal growth
● lift and divide irises as soon as flowering ceases (p.45)
● sow border carnations for planting out in the autumn
● spray roses with a combined insecticide and fungicide against common ailments
● rejuvenate top-heavy shrubs and climbers by hard cutting back now they are growing vigorously (p.48)

THE KITCHEN GARDEN

● sow lettuces in situ or in pots for planting undisturbed, and sow further successional crops (p.44)
● test early potatoes to see if first tubers are ready; continue

earthing up later kinds
● an early carrot variety sown now will usually miss attacks from carrot root flies
● water and mulch vulnerable crops before drought becomes a problem (p.45)
● dig up shallots and Japanese onions as they ripen
● thin and peg down strawberry runners to make replacements for older plants (p.44)
● sow perpetual spinach for cutting in winter and spring
● sow dwarf French beans now for cloching and picking in autumn
● cover summer raspberries with nets, and spray with derris if grubs normally infest berries
● watch out for the main wave of pests and diseases, and spray if necessary (p.47)
● pinch out sideshoots of trained figs to 3-4 leaves
● plant out marrows and squashes of all kinds on mounds of soil above a bucketful of rotted manure to each plant
● thin heavy crops of young fruit and support laden branches (p.48)
● pick peas regularly to maintain supplies, and sow more

UNDER GLASS

● damp down paths and staging daily to keep up humidity
● take cuttings of pinks and other perennial kinds of dianthus for rooting in pots in a cold frame
● pot up seedlings of spring flowers and grow on in shade outdoors
● sow cyclamen seeds for early winter flowers next year (p.61)
● take cuttings of geraniums, fuchsias and marguerites to train as standards (p.49)
● watch out for red spider mite and greenhouse whitefly, and introduce predators at an early stage (p.47)
● stand chrysanthemums outdoors after final potting
● water and feed achimenes in full bloom, and shade from the sun
● pick dead flowers and leaves from pot plants to prevent fungal diseases
● thin bunches of grapes to allow berries room to swell
● feed pot plants, hanging baskets and window boxes planted earlier
● paint the glass with a full coat of shading

Mid SUMMER

A lady looks as graceful with a hoe or rake, or with a wheelbarrow, or knife, and scissors, nails and shreds, nailing fruit, Roses or other flowers against a wall, as at croquet, archery, or lawn tennis, or any other of those innocent games, or useless frivolities, in which lovely women are expected to display to most advantage their beauty of face and grace of form. In fact, the very usefulness of the labour adds a fresh charm to the doers of it, and Tennyson's gardener's daughter could never have looked half so fascinating had she not been training and making fast that Rose-shoot round the window.

from The Villa Gardener, November 1875

WEATHER

Some of the highest temperatures are experienced this month, but the air remains relatively dry. Drought can become a serious problem while maincrops are still actively growing, although heavy thundery rain may save the situation (while also helping spread summer fungal diseases). Patrol plants under glass twice daily with a watering can, and damp down freely. Outdoors save laborious tasks for early morning or evening, and relax during the heat with a little summer pruning or training and making fast rose shoots.

THE FLOWER GARDEN

● thin dahlia flower stems for large blooms, leaving 4-5 per plant
● summer prune wisterias to concentrate energy on bud formation (p.57)
● gather everlasting flowers to dry for indoor arrangements
● cut out exhausted rambler rose stems and replace with the best of the new ones (p.52)

● in very dry weather mow lawns less frequently and leave the clippings uncollected
● plant late-flowering bulbs such as colchicums, sternbergias and autumn crocuses
● trim early summer-flowering shrubs such as rosemary, osmanthus and cotoneaster once blooms have faded
● remove rose suckers as they appear, but save some for budding your own plants (p.56)
● cut back and feed lupins and delphiniums after flowering to stimulate a second flush of bloom
● sow annuals for autumn colour, and transplant perennial and biennial seedlings to a nursery bed
● if fish are gasping at the pond surface in hot weather, aerate the water by spraying with a hose
● dig up, dry and clean tulips and any other spring bulbs to be stored over winter

THE KITCHEN GARDEN

● start gathering herbs just before they flower, and dry for winter use

● transplant leeks to dibber holes, water thoroughly and mulch with lawn mowings
● harvest soft fruit as it ripens; prune blackcurrants while picking, removing a third of the oldest stems
● train and tie in tomato stems frequently, and check for sideshoots which grow rapidly at this time of year (p.57)
● sow spring cabbage about mid-month, and again 3-4 weeks later for a long supply next season (p.61)
● start summer pruning trained fruit, currant and berry crops first, followed by cherries and plums, then apples and pears (p.57)
● remove any strawberry runners needed for new beds, and then burn or cut down leaves on fruited plants (p.58)
● sow parsley for late pickings and to pot up for winter use
● start earthing trench celery after scattering slug bait on heavy soils
● make a last outdoor sowing of a fast carrot variety (p.61)
● cut down a proportion of mint plants to stimulate young leaves for late use

UNDER GLASS

● feed and water cacti at regular intervals, and stand outdoors in a hot season (p.55)
● sow French beans in pots for use in mid-autumn
● take cuttings from geraniums for next year's bedding plants
● repot old cyclamen corms, water and stand in shade to resume growth
● there is enough natural heat now to root most kinds of soft cuttings quickly, especially those from houseplants (p.55)
● take tip cuttings of hydrangeas to grow as pot plants
● support ripening melons in nets and remove any leaves hiding them from the sun
● stop greenhouse tomato mainstems 1-2 leaves above the topmost truss
● sow mignonette for winter fragrance indoors; train the strongest seedlings as standards
● stand regal pelargoniums outdoors for a rest after flowering
● semi-ripe cuttings (p.56) from most garden shrubs root quickly this month in a greenhouse or on the windowsill
● start watering and feeding poinsettias to revive growth

Late SUMMER

"And pray, Antonia, who gave you leave to give my flowers away?"
"I thought flowers were meant to be picked, and you did say
Miss Crump looked dull, so I thought, Aunt Dove, this would just
please you. Why it gives her a touch of— of— Oh, I can't explain,
but she's like a flower somehow herself."
"Nonsense, Antonia!"
"If it is nonsense I shall give her just the free daisies.
May I pick the daisies in the park?"
"You must ask me another time, Antonia, for permission to pick
flowers. I don't say I shall refuse, but—"
"But some of them are Uncle Dove's flowers, aren't they? I heard
him say 'my gardener' this morning."
"Miss Crump, will you go on with the book we began till the
gentlemen come in, if you please?"

from Harum Scarum: Esme Stuart

WEATHER

High humidity and sultriness
can make this an enervating
month of torrid heat. The soil is
at its warmest and last minute
sowings spring to life if kept
moist, while bright summer
flowers give way to richer
colours, a hint of autumn.
Under glass give all the fresh air
possible, leaving doors and
vents wide open by day. Plants
and gardeners may wilt visibly
in the heat, but fortunately you
can spend much of the time
gathering flowers and crops,
saving your energies for autumn.

THE FLOWER GARDEN

● give hedges a last trim to
shape and water those planted
this year (p.65)
● deadhead annuals and
perennials regularly to prolong
flowering
● prepare a new lawn site for
sowing or turfing next month
● plant Madonna lilies in well-
drained soil
● give lawns a last application
of weedkiller and a low-
nitrogen feed
● start preparing ground for new

shrubs and hedges, and leave for
weed seeds to germinate
● pinch out the tips of young
wallflowers to encourage
bushiness
● order spring bulbs such as
narcissi for early planting (p.73)
● watch out for mildew on
Michaelmas daisies and spray
with a fungicide (p.65)
● layer border carnations and
root soft cuttings of pansies and
penstemons in a cold frame
● harvest lavender flowers
and trim bushes to a neat shape
(p.70)
● feed chrysanthemums and
dahlias for the best blooms
● plant winter aconites after
soaking the dry corms for
48 hours

THE KITCHEN GARDEN

● finish summer pruning fruit,
and cut out exhausted stems of
loganberries and other hybrids
(p.79)
● start picking the earliest
apples and pears for
immediate use
● sow salad onions for next
spring
● finish drying and ripening

shallots and garlic before storing
● sow Japanese onions to mature
next summer before maincrop
varieties
● water celery freely and
continue earthing up stems
● make last sowings of radishes,
together with an early carrot
variety in a cold frame
● Brussels sprouts and red
cabbages sown now and overwintered in a seedbed will crop
next year in late summer
● start blanching endive for use
2-3 weeks later
● strawberry runners planted out
now in rich soil make strong
fruiting plants for next year
● water and mulch runner beans
now that pods are developing
(p.69)
● cut down fruited summer
raspberry stems and tie in
replacements
● start digging beetroot for
storing in boxes of moist sand
or peat
● trim and pot up chives for
autumn and winter use indoors

UNDER GLASS

● sow schizanthus in pots for
early flowers next year

● pot up spring-flowering bulbs
as soon as they are available
● prepare conifer cuttings from
sideshoots with heels and root
in a cold frame
● pick off ripe fuchsia berries,
both as a crop (p.68) and to
encourage further flowering
● reduce watering hippeastrums
to encourage them to rest for a
few months
● start sowing a sequence of
winter lettuces to grow in the
frame or greenhouse
● order lilies for planting in pots
indoors (p.72)
● pot on winter begonias and
grow in shade outdoors until
next month
● plant freesia corms in 15cm
(6in) pots to flower in early
winter
● aerial layer tall houseplants
such as ficus and dieffenbachia
(p.72)
● pot or repot lachenalia bulbs
to flower in late winter (p.65)
● sow Beauty of Nice stocks and
grow on in pots for winter
fragrance under glass
● repot and water white arum
lilies after their summer rest
outdoors

Early AUTUMN

Dusk nestles down,
water and sky blending in a grey-green mist;
silhouettes of trees are etched
against a sunset of rose and amethyst;
the moon rising from the sea
glimmers on the storm-dark waves;
through the frosted rushes
ripe oranges gleam golden as stars;
free from cares
and affairs
I drink and dream at peace.

Po Chui. c.800

WEATHER

A soft, calm month – noticeably cooler at times, though more often by day, since the nights remain pleasantly mild until late in the month when frost may become a threat once more. While average rainfall tends to increase, this golden month of harvest is normally dry enough for you to gather in fruit, main-crop vegetables for storing and seeds to save for next year, and then purr with satisfaction before autumn arrives in earnest.

THE FLOWER GARDEN

- check all stakes, ties and supports, and secure climbing stems before strong winds arise
- continue planting spring bulbs as they are delivered
- begin raising the cutting height of mower blades
- sow seeds of crevice plants in mortar joints of walls (p.14)
- sow hardy annuals in situ or in frames for early colour next year
- paeonies are most likely to succeed if moved this month
- transplant biennials from nursery beds to flowering positions
- start digging up tender

perennials to overwinter under glass (p.87)
- prepare a nursery bed for hardwood rose and fruit cuttings, and start taking these late in the month
- prepare the ground for planting new shrubs and trees – evergreens first, followed by deciduous kinds in a month or two
- clear bedding from window boxes and replace with ever-greens or spring-flowering plants
- sow grass seed for new lawns on thoroughly prepared sites
- clean decaying foliage from ponds and cover with nets before trees start shedding their leaves
- spread a little lime where wall-flowers are to grow
- spray roses once more for blackspot and gather infected leaves as they fall
- you can spray perennial weeds with glyphosate on a still mild evening this month and hope for success

THE KITCHEN GARDEN

- gather in all mature crops for storing under cover (p.80)
- sow hardy cos lettuces outdoors, under cloches in cold areas

- transplant spring cabbage to fertile, limed sites
- sow hardy turnips to provide nutritious 'tops' in spring
- gather nuts, hops and wild fruits from the hedgerow (p.74)
- pull up outdoor tomato plants and suspend upside down under glass to finish ripening
- prune out fruited stems of fan-trained peaches and Morellos and tie in replacements
- cover autumn-fruiting strawberries with cloches to prolong their supply
- sow summer cauliflowers in a cold frame to transplant next spring
- plant autumn onion sets and garlic in a sunny fertile position
- tie grease bands on fruit tree trunks and stakes to trap pests
- cut and ripen marrows in the sun for a few days before storing
- order fruit on appropriate root-stocks for training on walls and arches (p.78)
- sow green manure such as win-ter tares on vacant ground (p.80)

UNDER GLASS

- sow hardy varieties of lettuce and radish in a cold frame or cool greenhouse border

- take cuttings of ivy in a frame or cool greenhouse (p.82)
- root tip cuttings of hebes in a cold frame as insurance against frost casualties
- early in the month plant potatoes in tubs for winter crops under glass (p.77)
- continue planting bulbs in pots, specially any for early blooms
- pot up summer-sown parsley plants for winter cutting
- rehouse greenhouse shrubs after their summer outside, and be ready to insulate containers left outdoors (p.83)
- bring in azaleas, repot in ericaceous compost and keep in a cool part of the greenhouse
- dig up healthy clumps of violets to force under glass (p.76)
- gradually water cacti less, and rehouse any standing outdoors
- ventilate cautiously at night, especially where grapes are ripening
- remove shading and wash glass to counter reduced light levels
- spray late chrysanthemums in pots with insecticide and rehouse
- pot up ageratum, petunias and mesembryanthemums to prolong flowering and provide cuttings in spring (p.87)

Mid AUTUMN

'Oh!' cried Marianne, 'with what transporting sensations have I formerly seen them fall! How have I delighted, as I walked, to see them driven in showers about me by the wind! What feelings have they, the season, the air, altogether inspired! Now there is no one to regard them, they are seen only as a nuisance, swept hastily off, and driven as much as possible from sight.'

'It is not every one,' said Elinor, 'who has your passion for dead leaves.'

from Sense and Sensibility: Jane Austen

WEATHER

Shorter days, chilly nights and the occasional touch of frost are all omens of approaching winter. By the end of the month it is noticeably an overcoat colder outdoors, and high winds may become a problem, swirling fallen leaves into heaps. It is a time for clearing, reorganizing and making everything secure, digging heavy soils to expose them to later frosts and planting new shrubs and trees. Given the perfect combination of sunny days and cool nights, it can also be one of the most vividly colourful months.

THE FLOWER GARDEN

● gather all leaves, especially from lawns, and stack to make leaf mould (p.84)
● finish clearing summer bedding and pot up anything that might usefully survive the winter under glass (p.87)
● continue planting spring bulbs, especially hyacinths this month
● dig up and divide large clumps of herbaceous perennials, but wait until spring if your soil is heavy (p.88)
● dig up gladioli and other

tender bulbs, and dry for storing
● cut down *Cobaea scandens* and thickly mulch the roots (p.87)
● start lifting dahlia tubers for store if blackened by frost
● box up early chrysanthemums to overwinter under glass
● collect ripe seeds (p.86), dry and store cool in airtight containers
● plant out pansies and pot a few to flower under glass
● dig up lilies to propagate from scales (p.82) before replanting
● prepare the ground for new roses, best planted next month
● choose shrubs for winter colour and shelter, and plant while the soil is still warm (p.88)
● cover damp-sensitive alpines with cloches or panes of glass
● lay turf for new lawns, or plant alternative species (p.92)
● scratch out thatch (dead fibres) from lawns with a wire rake
● take hardwood cuttings of roses, flowering currant and other shrubs

THE KITCHEN GARDEN

● start autumn cultivation according to the nature of your soil (p.84)
● prepare fertile, well-drained

sites for new fruit
● strike hardwood cuttings of soft fruit in a nursery bed
● test the soil to check if lime is needed (p.103)
● sow broad beans and round-seeded peas at the end of the month in mild areas (p.90)
● protect winter root crops with straw or leaves if the ground regularly freezes
● continue planting out spring cabbage in blocks easy to net
● finish harvesting keeping varieties of apples and pears
● cut down asparagus fern and mulch plants with manure (p.18)
● divide healthy rhubarb crowns and leave a few pieces on the surface for two months before forcing under glass
● finish digging winter carrots, beetroot and potatoes, and store under cover or in clamps (p.91)
● clear exhausted pea and bean vines, but leave the roots to rot
● pot up strawberry runners to force indoors from mid-winter
● finish earthing up celery and shape mound to shed rain
● cover late lettuce, spinach and French beans with cloches
● box up a few mint roots for supplies under glass

UNDER GLASS

● finish potting spring bulbs and stand outdoors for several weeks under a blanket of soil or leaves
● feed potted chrysanthemums regularly and ventilate whenever possible
● pick bunches of ripe grapes, and maintain warmth for any not yet ready (p.87)
● bring in greenhouse primulas and cinerarias from the cold frame
● watch out for fungal diseases, prevalent where the atmosphere is damp
● for early quality blooms, sow sweet peas in pots early this month (p.93)
● clear tomatoes and other crops as they finish, dig over borders and sterilize
● start forcing chicory in pots in a dark place
● dry off begonias and gloxinias, and store under the staging
● keep the atmosphere drier: cease damping down and water only in the mornings
● check heating equipment and materials for insulating the glass
● pot up late sown hardy annuals for spring colour indoors

Late AUTUMN

The roof came down to the floor all round, and all the beams and rafters were oak, and the floor went up and down like stormy water. The apples and pears had their places according to kind all round the room. There were bodlins and golden pippins, brown russets and scarlet crabs, ciffins, nonpareils and queanings, big green bakers, pearmains and redstreaks. We had a mort of pears too, for in such an old garden, always in the family, every generation'll put in a few trees. We had Worcester pears and butter pears, jargonelle, bergamot and Good Christian. Just after the last gathering, the attic used to be bright as a church window, all reds and golds.

from Precious Bane: Mary Webb

WEATHER

This month is often dull but never tedious. High pressure can delay autumn's demise by another few mellow weeks or wrap the garden mysteriously in a blanket of fog. Low pressure brings dramatic change: bracing, boisterous winds and horizontal rain, with temperatures edging ever downwards. Though there is little incentive to go outdoors some days, it is worth braving the elements to tuck the garden up for winter and conclude preparations for next year.

THE FLOWER GARDEN

● take a chance with woody cuttings from flowering shrubs, rooting the largest outdoors, smaller cuttings in a frame (p.96)
● continue planting new hedges or improving existing ones (p.103)
● overgrown deciduous hedges can be cut hard back now or in spring; tie down stems to fill bare patches
● transfer plants in moveable containers to a sheltered place,
and insulate those left outside (p.83)
● continue cutting down and weeding flower borders; mulch with manure or garden compost
● sow rose hips, hawthorn berries and other fruits outdoors or in a seedbox where they are exposed to frost
● now is the time to adjust planting schemes, moving herbaceous plants and shrubs to new sites (p.95)
● trim lawn and border edges to stay neat all winter
● plant tulips this month, either in beds or in naturalized drifts (p.100)
● plant roses in soil that has been improved according to their needs (p.103)
● dahlias may still be flowering, but must be dug up as soon as they are frosted
● prepare the site of a new pond, but do not line it until the spring (p.99)

THE KITCHEN GARDEN

● gather quinces and store on their own until ripe (p.94)
● topfruit can be pruned after leaf fall, except stone fruits (p.29)
● continue digging and exposing heavy soil to frost
● clear away spent plants, dead leaves, bamboo canes and other debris from the season's work
● clean up rhubarb crowns and cover with compost or old manure
● tidy up edges of vegetable beds and decide how to make full use of them (p.98)
● cut down autumn-fruiting raspberry canes, or leave until late winter if useful as a windbreak
● clear rows of horseradish grown as an annual crop (p.38)
● plant all kinds of fruit, except strawberries, in prepared soil
● remove fruit nets and roof netting from cages before snow arrives
● dig up Jerusalem artichokes, but only when needed, as they keep better in the ground
● perennial herbs can be divided on all but the heaviest soils
● stake Brussels sprouts 'lodged' after high winds
● when ground is frozen, barrow manure and compost on to ground to be dug

UNDER GLASS

● force chicory, seakale and rhubarb in a warm greenhouse
● feed cinerarias, cyclamen and other winter flowers in bud
● start prepared hippeastrums into growth
● sow a cold-tolerant tomato variety for earliest crops (p.97)
● pot up primroses from the garden and leave in a cold frame until late winter for forcing
● reduce heat and prune grape vines once leaves are shed
● prune greenhouse climbers such as plumbago and passiflora
● rest summer-flowering bulbs where appropriate, and order more for next year (p.100)
● check earliest potted bulbs for readiness to come into warmth
● keep mats and old blankets handy to insulate cold frames
● tidy and support winter begonias with thin canes and string (p.97)
● move active greenhouse plants and houseplants into the best light
● check source of draughts and fix insulation in place
● adjust heat, ventilation and watering according to the kind of plants heading for winter

Early WINTER

'The Queen entertained the children here, Christmas evening, with a German fashion. A fir tree, about as high again as any of us, lighted all over with small tapers, several little wax dolls among the branches in different places, and strings of almonds and raisins alternately tied from one to the other, with skipping ropes for the boys, and each bigger girl had muslin for a frock, a muslin handkerchief, a fan, and a sash, all prettily done up in the handkerchief, and a pretty necklace and earrings besides. As soon as all the things were delivered out by the Queen and Princesses, the candles on the tree were put out, and the children set to work to help themselves.'

The Honourable Georgina Townshend
Housekeeper to Q Charlotte and K George III. 1800

WEATHER
Frequent light frosts and even the first snowfall may appear this month, but rain is a virtual certainty – cold, penetrating rain that drives the hardiest gardener to seek the comforts of greenhouse work. With the soil often too wet to cultivate, tidying and pruning are the chief outdoor jobs that remain feasible. Or there is the simple and sensible country advice this month to 'keep yourself warm and sleep'.

THE FLOWER GARDEN
- finish raking autumn leaves for stacking or mulching
- continue planting deciduous trees and shrubs while conditions allow
- check *Iris stylosa* for early blooms and cut if required
- clean tunics and fibres from dried bulbs and store frost-free
- give new plants some kind of frost protection, as these are particularly vulnerable (p.109)
- repair lawn edges when the grass is not frozen or soaked
- mulch bulbs with leaves or straw where precocious growth shows
- clear snow from evergreens and wire in displaced branches
- roses can still be planted or heeled in until better weather
- late in the month lightly fork over bulb beds and dress with a general fertilizer (p.107)
- check deciduous shrubs while they are bare and thin surplus branches (p.29)
- in a mild season annual weeds might need hoeing
- keep frequently used paths clear of snow and slippery algae
- send lawn mowers for servicing and sharpening
- clean, overhaul and repair all tools, sprayers etc

THE KITCHEN GARDEN
- plant shallots after the shortest day if soil conditions permit
- prune brambles, cutting out fruited canes and tying in new ones
- lightly fork beside raspberry rows, removing invasive suckers
- cover dormant chicory, chard or turnips with leaves to blanch new growth (p.111)
- clear rootcrop turnips into store as these cannot stand frost, but leave those grown for their leafy tops
- dig up exhausted brassicas and stumps promptly to reduce pest and disease persistence
- continue winter pruning soft fruit and topfruit, except plums and cherries
- mulch celery with leaves or keep a few heads in a shed safe from hard frost
- sow sweet cicely seeds outdoors where they can experience frost (p.113)
- note where water lies after heavy rain and check drainage
- order seed potatoes and spread in trays to chit
- pick off mummified fruits which transmit disease from one crop to the next

UNDER GLASS
- sow geraniums in 21°C (70°F) for bedding plants next summer
- repot hippeastrums in fresh compost as they resume growth (p.107)
- wash and disinfect pots, trays, labels and glass ready for the new season
- ventilate on sunny days to refresh damp unhealthy air
- new fruit and climbing plants can be introduced to a greenhouse border, whatever the weather (p.111)
- collect rainwater for ericaceous plants such as Indian azaleas and camellias in pots (p.107)
- cut down chrysanthemums after flowering and keep cool
- save pips and stones from seasonal fruit to sow in pots (p.112)
- divide astilbes and pot up for forcing in a frame or greenhouse
- pinch out autumn-sown sweet peas after 3-4 pairs of leaves
- keep desert cacti and stored geraniums dry for the next three months
- continue bringing in potted bulbs with 5-7.5cm (2-3in) of leaf growth
- check houseplants have optimum heat, light, shade or humidity according to type (p.113)
- check dahlia tubers in store, trim decayed areas and treat with sulphur

Mid WINTER

The rain set early in to-night,
The sullen wind was soon awake,
It tore the elm-tops down for spite,
And did its worst to vex the lake:
I listened with heart fit to break.
When glided in Porphyria; straight
She shut the cold out and the storm,
And kneeled and made the cheerless grate
Blaze up, and all the cottage warm

from Porphyria's Lover: Robert Browning

WEATHER
The dead of winter and the toughest time for plants, when soils may be frozen or covered with snow for days on end. Most plants are dormant, but 'if vegetation does not move, that is no reason why man should not' according to one tendentious manual. In fact the average temperature is usually above freezing, with many fine days on which to press ahead with preparations for spring and the new season. When all else fails, sit in comfort and complete the seed orders.

THE FLOWER GARDEN
● remove lilac suckers and discard or transplant
● layer flexible branches of shrubs to make new plants by autumn
● delayed spring bulbs can still be planted and will flower in succession
● check trees and shrubs after snow and high winds, make necessary repairs and renovate neglected trees (p.120)
● build or repair rock gardens, clear dead or fallen leaves, and top up gravel screes and grit mulches

● divide congested bergenia clumps, replanting healthy sidestems
● lightly fork over soil between shrubs, working in compost, old manure or autumn leaves
● assess mid-winter colour in the garden, and plan additions (p.115)
● erect screens of net or sacking to protect young evergreens from cold winds
● continue pruning deciduous shrubs and overgrown hedges
● keep paths clean and passable, and plan any improvements (p.116)
● lawns continue growing in mild winters and may need a light cut, but avoid walking on the grass when wet or frozen
● in fine weather you can turf new lawns right up to early spring
● in the coldest weather, identify warmest and most sheltered areas of the garden for growing vulnerable plants (p.114)

THE KITCHEN GARDEN
● protect wall-trained figs against hard frost: cover them with straw and netting, or bundle branches in blankets
● sow summer cauliflowers and transplant seedlings to small pots

● spray fruit trees and bushes with a winter wash if pests are usually a problem
● plant Jerusalem artichokes when the soil is workable
● if severe frost is forecast, pull cabbages and Brussels sprout plants and suspend upside down in a shed for convenient supplies
● finish pruning fruit by the end of the month
● lime soil that was manured in autumn for brassicas
● check and repair supports and ties for trained fruit
● plan soil cultivation and improvements, as few types are naturally perfect or remain so for long (p.122)
● cover strong rhubarb crowns with pots or boxes for early stems
● if bullfinches and other birds attack your gooseberry buds, net bushes now
● warm a seedbed with cloches or a portable frame for earliest sowings of carrots and radishes

UNDER GLASS
● complete and send off seed orders, and make preparations for first sowings in ideal temperatures (p.119)
● sow onions after the shortest

day for the largest bulbs (p.117)
● take root cuttings of phlox, oriental poppies and other perennial flowers (p.122)
● box up roots of doronicum, violets and lily-of-the valley for forcing into bloom
● sow Charm and Cascade chrysanthemums for a long growing season (p.120)
● sow further batches of greenhouse lettuces and radishes
● sow broad beans in boxes late this month as an alternative to autumn sowing
● plant lilies in pots to flower fragrantly indoors
● buy seed potatoes without delay, and chit in trays
● adjust watering according to needs: some plants prefer dry dormancy, others such as oleanders (p.121) constant moisture
● start sowing tender bedding such as impatiens, begonias and annual carnations in warmth
● house potted strawberry plants and force in good light
● continue forcing rhubarb and chicory under glass (p.123)
● check all stored crops, bulbs and tubers are in good condition
● water cinerarias carefully and watch out for aphids (p.117)

Late WINTER

When the ground was partially bare of snow, and a few warm days had dried its surface somewhat, it was pleasant to compare the first tender signs of the infant year just peeping forth with the stately beauty of the withered vegetation which had withstood the winter, - life-everlasting, golden-rods, pinweeds, and graceful wild grasses, more obvious and interesting frequently than in summer even, as if their beauty was not ripe till then; even cotton-grass, cattails, mulleins, johnswort, hard-hack, meadow-sweet, and other strong stemmed plants, those unexhausted granaries which entertain the earliest birds, - many of the phenomena of Winter are suggestive of an inexpressible tenderness and fragile delicacy. We are accustomed to hear this king described as a rude and boisterous tyrant; but with the gentleness of a lover he adorns the tresses of Summer.

from Walden, or Life in the Woods:

Henry David Thoreau

WEATHER

It can be mild enough this month to sow outdoors and revel in the weak sunshine, or you might be shovelling snow and chipping the greenhouse door free from ice. It is often a beautiful month, though, when hoar frost embroiders every surface and the first spring bulbs raise their heads. But the weather may be irrelevant, for everyone is busy under glass getting ready for early spring.

THE FLOWER GARDEN

● continue planting deciduous trees and shrubs in good weather
● winter prune wisteria, buddleia and late-flowering clematis
● tidy the base of hedges and feed with general fertilizer 135g/sq m (4oz/sq yd) after hard pruning
● check variegated evergreens for any reverted green stems and remove at their base
● plant *Anemone coronaria* corms in rich soil
● tidy spring bedding, lightly

fork over the soil and topdress bulbs with a general feed
● protect delphinium and hosta crowns from slugs
● divide congested clumps of montbretia and replant in fresh soil
● move clumps of snowdrops while they are in active gowth
● start clearing neglected areas of a new garden warily, and wait to see what will appear (p.126)
● prepare the ground for sowing or turfing new lawns in spring (p.129)
● hellebores can be moved carefully immediately after flowering
● make sure mowers have been serviced ready for the new season

THE KITCHEN GARDEN

● take care with early sowings, testing that the soil is warm enough for germination (p.127)
● sow early brassicas, salad plants, broad beans and lettuce under cloches or in a frame
● thin growth on hazelnuts to leave an airy structure (p.127)
● plant new rhubarb crowns in well-manured ground

● sow parsley in pots or under cloches to transplant later
● check wall-trained peach and apricot stems are tied in and be prepared to protect early blossom (p.132)
● feed overwintered crops with dried blood to stimulate new growth
● plant garlic now rather than in autumn in cold districts
● go over your cropping plans, checking soil preparations, seeds and rotation (p.125)

UNDER GLASS

● sow half-hardy annual flowers in 15°C (60°F)
● sow tomatoes for planting in late spring in cool greenhouses
● ventilate houses on mild days and make sure growing plants receive maximum light (p.129)
● sow *Solanum capsicastrum* for decoration next winter
● pot on spring-flowering plants, prick out seedlings and pot up rooted cuttings without delay
● prune greenhouse climbers if not already done, and mulch with decayed manure (p.132)

● sow cannas after filing a notch in each seed and soaking in warm water for a day
● revive overwintered chrysanthemum stools and take cuttings as soon as shoots are long enough
● pollinate early fruit blossom under glass
● sow celery and celeriac, and transplant singly into pots
● melons can be sown now in pots for heated greenhouses
● there is still time to pot up violets to flower indoors (p.134)
● clean out water tanks and cans, as dirty water spreads damping off disease
● revive fuchsias and geraniums to provide spring cuttings
● pot up achimenes corms and start into growth (p.127)
● fork over last year's growing-bags, add fertilizer and sow early salads or use for cuttings
● water plants more often, but only in the morning, and avoid wetting foliage
● sow dahlias, petunias, salvias and African marigolds
● sow sweet peas in pots if not done in autumn

Glossary
of common English names

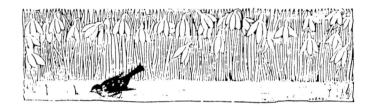

Gardeners often use different popular names for the same plant, and these may vary even between neighbouring districts; British county names for the commonest wild flowers, for example, are themselves a complex study in folklore and dialect. Since botanical names are more precise and understood internationally, this glossary lists the Latin counterparts for common names mentioned in the text. But beware — even these are variable, because a Latin name is not fixed by any single authority and its validity depends solely on general acceptance by botanists.

A

asparagus pea, *Tetragonolobus purpureus*
  (syn *Lotus tetragonolobus*)
arum lily, *Zantedeschia aethiopica*

B

bay (sweet), *Laurus nobilis*
beech, *Fagus sylvatica*
bergamot, *Monarda didyma*
birdseye primrose, *Primula farinosa*
birdseye speedwell, *Veronica persica*
black medick, *Medicago lupulina*
bluebell, *Endymion non-scriptus* (syn
  Hyacinthoides non-scripta)
bogbean, *Menyanthes trifoliata*
bracken, *Pteridium aquilinum*
bryony (white), *Bryonia cretica*
bullace, *Prunus institia*

C

campion, *Silene* sub-species: eg red campion,
  S. dioica
castor-oil plant, *Ricinus communis*
catmint, *Nepeta cataria*
chickweed, *Stellaria* sub-species: eg common
  chickweed, *S. media*
Chinese lanterns, *Physalis alkekengi franchetii*
cinquefoil, *Potentilla* sub-species: eg hoary
  cinquefoil, *P. argentea*
coleus, *Coleus hybrida* (syn
  Solenostemon scutellarioides)
comfrey, *Symphytum officinale*
common (lawn) daisy, *Bellis perennis*
cornflower (annual), *Centaurea cyanus*
cotton lavender, *Santolina chamaecyparissus*
couch grass, *Elymus* (syn *Agropyron*) *repens*
cow parsley, *Anthriscus sylvestris*
creeping buttercup, *Ranunculus repens*
croton, *Codiaeum variegatum pictum*
cuckoo flower, *Cardamine pratensis*
cup-and-saucer vine, *Cobaea scandens*

D

dandelion, *Taraxacum* sub-species
day lily, *Hemerocallis* sub-species and cultivars
dewberry, *Rubus ursinus*
dog violet (common), *Viola riviniana*
dogwood, *Cornus* sub-species and cultivars
dwarf box, *Buxus sempervirens* 'Suffruticosa'

E

elderberry, *Sambucus nigra*
enchanter's nightshade, *Circaea lutetiana*
evening primrose (common), *Oenothera biennis*

F

fescue, *Festuca* sub-species
fool's parsley, *Aethusa cynapium*
forget-me-not, *Myosotis palustris*
foxglove, *Digitalis purpurea*

G

Georgius the Fifth = purple toadflax,
Linaria purpurea
germander, *Teucrium chamaedrys*
golden rod, *Solidago canadensis* and cultivars
good King Henry, *Chenopodium bonus-henricus*
grass of Parnassus, *Parnassia palustris*
greater celandine, *Chelidonium majus*
green alkanet, *Pentaglottis sempervirens*
ground elder, *Aegopodium podagraria*

H

hawthorn, *Crataegus monogyna*
hazel, *Corylus avellana*
heartsease, *Viola tricolor*
hemlock, *Conium maculatum*
herb robert, *Geranium robertianum*
hollyhock, *Althaea rosea*
hop, *Humulus lupulus*
hornbeam, *Carpinus betulus*
horseradish, *Armoracia rusticana*
hyssop, *Hyssopus officinalis*

I

ivy-leaved toadflax, *Cymbalaria muralis*

L

lady's mantle, *Alchemilla mollis*
lady's smock, *Cardamine pratensis*
larkspur, *Delphinium consolida*
lawn chamomile, *Chamaemelum nobile*
lemon balm, *Melissa officinalis*
London pride, *Saxifraga umbrosa*

M

marguerite, *Argyranthemum* (syn
  Chrysanthemum) *frutescens*
marsh marigold, *Caltha palustris*
meadowsweet, *Filipendula ulmaria*
Michaelmas daisy, *Aster amellus, A. novae-angliae*
  and *A. novi-belgii* cultivars
mignonette, *Reseda odorata*
mind-your-own-business, *Soleirolia soleirolii*
mistletoe (European), *Viscum album*
morning glory, *Ipomaea purpurea*
mother-in-law's tongue, *Sansevieria trifasciata*
mountain avens, *Dryas octopetala*

N

nasturtium, *Tropaeolum majus*
nightshade, *Solanum* and *Atropa* sub-species: eg
  deadly nightshade, *A. bella-donna*

O

obedient plant, *Physostegia virginiana*
oxlip, *Primula elatior*

P

perennial sweet pea, *Lathyrus latifolius*
periwinkle, *Vinca minor* and *V. major*
pink, *Dianthus* sub-species and cultivars: eg
  maiden pink, *D. deltoides*
Portugal laurel, *Prunus lusitanica*
pot marigold, *Calendula officinalis*
primrose, *Primula vulgaris*
privet, *Ligustrum vulgare*

Q

quaking grass, *Briza maxima*

R

rosebay willowherb, *Epilobium angustifolium*
rosemary, *Rosmarinus officinale*
rue, *Ruta graveolens*
rye grass (perennial), *Lolium perenne*

S

scarlet pimpernel, *Anagallis arvensis*
silverweed, *Potentilla anserina*
snakeshead fritillary, *Fritillaria meleagris*
snowdrop (common), *Galanthus nivalis*
soldiers and sailors – lungwort,
  Pulmonaria officinalis
speedwell, *Veronica* sub-species: eg germander
  speedwell, *V. chamaedrys*
stinging nettle, *Urtica dioica*
stonecrop, *Sedum* sub-species: eg biting
  stonecrop, *S. acre*
sweet woodruff, *Asperula odorata* (syn
  Galium odoratum)

T

tamarisk, *Tamarix gallica*
toadflax, *Linaria* sub-species: eg common
  toadflax, *L. vulgaris*
tobacco plant, *Nicotiana sylvestris*
tormentil, *Potentilla erecta*
traveller's joy, *Clematis vitalba*

V

valerian (red), *Centranthus ruber*
variegated hop, *Humulus lupulus* 'Aureus' (hardy
  perennial), *H. japonicus*
'Variegatus' (hardy annual)

W

wallflower, *Cheiranthus cheiri*
water forget-me-not, *Myosotis scorpioides*
wild thyme, *Thymus serpyllum*
winter aconite, *Eranthis hyemalis*

Z

zebra grass, *Miscanthus sinensis* 'Zebrinus'

Glossary
of gardening terms

A

Annual A plant that completes the cycle of its growth in one year and dies after it has flowered and produced seed

Attar Oil from flowers

B

Biennial Similar life cycle to an annual, but needs two growing seasons to complete it

Blanching Excluding light from vegetables such as celery and rhubarb in order to whiten the stems or leaves and remove the bitter taste

Bolting Running to seed prematurely

Brassica Any plant of the genus Brassica, such as cabbage, swede, turnip

Break A branch or fork. To make a plant 'break' means to produce a branch or fork when otherwise it would not do so

Broadcast To scatter seeds evenly all over the surface of soil

Bromeliad Any of a family of tropical American plants, usually rosette in form with a central 'urn' of leaves filled with water

C

Calcifuge Disliking lime or chalk in any form

Calyx The outer protective part of a flower which persists at the top of the fruit, eg tomato

Cambium layer Botanically this name may be given to any plant tissue other than that at the growing points which retains the power of growth. When the term is used horticulturally it is confined to the very narrow layer of active tissue which exists between the bark and wood of dicotyledons

Catch crop A quick-maturing crop grown between rows of slower-growing species or sown and harvested in the brief time between one crop being picked and the next being sown

Cordon A plant grown on a single main stem, achieved by strict pruning. Double and triple cordons have two and three stems respectively

Corm An underground storage organ formed by a thickened leaf base. Unlike a bulb, a new corm is produced annually above the old one, which gradually shrivels away

Crown The bottom of a perennial from which shoots and roots arise

Cultivar A variety of a plant produced from a natural species and maintained by cultivation

Cutting A portion of a plant stem that may be induced to form its own roots

D

Dibber A tool used for making holes in soil

E

Earthing-up The process of drawing soil towards and round plants

Epiphyte A plant which can live without having its roots in soil, eg many bromeliads and orchids

Ericaceous Lime-free compost - when used to refer to compost

Espalier A type of tree trained with the support of wires, often against a wall. The main stem is vertical with pairs of branches extending horizontally at regular intervals

F

Floriferous Bearing or capable of bearing many flowers

Forcing Hurrying plants into growth by use of heat or some other means

Frond The 'leaf' of a fern

G

Grafting A method of propagation whereby a union is made between one plant and another or even between two branches of the same tree or shrub. It may occur naturally

H

Haulm The stems of certain plants are given this name, notably those of potatoes and sweet peas

Heart wood The innermost and hardest wood of the branch or trunk of a tree

Heel The base of a sideshoot which has been torn away from the stem to be used as a cutting. Cuttings often root more readily if a heel is attached

Husk The external covering of some fruits and pods

L

Layering The name given to a particular method of propagation in which a shoot or stem is induced to form roots while still attached to the parent plant, after which it is severed and replanted to form a new plant

Legume A botanical term used to describe the particular type of seed-pod found in members of the pea family

O

Offset A young plant that is naturally produced by mature (or 'parent') plants and can be detached and used for propagation

P

Perch see rod

Perennial Any plant that continues to live for an indefinite number of years and to flower each season

Pinching out Removing the growing point of a stem to encourage bushy growth

Pole see rod

Pricking out Transplanting seedlings for the first time to larger trays or individual pots

Propagation Increasing or raising new plants, either from seed or vegetatively, ie from cuttings, offsets or suckers

Prothalus The small flat green disc of tissue that bears the reproductive organs of pteridophytes

Pteridophytes A plant, such as a fern, reproducing by spores rather than seeds

R

Raceme Elongated, unbranched flower clusters in which each flower is attached by a stalk to the main stem and in which the lower flowers open first

Reversion Return to the original uncultivated state

Rhizome An underground storage organ composed of a creeping stem

Rod A measure of area, 1/160 of an acre, that is synonymous with pole and perch

Rootstock The name for the plant on to which another is grafted

Runner An aerial stem which roots at the tip when it touches soil, to make a new plant

S

Scarify To break up and loosen soil or plant fibres eg turf to a shallow depth

Self-fertile Used to describe a plant that does not need a pollinator to set fruit

Self-sterile Used to describe a plant that does need a pollinator to set fruit

Set A term applied to certain tubers and corms used for planting

Shell The hard outer layer of some fruits

Shuck The outer covering of something, such as the husk of a pea pod

Specimen plant Any plant which is grown prominently so that it can be viewed from all sides as distinct from being grouped with other plants.

Spike A flower cluster very closely resembling a raceme but differing from it in having individual flowers which are stalkless or nearly so

Spit A spade's depth – about 25-30cm (10-12in)

Spore A minute particle by which ferns reproduce themselves

Sport Any variation from the normal in the character of a plant may be termed a sport, but in garden practice the term is usually reserved for variations which occur apart from seed

Spur A small lateral branch of a fruit tree which bears flower buds

Standard Any tree or shrub with a single bare stem below the first branches. Certain shrubs may be trained to form standards

Stock A name given to the part of a grafted or budded plant which produces roots, or to plants grown specifically for the purpose of providing roots for budding and grafting

Sucker A shoot that arises from below ground level and which in some species can be used for propagation

T

Tap root The first root produced by some seedlings which is usually undivided and grows straight down into the soil. The term is also used more losely to denote any strong root growing downwards

Topfruit Fruit that naturally grows in the form of a tree

Triple dug Dug two spits deep with the third spit loosened with a fork

Triploid A plant with 50 per cent more chromosomes than is normal for the species to which it belongs; usually poor pollen source and needs two compatible neighbours to fertilize its flower and set fruit

Truss A cluster of flowers or fruits

Season and month charts

NORTHERN HEMISPHERE

January	Mid-winter
February	Late winter
March	Early spring
April	Mid-spring
May	Late spring
June	Early summer
July	Mid-summer
August	Late summer
September	Early autumn
October	Mid-autumn
November	Late autumn
December	Early winter

SOUTHERN HEMISPHERE

January	Mid-summer
February	Late summer
March	Early autumn
April	Mid-autumn
May	Late autumn
June	Early winter
July	Mid-winter
August	Late winter
September	Early spring
October	Mid-spring
November	Late spring
December	Early summer

Index

155

The Publishers would like to thank the following organizations and individuals for their kind permission to reproduce the photographs in this book.

Jacket cover: Jane Gifford
Back cover: Robert Harding Syndication Ltd:- IPC Magazines, 1991: top left; Harry Smith Horticultural: top right; Reed International Books: bottom left; Insight:- Michelle Garrett: bottom right

Endpapers, front and back:- Reed International Books

Anthony Blake Photo Library:- Anthony Blake: 51;
Gerrit Buntrock: 67b; Lucy Mason: 18r
Biofotos:- 91
Bridgeman Art Library:- 11tr, 63t, 95t, 111, 134l, 134r
Eric Crichton:- 11br, 21r, 22, 23c, 24t, 28, 31, 32b, 34, 35, 47, 48, 51, 53t, 53b, 65b, 68, 70, 75b, 85t, 87b, 90b, 93t, 96, 101, 105b, 107c, 107b, 119, 120, 127c
Garden Picture Library:- John Bouchier: 125b; Linda Burgess: 71, 81; Brian Carter: 98, 105t; Geoff Dann: 106t; John Glover: 95b, 115t; Lamontagne: 32t, 102b; Gary Rogers: 25; Nigel Temple: 108; Brigitte Thomas: 109t, 125t; Micky White: 128t
John Glover:- 8tl, 13c, 16, 33t, 33c, 37r, 41, 65t, 76, 82b, 90t, 97t, 100, 107t, 110, 112, 117t, 117c, 130, 133b, 136, 138, 140, 141
Jerry Harpur:- 27t, 42t, 45, 49, 52t, 53c, 54, 60, 66, 75t, 94b, 99l, 99r, 118, 131, 132, 142, 145, 146, 147, 149
Insight:- 37, 39, 43, 86b, 129; Michelle Garrett: 8tr, 15t, 15b, 46, 57, 61l, 61r, 67, 79t, 123b, 128b
Andrew Lawson:- 8bl, 8br, 14tr, 18b, 27b, 38, 42b, 72, 73, 76b, 77c, 78, 79b, 82t, 85b, 86t, 97c, 97b, 102tl, 102tr, 106b, 109b, 113, 115b, 116t, 116c, 121, 133, 135t
Marianne Majerus:- 12t, 14, 19, 89, 126t, 143
John Miller:- 56, 126b
National Trust:- 92
Clive Nichols:- 139, 148
Reed International Books:- 12b, 13t, 13b, 23t, 33b, 43t, 43c, 64, 65c, 77b, 87t, 87c, 117b; Bob Gibbons: 123t, 135b
Robert Harding Syndication Ltd:- IPC Magazines, 1991: 44, 52b, 67c; 1992: 59, 63b, 116b, 144
Harry Smith Horticultural:- 2, 23b, 69, 77t, 127t, 127b
Mark Williams:- 122t, 122b

160